Take a Seat

One Man, One Tandem and Twenty Thousand Miles of Possibilities

Dominic Gill

FALCONGUIDES

GUILFORD, CONNECTICUT
HELENA, MONTANA

AN IMPRINT OF GLOBE PEQUOT PRESS

For you.
May you always extend your hand to a stranger.

If evil were ubiquitous
If to trust resulted always in a fall
If a friendly face were hard to find
Bad news would not be news at all.

FALCONGUIDES®

Copyright © 2010 by Dominic Gill
First published in Great Britain in 2010 by Mainstream Publishing
Company (Edinburgh) Ltd.
First FalconGuides edition 2010

This book is a work of nonfiction based on the life, experiences, and
recollections of the author. In some cases, names of people, places, dates,
and sequences or the detail of events have been changed to protect the
privacy of others. The author has stated to the publisher that, except in such
respects, not affecting the substantial accuracy of the work, the contents of
this book are true.

Library of Congress Cataloging-in-Publication Data is available on file.

ISBN 978-0-7627-7069-4

Printed in the United States of America

10 9 8 7 6 5 4 3 2 1

96.6092
7475t

Contents

Acknowledgments

A few weeks ago, I got home from giving a lecture to a room full of teenagers in Blackburn. It was dark and wet, but, knowing it would wipe my tiredness away, I quickly changed and went for a run along rows and rows of terraced houses. The air was damp, perhaps two or three degrees above freezing, and I could smell coal smoke that took me immediately back to cycling through Lota in central Chile. As I ran through the darkness back to my house, breathing hard, I heard a robotic rendition of 'Greensleeves' coming from an ice-cream van nearby. I was most definitely in England.

Over the year and a bit since I'd returned to the UK exhausted, my hunger for adventure had returned, and it was time to think about feeding the addiction. It was December already, and I planned to set off again on another trip in July. Six and a half months isn't long to organise an adventure, and funding wouldn't appear by itself, so I sat down to write emails to contacts in the States.

But as usually happens when I try to do some work, I got sidetracked. I began reading emails from friends I'd made in the Americas, and I thought about the stories I'd told that day in Blackburn. About the old man pedalling an excuse for a bike in the middle of the Bolivian desert in order to look after a handful of baby llamas. About the hundreds of hosts I'd had, often in the most unlikely places. About the shouting children who had treated my tandem as a fairground ride, urging me to take them a block further down some muddy street in the mountains. About the encouraging emails I'd received from family or well-wishers.

In short, I spent the evening in a nostalgic stupor, staring longingly up at the bike trailer hanging from my kitchen ceiling, the only visible link to what felt a little like a past life, a life where I had rubbed shoulders with more people than it's possible to imagine. So many of them had loaded their bags onto that contraption, which now serves only to scalp me on the rare occasions I crouch under it to get the vacuum cleaner. Dozens of kids had helped themselves to a ride on it and thousands of dogs had chased it as if their life depended on it.

I couldn't hope to show the thousands of people – or dogs – involved in this journey the thanks they deserve; after all, most of them will be too busy surviving to remember me, let alone see this book. But since every conversation, every email, every hug or smile helped me to carry on, the best I can do is to tell *you* that I'm grateful for your help. There is, after all, if you're reading this, a distinct possibility that you had some part to play in my journey, whether it was a wave from a car window, palatial hospitality or something in between. I'm sorry if your name doesn't appear in the text, but whether you can get a refund for this ineptitude depends on where you bought the book, I suppose.

There is perhaps only one person I can thank properly using the written word: my literary agent Humfrey Hunter, without whom this book might well never have been written. Thanks to him and Mainstream Publishing, I have been able to share my story.

And thank *you* for reading it.

Introduction

Fresh out of school back in 1999 I'd ridden a bicycle from Vancouver to San Francisco with a good friend of mine. I was living in Vancouver at the time and thought it would be fun to do some kind of human-powered road trip. We decided to do the trip on a tandem – for ease of rental as much as anything else. Neither of us had ridden one before for more than a few minutes, but sure enough, two weeks after we set off and 1,400 miles later, Mark and I cycled over the Golden Gate Bridge on a bike that looked like something out of wacky races. A pair of Mark's Union Jack boxers fluttered limply from a stick on the trailer by way of a flag, the frame had begun to flex ominously and the tires, mounted on rims that were impressively buckled, were reinforced with dollar bills that showed through tears in the rubber. But we'd done it, and I'd learned that bicycle travel was perhaps the best way to get to know a country while moving quickly enough to feel like you're getting somewhere. During the two-day train journey back to Vancouver, Mark and I dared to discuss the possibilities of pedalling a little further together.

For the time being, however, we went our separate ways. I went to university to study Biology then tried to establish a conventional career for myself back in London. I ended up moving to Oldham, in Lancashire, where I had climbing and mountain biking on my doorstep to keep me happy at least outside the nine-to-five during the week. But after a few years of trying to shoehorn myself into a desk job I thought I *ought* to be doing, the pull of adventure became too strong to ignore.

It was time to change tactics; all I knew for certain was that I loved the outdoors, I loved physical challenges and I loved videography. So I decided to combine those things and revisit my dream of cycling from Alaska to Argentina, with the added project of filming a documentary along the way.

But by now it was five years later, and Mark had entered the world of academia, found himself a good job and gracefully sidelined any larger dreams he had had of further bike tours. So, having lost the one partner I would have wanted on my tandem, I set about planning a solo adventure down the entire landmass we'd pedalled just a fraction of. It was February 2006, in June I would be 26, and since June was the best month to be in northern Alaska, on account of milder temperatures, I decided to set my birthday as my departure deadline, thinking the entire trip would probably take about 15 months. I called my girlfriend out in northern Canada to discuss my exciting plans – plans that didn't include her other than perhaps for a few weeks here and there. I was sufficiently self-absorbed, however, to think she might be excited about the whole idea too.

I wrote and sent off a film pitch with little clue as to how to go about it, and to my surprise a response came inviting me to come for a chat in the production offices of Ginger Television. 'Sounds like a great trip,' Ed said to me from the comfort of a plush sofa in the corner of a stuffy yet open-plan office. 'But just you on a bike . . . it's missing something – it's not interesting enough,' he continued, not so subtly rubbishing my grand plan full of bravado and endeavour. Trying not to sound annoyed I asked him drily what he'd suggest. He said nothing for a few seconds and stroked the barely present whiskers on his chin.

'I dunno . . . what about . . . going on a tandem and picking up random strangers – d'you know what I mean?' he said in his heavy London accent, grinning slightly, evidently pleased with the idea. I grinned too, but it felt like more of a grimace. Logistically I doubted whether a journey like this was possible. Why the hell would someone want to jump on the back of a bike with a complete stranger simply to lighten his workload? I walked out of the office shortly after Ed's suggestion, thinking little more about it. I had to think of something

INTRODUCTION

else to spice up my journey and I had to think of it fast. After all, I'd already taken out a 'home improvement' loan to cover the costs of the journey. But Ed's tandem idea was ridiculous.

Over the next two weeks, desperately trying to think of a better plan whilst sitting at my desk, I begrudgingly began to realise that Ed's idea, if it were possible, was actually quite a good one. I found a recent email from him on my computer, clicked Reply and typed three simple words: 'I'll do it.'

1

Anywhere but here

The man sitting next to me didn't want to talk. As soon as he wedged himself into his seat, I glanced sideways, desperate for at least a nod or a smile. Maybe he'd crack open a few stories about the country we were heading towards, or give me advice about how to handle the road south – failing that, stories of bear maulings or lonely riggers and their vicious ways with fresh-faced strangers. Anything would do. I just wanted something to take my mind off the life I was running from, and the one I was choosing to embrace in its place.

But he ignored me. Repositioning his half-mesh trucker's cap and pushing his slightly yellow-tinted glasses down his nose, he pulled out a hunting magazine and buried his face in it, leaving me to look out of the window at an empty Alaska 20,000 feet below. My stomach tightened as I realised I'd be down there soon, going back the way I'd come, on a seat that wasn't nearly as comfortable as this narrow economy-class armchair. Force of habit caused me to reach under the cushion and feel for the questionable security of the lifejacket complete with light and whistle for attracting attention.

The macho man in me – the part that had decided to cycle the length of the Americas – had vanished hours ago, and now the idea of setting off alone into that wilderness gripped me with a numb dread. Right then, if I could have clicked my fingers and been back at home or on a flight to see my girlfriend – the one that had decided that she was better off without me shortly before I'd left – I would have done it in a heartbeat. The more my tenacity wavered, the more I thought about my 'ex'. I'd be cycling through the wilderness in northern Canada that made up a small portion of her backyard, and I knew cycling through that land of stunted spruce trees would hurt badly. I couldn't blame her really, though. I mean, what was the point of staying with a boyfriend planning to spend the next 15 months – and that was a secretly conservative estimate – cycling slowly further away from you?

That rejection mixed with fear of the impending unknown blended into a powerful concoction of self-pity. What on earth was I thinking? When I had told my father what I was planning to do, he had written a letter asking me not to go. A letter meant it was a serious request, and sitting on the plane sick with uncertainty and very definitely the odd one out I wished I'd followed his advice. He said that I'd mix 'with people that march to the beat of a very different drum', and I guess he meant that by setting off alone on another continent I was upping the likelihood of meeting someone who would either kill me or, if I was lucky, just rob me blind.

I roused myself from those blurred and painful thoughts and glanced around the cabin. Most of the passengers were heading to work on the oil rigs while the rest were heading home to the small indigenous communities on North Slope, near Prudhoe Bay, the end of the road at the top of North America. The dark and beautifully lined faces of the elderly indigenous people mixed with the tough, stubbly complexions of riggers there for a few weeks of hard labour before returning to families down south in 'lower 48' (the 48 contiguous US states, i.e. those below Alaska, and not including Hawaii).

One old lady, her features well hidden by deep age-earned wrinkles, was helped respectfully onto the plane by the cabin crew when boarding in Anchorage and had two blankets tucked around her stick-like thighs as she nodded thanks to the stewardess. She spoke no English, only her native Athabaskan tongue. I looked at the others and nearly all of them, old ladies and stubbly riggers alike, had a slightly swollen cheek hiding a saliva-soaked wad of 'chew' nestled next to their gum. In the older ones, a smile or yawn would reveal an incomplete set of teeth the colour of the old yellowing pub ceilings back home. The more I scanned the aisles the more I felt too fresh-faced, too green to be on this northbound flight with these old timers. It was fitting maybe, given I really *was* the odd one out, the outsider, arriving only to hightail it south. Penned in on this flight, before I'd even arrived at the beginning of my journey, I'd never felt so alone. This was the first time that I realised any friendly hand I had had to hold was growing further out of reach. I wouldn't be going anywhere near home until after I'd arrived in Patagonia, an unimaginable 20,000 miles away. Or until I gave up.

The more I thought about it and the more I stared down, the more I questioned why I'd opted to start alone on my tandem bicycle. I cursed my egotistical and ambitious idea of making a documentary about my trip. No one had ever travelled halfway round the world on a tandem looking for company in the form of strangers, and that made it interesting, different and very definitely more challenging. Leaving alone and finding friends was the whole point, all in the name of documentary film-making – all thanks to Ed's well-honed imagination. In the comfort of my small terraced house in Oldham, staring at a world atlas and pictures of bicycles, it had seemed so exciting, and I'd felt brilliantly foolish and strong. That was during the planning stage. Now, sitting in a plane above Alaska, I still felt foolish, but also weak – I craved a companion to help me through like nothing before.

My clammy breath began to cloud the plexiglass, my face pressed up against it as I imagined life in less than 24 hours. Life down there.

As we descended slowly and the overhead lockers wobbled in the turbulence, the Arctic tundra crept closer, now a drab but still icy midsummer brown. I had a bulky video camera wedged conspicuously between my legs. With good intentions of comprehensively documenting the opening stages of this journey, I fumbled for the record button on the back. I stared at the little red light on the front, trying to think of something suitably profound. My mouth opened but nothing came out. I just stared at the lens before replacing the cap and fixing my gaze on the seat in front of me as we bumped onto the huge runway, my normal flight anxiety dwarfed by a greater fear about the forthcoming journey.

This was the service center for the oilfields up here, which accounted for the acres of tarmac and ugly warehouses I could see speeding by, no doubt housing drilling machinery. This was the source of what a huge chunk of the States' gas-guzzling culture depended on. I had been warned that it was a bleak and loveless place, but it was worse than I'd imagined, grey and seemingly void of natural life.

So this was it. Touchdown. It felt like the door to everything I'd known up till now had been closed behind me and locked.

Cold air rushed through the cabin and my brain defaulted to more practical and immediate concerns as seat belts clicked open and signs overhead pinged off. Had the pilot said it was 37°F or 39°F? I couldn't remember, but with only a T-shirt and a thin fleece, the wind bit into me as I passed the smiling cabin crew and walked down the steps onto the tarmac. It was coming from the north, where 1,200 miles away a deep crust of sea ice floated over the North Pole.

Despite the cold, I dawdled towards the tiny terminal building, looking around. To the north on the level horizon, tiny chimneys from the drilling rigs stuck out, with sooty smudges of smoke above them. To the south, the hardy stunted grass poking out of the earth had been scraped away to make room for the Dalton Highway and the oil pipeline that divided the land in two. There was no getting lost on the roads up here; the Dalton – more of a track than a highway – was the only option. The terminal building and collection of drab warehouses were the ugly oasis in this desert.

When my cheeks stung with cold and my hands started numbing, I walked through the double doors wondering what I would do if one of the three boxes of bike equipment had been damaged or gone missing. Simple – it would be my last chance to back out of this journey for respectable reasons. I'd be lying if I said part of me wasn't hoping one of the boxes hadn't made it.

But in the grey waiting area, there they were, all three of them, carefully stacked in the corner awaiting collection. I got out my knife and set to work putting the shiny new tandem and trailer together. I had an hour until the airport closed for the night, and, never having assembled or loaded the set-up before, time was short. As I worked feverishly, putting unfamiliar nuts and tubes in the right combination and reassembling a ridiculously long bicycle, a small crowd of airport staff gathered silently around, clasping cups of coffee and watching the spectacle.

The bags would have to be unpacked and repacked before the contents were properly organised, but there it was: the bike, trailer and all my equipment together as a unit for the first time, propped awkwardly against the only check-in desk. A couple of staff had hung around and waited as I nervously wheeled the 14-foot machine into the daylight. The big-boned man holding the door open handed me a small polystirene box from the canteen. 'Leftovers, no one seemed to want it,' he said in a friendly American drawl, and I thanked him, genuinely grateful for a tiny and normally insignificant bit of dialogue, not to mention the food. I was starving. I hadn't eaten properly all day, and my supplies were supposed to have been delivered to the post office up here. I asked him for directions, and he said that if I hurried I might catch Les Dunbar, the post lady, before she closed up shop for the day.

Leaving the bike outside the airport, I jogged round to the next warehouse and a small door next to a sign reading 'Welcome to Deadhorse, Alaska, the End of the Dalton Highway'. I'd forgotten that Deadhorse was the name of this little industrial settlement near Prudhoe Bay. The cartoon of an upturned horse expiring got twisted in my brain until the horse was a bicycle and a skeletal rider, wheels and skinny legs upturned, frozen in the tundra.

'Well hi there!' a loud, gravelly American voice that I guessed belonged to Les boomed out from behind some shelves in the tiny post office.

'Hello,' I said, my English accent sounding weak in the air. 'My name's Dominic; you haven't got a parcel here for me by any chance?'

I had no idea what I'd do if she didn't have it, but Les rummaged behind the counter and produced a large box.

'You're the cyclist that called a few weeks ago?'

'Yup,' I said, puffing out my chest, trying to look athletic, before I noticed a pinboard behind the counter half full of old postcards and photos, some from tanned, strapping travellers at the end of their journeys, addressed to a Miss Dunbar. Evidently, she was something of a legend: the post lady at the end of the world, a guardian angel to many a stricken traveller over the years, perhaps.

Ripping open the box she'd plonked in front of me and peering inside, I gulped. How was that small pile of foiled packed rations going to last ten days? I must have miscalculated my order back in the comfort of my house, more interested in my flashy new rain gear or sleeping bag than calorie counting.

'Great, that's it!' I said, not feeling great at all.

'Say, why don't you swing by tomorrow for a photo before you head off?'

I left the very welcoming Les Dunbar – the Angel of the North – promising to see her before I headed south the following morning.

It was nearly 9 p.m., and I was running on empty. Opposite my bike, on the other side of a large stretch of dirt, a couple of oil tanker trailers stood idle and dirty in a kind of never-ending parking lot. I cycled, wobbling disconcertingly, towards them and found that they'd shelter me from the worst of the wind, but there was no way I was getting my tent pegs into the stony ground. I cast around and found two old iron girders to anchor my tiny nylon home.

My first encampment of the journey looked pathetic in the shadow of the dirty tankers. The site was grey, mud spattered and depressing, doing very little to buoy the sinking feeling in my stomach. As I prepared to sit down and tuck into the leftover corn-beef hash in the polystirene box, a mangy fox loped silently by, stopping stock-still for a moment to look at the stranger in town before dipping his head and skirting round the tanker and out of sight.

The food was cold, but I gratefully spooned it down as my thoughts drifted keenly away from the surrounding nothingness.

I had done my best to say goodbye to my friends back home and had organised a farewell party at a club in London at the beginning of June, two weeks previously. Touched by how many people came to see me off, I danced happily – though badly – with renewed confidence and high hopes.

I carried on dancing as one by one my friends trickled off home. By the time the club was winding down, I found I was on my own.

I'd foolishly assumed someone would invite me back, but my friends had all disappeared, and with them any prospect of a bed for the night. Stepping into the illuminated night air sober and tired, the doubt and self-pity that I'd danced away encroached once again, and the yawning unknown of my immediate future engulfed me in the dirty streets of London's West End.

I walked off without caring where I ended up, and arrived some time later at St. James's Park, where I crawled into a small patch of uncut grass next to a hedge and lay dozing until the sun coloured the sky over Knightsbridge and the street light behind me clicked off.

However depressing those early morning hours were, St. James's Park had been more inviting than what surrounded me in Deadhorse, Alaska, dirty and for the most part dead.

I scraped the polystyrene clean with my spoon, looked into the lens of my video camera and began to talk.

Why was I doing this if I was so unwilling?

Doubts continued to harass me, and I only had one barely acceptable answer: because I'd planted the seed and dared to dream of the possibilities. It was too late after that; I would risk a life of regret if I didn't try.

I'd always been like that. I suppose it was my mother who instilled it in me. She taught me to climb when I was 12 and in the process opened up a new world for me. But soon after that she died on the way to the Himalayas, where she intended to live out some of her dreams, as she encouraged me to do. She had done what must be the most difficult task for any loving parent and unfurled her protective wing, actively encouraging me to go and explore, come what may.

I remember being allowed to ride in the front seat of the car for the first time when I was eight years old. The handbrake caught my attention as I sat there on the way to see my godmother.

'What would happen if I pulled that?' I piped up inquisitively, looking for something to occupy myself.

My mother looked at it, then looked at me and said, 'I don't know. Why don't you find out?'

I couldn't believe it, expecting a harsh 'Don't touch that!', so I yanked on it, and the car dipped and groaned as the brake dragged and slowed us aggressively until she released it and we carried on. I remember laughing, excited, and for the first time I began to understand her teaching methods.

By the time I was nearly 13, she had taught me as much as I can imagine any parent teaching a child in a lifetime. And then she disappeared in an aeroplane, leaving me to get on with it.

I looked at my watch; it was 10:50 p.m. It was June, and the sky was still the same leaden grey as when I had landed. The sun was nowhere to be seen, but this far north the dark was weeks away from making an appearance. I brushed my teeth and spat the white froth into the dirt before zipping myself into my sleeping bag and shuffling about until I was comfortable, staring up at the green-yellow fabric and listening to the flysheet fluttering in a weak, persistent breeze.

Eight hours later I got up, having been awake for some time trying to find reasons to remain in my tent. The morning was no different from the night before, the same grey light pressing down on the landscape, allowing no room for optimism. Yesterday's depression and worry had not left me, but once up I was keen to try and leave it behind, quickly stuffing my tent and mat into a slightly reorganised pannier bag and cycling off to Les Dunbar's mail room, the trailer wheel juddering disconcertingly and the bags jumping up and down in their brackets over the corrugated surface. The sky seemed to be darkening slightly, but it wasn't raining, nor would it, I hoped. The view was simply oppressive, and whilst the sky was maybe the biggest I'd ever seen – a vast expanse of grey – it seemed uncomfortably close.

After posing for an 'official' photo next to the ominous Deadhorse sign, I was waved off by Les for the first unsteady pedal strokes of my journey. The bike weaved from side to side before I sped up enough to balance and travel in a straight line. It was June 16, 2006, and after months of looking dreamily at maps, my journey had finally grown wheels.

2

In blind hope of company

DAY 1: 0 MILES

I looked back and tried a wave, snatching the handlebar back quickly as the bike lurched across the dirt. That was the last time I looked over my shoulder at Deadhorse, preferring to concentrate on avoiding the larger stones ahead of me. The track was perfectly straight and, without a single deviation, it met the almost convex horizon, forever away. My hands started to tingle as they were bombarded by the judders and rattles resonating through the bike. Every single small sensation was new to me. I was cycling a bike I'd barely ridden before, with a heap of gear I'd failed to test, in a landscape that reminded me of nothing I'd ever seen. But despite my poor preparation, my nerves fell further behind with each yard as pragmatism and the effort of progress took over.

Half an hour later, I almost felt the tiniest bit optimistic – after all, I had actually started to move towards my goal, though the horizon gave nothing away. The sky was the same leaden monotone and the wind was still keen and cold, but it was coming from the north and pushed me gently south, as if it knew I needed the encouragement. Every few hundred yards, I would become wise to another idiosyncrasy of my unusual machine. I could begin to predict how it would react when the front wheel skipped off a stone or the trailer slipped sideways into a pothole. The line I pedalled got slowly straighter as I mastered the art of tandem cycling solo. It wasn't until a nondescript but clearly marked mile 26 that I saw another moving object. An oil tanker heading south

19

overtook, spitting gravel at me as the driver saluted my stupidity with a friendly blast on the horn.

A little way off to my left and hidden well in the drab Arctic tundra, I spotted a small herd of caribou, looking in my direction, ears twitching. I slowed a little to watch them, pleased to have company of sorts, even if conversation was limited. Every time I looked up from the bumpy ride, there they were, necks stretched, peering at me unblinking and following at a safe distance, sometimes running and overtaking me, then sniffing the air and waiting. I talked at them regularly for maybe 5 miles until at last the novelty wore off and my newest friends fell behind to graze some more.

When I next looked back, Deadhorse had disappeared, the warehouses and smoke stacks hidden behind almost indiscernible hummocks in the tundra. The only evidence of industry I could see was the pipeline, built on stilts and snaking its way south with me. Around a million barrels of oil poured their way south each day. Les at the post office had told me it took each litre about eight days to reach the Valdez oil terminal on the coast. I tried to ignore the fact that the oil was going quicker than me. But then I reasoned, I'd go that quickly if I had a multi-billion-dollar industry behind me rather than the 'home improvement' loan I was supposed to be using for a loft conversion. Stopping a while later to rest my unaccustomed hands and buttocks, I clambered onto the huge pipe. Weird, I thought while sitting on the highest thing for miles. Here was one of the world's most important arteries, unguarded yet imposing. The post lady had told me about a local drunk from a community further south who, after weeks of late-night drinking binges and tens of shots from his hunting rifle, had succeeded in holing the pipeline, though no one discovered the leak until weeks later, when hundreds of thousands of litres of oil had polluted the soil and melted the permafrost.

In the afternoon, after I had stopped again for some fairly tasteless ration-pack cheese and biscuits, the monotony was broken by the dust cloud of a small approaching vehicle. A minute or so later a dusty red hatchback pulled over, a little way ahead of me still, and before I wondered who the hell was stopping in this nothingness, I could hear the motor drives of the occupants' cameras whirring away. Tourists

– bingo! I thought to myself as I pulled up alongside, keen to say hello and talk to someone for the first time in five hours.

'Hey there,' I said, smiling. 'Where are you headed?'

It was a stupid question, not just because this road only led to where I'd come from but also because the couple smiling and nodding attentively at me clearly didn't understand a word. My heart sank when I realised that any wholesome chat was out of the question – these people were Japanese and, though keen to converse, their English extended to 'herro', 'yes' and 'thank you', and not always in any logical order.

Trying to salvage something from this encounter, I pointed to my video camera and made the charades sign, rotating my wrist and holding an imaginary camera lens. After a minute of gesturing, the beaming man nodded attentively, took my camera and brandished it enthusiastically as I cycled 100 yards up the road to cycle past again. Given the Japanese stereotype, I figured this guy would certainly be video savvy, so I was surprised to see him apparently shooting some quite detailed footage of the red hatchback parked up in the dirt as I cycled slowly passed. I made another U-turn in the dirt with my ungainly machine and rejoined the couple. My camera, like a trophy, was proudly presented to me, still recording and pointing at the ground. I thanked them before packing my camera and cycling slowly away waving while they kept me in the cross hairs of their own snapping cameras.

At 10 p.m., it was my growling stomach that forced me to a halt, my brain having no time cues in the same grey sky as the morning. I had covered 55 miles. Not bad for a breaking-in day, I thought, and anyway, what's the hurry? I settled down to cook the first of my dehydrated rations after collecting water from the river that meandered shallow, never far from the road.

After pouring the pitiful amount of food out – Mexican rice and chicken that looked a little like dry porridge – I read the back of the foil packet. Nine hundred calories? I quickly looked at the equally Lilliputian breakfast and lunch packets and found that in order to reach Fairbanks – eight days and 400 miles away – without restocking, I'd need to subsist on a pitiful 2,300 calories a day. That's about the amount I'd need simply to survive my old mundane office job, and even then I'd sneak out for a pork pie mid afternoon. Shit, I thought as I scraped my small pan as clean as I could get it. Compulsively greedy and ignoring my instinct to save what I had, I broke into the next day's biscuits.

I camped on an access track about 100 yards from the Dalton Highway, used to service the pipeline. As I packed away my compact gas stove, the sound of a truck travelling north behind me slowly died away, taking the light breeze with it. The tent's door flapped lazily behind me, and a mosquito whined close to my ear, causing me to slap irritably at my face and peer at my hand for evidence of a confirmed kill. Soon there would be too many I thought, and begrudgingly crawled into the tent to write the first day in my journal.

A little later, half in my sleeping bag, I stared up at the criss-cross nylon ceiling, letting memories of the immediate past and good company swill around in my mind until I dozed off, hands and bum vibrating with the aftershock of the bumpy road.

The next morning I woke early, the tent fabric bright with light. The sun was shining for the first time so far, and the depressing scene became immediately attractive. Looking to the south, I could see a tiny bumpy line on the horizon – the Brooks Range – the first hills, and with them the first real test. Quite safely assuming I wouldn't have a stoker – the name given to the person on the second seat – I would be there in two days, three at the outside if I fell short of my modest daily goal of 50 miles. There, on the Atigun Pass, I'd find out how manageable this giant machine would be to pedal uphill solo.

That morning, the vibrating monotony was interrupted once more by a vehicle approaching from the south. An old red Chevy pick-up sidled up next to me on the empty road and, once the dust cloud had cleared, the nearside window was rolled down by an old man with a white moustache and a Stetson. Over his far shoulder, I could see a little boy sitting in the passenger seat, the seatbelt tucked under his armpit to stop it biting into his neck.

'Well hello there,' he said, his friendly face reminding me slightly of Murdoch from *The A-Team*. 'Boy, you must be on some adventure!' he continued, seemingly speaking as much for the little boy's benefit as for his own.

The old man and his grandson were on a 'once-in-a-lifetime adventure' he told me, having driven up from the States, over 2,000 miles away.

'Don't get many opportunities to go on a trip with your own grandson. You gotta grab 'em,' he said, clenching his fist in front of him. He'd waited nearly his whole life to make this journey, and I got the feeling as we talked he was pleased to have found someone taking the plunge with a bit more time in hand.

'Man, you must be a little thirsty or hungry or something doing all that pedlin'.' He got down and opened the tailgate of the truck. I looked at his features as he produced a small coolbox full of sugary refreshments. He had sharp blue eyes full of energy and enthusiasm, his moustache and hair were a bright white, and his broad smile revealed equally white teeth. His smile – and this is less common than you might think – really seemed to suggest he was happy.

After I had gratefully retrieved a Gatorade from the box, he held out his hand. 'Well, we better be gettin' on up to the end of the world,' he said, still smiling, and as quickly as I'd met them they had disappeared north in a cloud of windblown dust. I couldn't shake that smile from my thoughts. It made me smile, too, and I pedalled off with the image in my head of his grandson staring at me, mouth open, from over the truck's back seat.

Long after the unlikely couple had disappeared and after another oil truck had kicked up stones that narrowly missed my unprotected head (I'd got lazy with my helmet halfway through the first day), I was still thinking about that last conversation. The cycling became easier as my mind became absorbed in the meeting, in their journey, in a very brief period of camaraderie and companionship. As my journey continued I would find my 'positivity meter' creeping a tiny bit further out of the red with each snippet of new friendly curiosity. For a few brief minutes as I pedalled slowly away from those fleeting conversations, I didn't feel so alone; the glass was half full, and I sensed the company of at least a handful of other people in this barren wilderness.

TAKE A SEAT

For ten, fifteen minutes at a time over the next few hours I zoned out of my immediate situation and into another, daydreaming about cycling along Mexican beaches dripping with sun and coconuts, meeting other altogether different people, or sitting round a campfire with a friend sharing a beer. But whenever I hit a large stone or the wind forced me to don another layer of clothes, I was back at the beginning, a long way away from the nearest piña colada, let alone Mexico. Looking around me, the palm trees would melt away, my companions vanish, and the tundra would once again become starkly oppressive.

During those first three days, the Brooks Range slowly crept closer, and on the evening of the third, approaching midnight the mountain's shadows fell on my camp.

Then it was as if the period of grace was over. The rolling hummocks became steeper, and the troughs between them sometimes had small streams running along them. I realised at this point that my food was running out. I'd been consuming it steadily at a rate of about 3,500 calories a day just to keep going, and after each meal my body would crave more. This worry nagged at me as the headwind increased and the road steepened. My speed would drop from a pathetic 13 miles an hour in the buffeting headwind on the flat to a snail's pace 4 or 6 if I was lucky, as I toiled up innocuous-looking angles feeling hopelessly underpowered. I could feel my temper creeping slowly out of its box until, halfway up the sixth hill, I stopped abruptly and bellowed into the wind. There was no satisfying echo; the wind sucked the sound north and I let my temper bubble over. There was nothing within arm's reach to grab and throw into the dirt. Instead I screamed out again, feeling my face redden and a vein in my forehead pulse.

'For fuck's SAKE!' I said loudly, before regaining some degree of composure and looking down the road, seeing it disappear as it topped the small hill that I knew would be followed by another, and another, and probably another after that.

I lost my temper several more times on those hummocks, sulking like a spoiled child then pedalling off again. No trucks stopped to inquire what the hell I was doing, in fact I didn't see a single one, so I couldn't solve my food problem by begging scraps off a driver. But late in the afternoon, and before thoughts of camping entered my mind, I saw a pick-up parked up on a small service track half a mile ahead of me. It must, I thought, belong to pipeline service engineers, or maybe scientists based at a field station somewhere in the tundra. As I drew closer, I formulated a plan. Every time I saw a parked vehicle, I could leave a note.

I leaned my bike against the large hood of the truck, opened the box attached to my handlebars and tore out a blank page from my journal.

> HELLO, I AM A CYCLIST WHO IS TRAVELLING
> SOUTH ON A TANDEM BICYCLE.

I stopped writing and wondered whether I should go into any kind of explanation as to why I was on my own on my tandem. In case the recipient might think I was joking, I kept it simple.

> IF YOU SEE ME, PLEASE STOP AND SAY HELLO. I
> AM SHORT OF FOOD AND WOULD GLADLY TAKE
> ANYTHING YOU MAY NOT NEED. THANK YOU!
> DOMINIC THE CYCLIST

Then, given that the reason for toting around this ridiculously long and overweight machine was to pick up strangers for a ride, I added:

> P.S. IF YOU KNOW ANYONE WHO WANTS TO PEDAL
> SOUTH ON A BIKE, I HAVE A SPARE SEAT!

That should do it, I thought, as I lifted the windscreen wiper and laid the note underneath. Then, looking up at the sky and thinking that rain might ruin my message, I tried the door. The latch clicked and the door creaked rustily open. I dropped the note on the dirty leather seat, pushing the door closed quietly, hopeful I'd see truck and driver within half an hour or so. Getting stuck into the next short hill minutes later, I looked forward to what would hopefully be the first meeting of the day.

But the truck never came, and I didn't see another vehicle until the evening while I was sitting outside my tent wondering whether to have the risotto or Mexican rice. An oil tanker rolled along the now sunlit road about half a mile from my campsite on the banks of a river. I got out my harmonica while the stove spluttered and roared. Blowing a few chords, I felt self-conscious in the silence, the wind having dropped to nothing, as it seemed to do in the evenings. I needed some practice before I could play anything that didn't offend anyone, and I packed it away again, deciding instead to write up my journal – a discipline that I figured might pleasantly distract me during lonely evenings – and lounge in the comfy moccasins my ex had made me, while enjoying the low, warming sun.

I felt a long way from my temper tantrum earlier in the day in the cold, maddening headwind, but looking to my right I saw the real mountains less than 10 miles away. The road contoured round the base of the mountains and disappeared around a large foothill, leaving me to imagine the severity of the next day's ascent. I'd eyed the Atigun Pass warily on the map. The first big obstacle.

'If you can pedal up that, you'll be all right further south,' I remembered a friend who had travelled this route telling me back home. *If* I can pedal up that, I thought anxiously as the sun edged the mountain tops in gold and left me in the shade.

By morning, the wind had returned with a new-found enthusiasm, ripping into the tent from what, as far as I was concerned, was the wrong direction. I crawled outside to see clouds gathering near the mountain tops. Back on the Dalton, after slogging my way up a small hill, I turned back to see the last two days of the journey etching a line in the carpet of tundra to the north.

At about 10 a.m., once I'd rounded the base of the hill, I saw what I'd been dreading. The road snaked away to the head of the valley and, cutting back on itself, climbed steeply up to a notch in the ridge line. The clouds were low, but I could see streaks of snow in the high gullies where the sun couldn't reach it. Just the sight of it caused me to collapse in the dirt, letting the bike fall heavily on its side. I got up again quickly, unpacked my stove and found a mossy crevice nearby to retreat to as the odd raindrop flecked my jacket. After coaxing a flame out of my blackening stove, I retrieved one of the few remaining foil food packets without looking at the contents. Fat windblown drops of water hissed on the stove's heat reflector as the rain fell more heavily.

I let myself escape this misery at least mentally as I thought back to my childhood when, on walks with my headstrong and independent mother, I had had a similar feeling of being unable to continue. I used to sit down on the footpath and fiddle with a perishing edge of my boots, my mother striding ahead and ignoring my feeble cries of 'Wwwaaaaaiiiiit!!!'

For less than a minute, I would sulk, perhaps cry a little, until I realised she wasn't coming to carry me. Then I would groan, stand up again, maybe ripping some grass out of the turf in outrage, and stamp heavily off in pursuit, catching up of course, eventually. I'd shout at my mother, 'Why didn't you wait for me?!' with that look of infuriated disbelief that only a defiant six year old can have. She would smile, take my hand, and we'd head off once more after some chocolate. Everything would be all right again.

No one was going to carry me up this hill either, I knew that, but I pouted and groaned all the same as I stirred the rice. I ate and crouched over the stove as the flame weakened and died, trying to profit from what little warmth it afforded. Then I picked the bike up with difficulty and continued into the wind and rain, which had taken no notice of my small pity party.

I set myself targets in order to coerce myself along. 'Cycle to that small marker post and then you can rest,' I'd tell myself. When I reached it, I'd set a new target without stopping. In that way I progressed slowly round the final sweeping bend to the switchback where the dirt ramped up five degrees for the ascent. I stopped for a breather and a quick painful look uphill, but leaning into the pedals a minute later I stopped abruptly. With no partner sitting behind me, my rear wheel was so far from any significant weight that it spun and skittered, losing traction as I tried to pedal. Even pedalling delicately I'd advanced only a yard or two before the wheel spun and I jolted to a standstill. It took ten minutes and 50 or 60 yards of stop–start progress for me to realise I couldn't climb the hill like this. But my anger and frustration had now given way to pragmatism, and I leaned the bike against the barrier while I thought about the 200-pound, three-wheeled problem.

I tried strapping the trailer's contents on top of the rear pannier bags, hoping the extra weight might do the trick. It didn't. It was time to start pushing.

With one hand pulling at the seat post and the other pushing at the handlebars, I moved off, my shoes now slipping on the road surface as I strained forward inches at a time. The rear handlebars dug uncomfortably into my back, and I would catch my ankles on the rear pedals every time my feet skidded from under me.

I began to see red for the second time that day as I leaned the bike back against the barrier only 6 yards further up hill. It dawned on me painfully, after removing the rear pedals and handlebars and trying to push once more, that my equipment and my bike were not going to reach the top of this hill together. After experimenting, I found that while the straps bit uncomfortably into my shoulders I could carry the trailer bag on my back and, using the bungee cords, secure the smaller panniers, on my front. Head down, I plodded slowly to the second switchback, sweating heavily. I looked down on my bare-looking bike about 50 vertical yards below me and gauged I was a little over halfway to the top. Fifteen minutes later I was there, standing on top of the Atigun Pass, with those streaks of snow I'd seen earlier now ending at my feet and arcing up to the little rocky summits above. I wanted to sit down, but I just dumped the bags and headed straight back down for the second load. I was still, despite days on the tundra, in my urban mindset, nervous about leaving the bike lest someone should ride away on it. With hundreds of empty square miles now laid out behind it, that worry seemed suddenly ridiculous.

It took me 20 minutes to shuttle the rest of my luggage to the summit, then I ran back to the bike and trailer, now empty apart from the handlebar box containing my wallet, MP3 player and other valuables, as well as my map and compass.

Moving the bike a few yards, to a less gravelly patch of road, I was able to ride again. The rear wheel still skidded occasionally, but I could control it now and pedalled sensitively up, round the last switchback, to reunite with my small cache of equipment at the top. I slumped on the handlebars, breathing hard, before looking up and realising that the skies had cleared, the spitting rain had stopped and the wind was no longer testing my patience.

This time, after leaning the bike against my bags, I sat down on a mound of soil and snow to take in my new surroundings. My view both to the north and south was uninterrupted for more than 100 miles, with the Brooks Range walling me in to the east and west. It was like sitting in a notch on a wall between two worlds. To the north, the land stretched away flat, grey-brown with only the pipeline, the road and a shallow river breaking the monotony. To the south, looking down, I could see the first stunted spruce trees appear and turn gradually into a spiky dark-green carpet broken by a smoother, less rocky Dalton Highway than the one at my back. The landscape looked warmer and friendlier, and the third dimension of the evergreens was a welcome change. Even from up here, I felt less cold just looking at the road ahead. The mountains seemed to form a barrier that prevented the bitter and monotonous force of the Arctic from pushing further south. Despite the gargantuan effort of getting my steed to the top of a hill, and despite the knowledge that those hills would be dwarfed by others further south, I felt a little hopeful, a little like I might not throw in the towel for a day or two longer.

For only the second time on this journey I reloaded the bike, took a few gulps of water and trod lightly on the pedals, looking forward to the long slope down towards the trees. But as the track began to drop I heard the growling of a vehicle approaching, and a second or two later I could see a small truck or jeep climbing up to the col from the south. I coasted at walking pace, holding off on the descent for a minute, not able to resist the possibility of talking to someone.

The engine throbbed like something twice its size as it reached the col, and we mirrored each other, circling in the dirt and coming to a stop like two mismatched wrestlers.

I could see from where I was that it was an old Land Cruiser missing doors, windows and roof but with an axe strapped to the bumper, like something out of Desert Storm. The occupants too, all three of them, fitted the image, jumping down off the truck, dusting themselves off and removing their goggles, leaving dust-framed panda eyes on their faces.

I pulled up alongside and beamed with happiness at being face to face with someone, anyone!

'Hi there,' I offered up as an introduction, hoping they spoke English and weren't planning on using their axe on me.

'Howaryadoin?' the nearest said, sporting an impressive handlebar moustache and a USA bandanna. 'Nice rig,' he added, looking at the full 14 feet of bicycle I'd just finished dragging up the hill.

I introduced myself to Charlie, Jimbo and Billy, shaking hands and enjoying it. These boys, I learned over the next few minutes, had travelled from New York down into Mexico, then on up to here, where, once they'd arrived at the end of the world, they'd hightail it back for the 4th of July celebrations in New York.

Compared to me, that made them veterans in the world of overland travel, and despite being younger, they looked gnarled and weathered by the sun and wind. Then the boys asked about my journey – what I was carrying, where I was going and why I had a small hunting knife, easily accessible, strapped to the top tube of the bike.

Mmm, why had I chosen to put my knife on show within arm's reach? Truth was that while it was handy to have something to cut inner tubes, cheese and shoelaces, there wasn't a good reason other than I thought it looked good, perhaps a sign that I was ready to defend myself should the necessity arise. I guess I knew that there was nothing to defend myself against. If a bear took a dislike to me I'd be better off with a broom or a prayer book. Still, there it was, and I liked it.

After I mentioned my food shortage, Jimbo wandered to the back of the truck and rummaged around in their bags, returning with a few dusty beers and a large can of soup. Barely wiping the dust off the beers we celebrated our meeting, and I gratefully stashed the soup in my front pannier for later.

Then I surfaced from the novelty of conversation and came to my senses, remembering the dead weight of the bicycle and the pristine stoker's saddle.

'Any of you boys want to ride south with me?' I asked, not hopeful since the boys were headed north. But Charlie looked at the others.

'I'd kill to get out the back of that truck for a while,' he said, my face instantly brightening at his words.

'How about we meet up on our way south?' he continued, the idea now being seriously considered. Thinking it through we realised we'd both have to visit Coldfoot, a tiny community home to the only gas station this side of Fairbanks. I'd need to stop to beg for extra food and gas for the stove while they would need to fill up on diesel – it seemed as good a place as any to meet up in the evening of the next day.

'Brilliant!' I blurted out, feeling childishly excited. I wanted to jump up and down and hug them, being so close to making my stupid plan a reality. Days on the road felt like a lifetime, and I was dying for some company, an ear to chew off at least.

I saluted the crew as I headed south, already looking forward to meeting again the following day. Smiling to myself I coasted fast down the mountain into a greener, warmer land. Distracted by the sight of a public toilet, perhaps the most northerly on the continent, I missed the first stunted little spruce tree I'd been told to look out for. But sitting happily on the surprisingly plush outhouse loo, I savoured the novelty of perching on a throne rather than squatting on tired legs in the tundra.

The clouds and the cold northerly wind were left behind the wall of the Brooks Range, and sitting next to my little green tent on the banks of a placid river I was content. I got my harmonica out and played for a little, this time making an effort to sound like those lonely cowboys I'd seen in films sitting next to a campfire. I warmed the soup the boys had given me, not bothering to pour it out of the can into a pot and singeing the label that told me it was super chunky chicken and vegetable. That, I thought, sounded manly enough to sustain me at least until the brown rice and carbonara that followed a few minutes later. I had given up caring about conserving my food, seriously hoping I'd be able to scrounge some more at the isolated petrol station only a long day's ride away.

31

The trees changed the feeling of the road completely. They blocked the evening sun and threw their long ragged shadows across the highway. The spruce harboured animals, too, and for the first time on my journey the air was alive with insects and the rustling of rodents. As the evening drew on, above the whine of hungry mosquitoes I heard the throaty, almost tuneful, conversation of a pair of ravens nearby. It felt somehow more comfortable now I was surrounded by more than just the wind pestering my tent. Briefly, as I lay there, I thought about bears, an animal I'd have to be aware of up here, especially since berries – their normal diet – had been scarce that summer.

Perhaps I was a little too laid back, perhaps not – I was quite used to these hulks since living and working as a trail guide at an isolated lake in northern Canada some years earlier. Either way, this new element interested me without causing me any real worry and I drifted off to sleep easily, only ensuring beforehand that my food was a few feet away from the tent. Tomorrow, I thought dreamily, was going to be good. Company at last. All I had to do was reach Coldfoot, another 80 miles south.

At about 4 p.m. the next day, in an area of highway where the trees on one side had given way to scrubby tundra once again, I sat heavily on the road, starving but with nothing other than a few small bags of rice to eat and no spare water to cook them in. My strength had sweated steadily out of me and leaked away through my pedals.

I only faintly registered something approaching from the north, preferring to hang my head and let sweat drip off the end of my nose. As it got close, though, I looked up to see it was a white minivan that 100 yards away seemed to be slowing down, the cloud of dust keeping pace and then enveloping the van as it stopped a few yards away from me. I stood up, most of the vehicle's dust cloud sticking to my sweaty face as the driver, clad in a khaki shirt and jeans, got out and greeted me.

'Hi zere!' he said, smiling, in a thick French accent.

'Hi,' I said, wiping the dust off my mouth. Through the tinted windows of the van I could see a small collection of elderly faces, cared-for and clean-looking, smiling out at me. A little hope elbowed its way over my exhaustion. Hope based around one little word . . . food.

The man introduced himself as Patrick, a tour guide. I shook his hand weakly, and wasted no more time on pleasantries.

'I don't suppose you have a small bag of trail mix or some old bread you can spare, do you?' I said. 'I'm hungry,' I added, as if it wasn't obvious.

'I'm sure we 'ave somesing in 'ere,' Patrick said encouragingly, and poked his head through the van window, speaking a few words to the immaculate tourists brandishing cameras on the other side of the windscreen. Seconds later, I swear I could hear cooing like a gaggle of aunts worrying about how thin I'd got, and within a minute bunches of grapes, bags of berries, nuts and a small pot of chocolate mousse were thrust out of the window. Evidently these kindly pensioners had had a whip round! Dribbling slightly, I placed my booty down in the dust and thanked the occupants, who seemed pleased to have come into such close contract with a bona fide grubby traveller. It was easy to forget during long, lonely hours in the saddle that my ungainly charge and by now dishevelled appearance cut a novel picture for those wooshing past in air-conditioned boxes for their 'Arctic experience' day trip.

I managed, just, to wait for the dust to be kicked up by the van and my saviours to disappear south before, like a shipwreck survivor, tucking into the fresh berries and bananas, all good intentions to ration the goodies vaporising in a feeding frenzy. Five minutes later, I sat in the same place feeling a little bloated, the dust around me now littered with banana skins, plastic wrappers and cherry pips. Despite a severe bellyache, I felt happy again, and with the exception of a few rushed and unscheduled stops in the bushes, I progressed smoothly to arrive in Coldfoot as the lengthening shadows clouded with mosquitoes and the sun painted its line along the tops of the shadowy trees.

3

Four legs good, two legs bad

DAY 5: 250 MILES

'Mate, what the heck is that??'

'Did someone fall off?'

'You hoping to get lucky?'

I leaned the bike against the wooden siding listening to the shouts of a rough-looking bunch of workers clutching stubby bottles of Bud. They beckoned me over, and I gratefully sat down on a cheap plastic chair to join what sounded like an Antipodean drinking circle. After a record 71 miles in one day I was exhausted, but with a yearning to talk overcoming my fatigue I headed straight for what looked like the bar. Trucks sat idling in the Coldfoot clearing, and generators chugged away behind tatty prefabricated buildings. This no-frills trailer park was home to a small number of staff, pipeline workers and perhaps, during the high season, a tiny trickle of tourists.

I sank into the chair, frivolously ample in comparison to my sweaty saddle, and listened to the Kiwis' story (I worked out they were New Zealanders before they told me, when one of them said something about 'potato chups'). They were electricians, over to work on the oil-pumping stations here in the middle of nowhere. It was difficult to distinguish them from their North American counterparts, since they too were big, stubbly, brash and friendly, with filthy baseball caps sometimes perched at a jaunty angle on their heads.

A beer landed in front of me without me having to ask. Never has a cheap American bottle of filth tasted so sweet. The first barely touched the sides, the second did but only briefly, and a few minutes later I sat in a contented, though salty and glassy-eyed, stupor. Only a little later, standing at the bar, I barely had to mention the word food before an elderly couple sitting at a rough wood table looked over and offered me their plates; they were full, they said. So, after my liquid refreshment, I tucked into the juicy, fatty leftovers of a steak with mashed potato with my wallet still wedged in my pocket. I paid in a way, but only by answering the questions fired at me about my journey.

'Yours is the rig out there with that trailer?'

'Uh huh.'

'You left someone behind?' came the inevitable response, followed by a smattering of appreciative chuckles from those listening in. I made a mental note to get used to that quip – it would doubtless be used again. An old man pointed out to me the same evening that Harley Davidson made a T-shirt occasionally seen on old pot-bellied bikers that reads on the back: 'If you can read this, the bitch fell off.' He suggested I got hold of one. I thanked him for his advice and didn't bother asking him how many people he thought might be discouraged from riding with me if they had to stare at that slogan.

After buying a round for the Kiwis, I heard the throb I'd been looking forward to – the dull, mature growl of an old truck.

Stepping out onto the small deck, I saw the dusty Land Cruiser roll in and park up, the brakes squeaking as they jerked to a stop next to the tandem. The boys jumped down and we slapped each other's backs and recounted our respective stories since the Atigun Pass. They'd stripped bare to swim in the Arctic Ocean. I'd begged berries off elderly tourists. They'd occasionally seen my tire tracks in the loose earth. I'd cherished every last chunky little morsel of the soup they'd given me. It felt good to share stories with people who already knew at least something about me.

Before Jimbo, Charlie and Billy gave the evening a second wind, I fixed my food deficit problem. I persuaded the initially frosty head of the little kitchen to sell me some raw materials: onions, cheese – a huge block of it to replace the fat I had already lost – rice, pasta, cookies, apples, tomatoes, porridge oats and sugar. It all added up, and the bag threatened to rip as I carried my booty back to the bike now parked next to the boys' jeep on a patch of grass at the far side of the clearing.

Once I'd rejoined the circle, the boys had of course succeeded in hijacking the redneck drinking session. Charlie and I talked, slurring heavily, about leaving after breakfast the next day while Billy and Jimbo waited at Coldfoot for much-needed diesel to be delivered. Kinda funny, I thought after I'd crawled clumsily into my tent and struggled to find the right end of my sleeping bag, that in one of the few oil hotspots in the world, diesel was hard to come by.

I was woken not by the sun or the heavy breathing of a bear sniffing the half-pound of cheddar stashed in my tent vestibule but by the persistent droning of the Coldfoot generator. It thudded in my skull like a hammer. My right ankle hurt, my mouth was crusty and, wiping a white streak of dribble from my cheek, I remembered the Budweisers.

I crawled out of my cocoon and groggily felt my way to the dripping shower room in the tired, faded building the Kiwis had laughingly called the hotel. Despite the shower room resembling something out of a refugee camp, I enjoyed the effortlessness of washing under a weak stream of tepid water. Up until now, I had taken advantage of every frigid river I camped by, where I'd wash as quickly as possible before my balls retracted irreversibly.

Billy was lighting a fire when I got back and before long had cooked peppered ham, eggs and pancakes and stood at the ready with a large plastic bottle of syrup. Squatting next to the fire, my slight nausea was replaced by greedy hunger, but heavy snoring from within the yellow dome tent next to the jeep told me Charlie still had a way to go before breakfast.

'Up and at 'em!' I shouted enthusiastically, shaking the thin nylon before stripping the bike of anything the boys could carry until we met up in the evening. It was June 21, my sister's birthday and the summer solstice, and while Stonehenge was a long shot, we had agreed that we would reconvene between 50 and 70 miles south, hopefully finding a creek to camp by, and hold a solstice celebration.

Charlie made his debut wearing his US flag bandanna and, stood next to the bike's back seat awaiting instructions.

'Get on,' I said, not quite sure how to initiate a tandem cycling lesson. He did what I said, after which I issued further instructions. 'Put both your feet on the pedals.' He did that too, though tentatively, instinctively wanting to touch the ground. With the weight on the back, the bike suddenly awoke and my arms struggled for a few seconds to stabilise it as I edged onto my seat and put one foot up on the pedal.

The boys cheered as we cycled off, zigzagging disconcertingly across the grass until equilibrium was established. There was power going through the back pedals, which felt good, though my arms began to work harder to balance the increased load subtly bobbing from side to side. After an acclimatisation lap of the jeep, Charlie and I set a course for the Dalton Highway, pedalling across the dusty parking lot to the junction, turning right behind a stand of spruce trees and back onto the long strip of dry mud.

This was, I guessed, how a tandem should feel. We were travelling a couple of miles an hour faster than I would on my own, and I could feel Charlie moving independently, making the bike shift and flex a fraction.

We talked as we cycled, a novelty I couldn't imagine tiring of. Charlie was a carpenter who spoke with the friendly, confident twang of a New Yorker. He and the boys had been on their travels for months. We talked about his home and his journey and adventures. It was rolling their Land Cruiser on its roof in Mexico that had given it its stripped-down look, Charlie explained, knowing I'd taken a shine to the lack of doors and roof on their vehicle, as well as the skull-and-crossbones licence plate. I had comparatively little to say with regard to my own voyage. It had, after all, begun less than a week before. But that didn't stop me talking – I was in 'transmit' mode after a week of almost constant silence.

A system soon developed whereby we'd rest every 8 miles or so to allow blood to flow back into Charlie's arse. The hard, brand-new leather saddle was taking its toll on a bottom used to the comparative comfort of the Land Cruiser's back seat.

Time seemed to go by more quickly with company. By the time we'd exhausted one topic of conversation, we were somewhere else. The carpet of trees on either side was occasionally now interrupted by a lake backed by steep valley sides, and sometimes the pipeline would appear again from a culvert or behind a stand of spruce, which were bigger now. A heavy cloud sometimes emptied on us, and then the wind harried our clothes until we were dry again, just in time for the next short downpour.

We stopped briefly 30 miles south of Coldfoot and the jeep hadn't caught up with us. We were more than halfway to our solstice celebration, I said confidently, where a fry-up and a fine bottle of Scotch were on the cards. The words caused Charlie's face to brighten visibly, allowing him to forget his throbbing arse for a second, and before long we were off again, my arms still learning how to counteract the weaving effect of a second rider. But I was happy, really happy, that Charlie was there. I had company, and the tandem idea no longer seemed as stupid as it had done at the windswept Deadhorse Airport.

Over the next 20 miles, stops became increasingly frequent to allow the worsening pain in Charlie's backside to subside a fraction before we eventually rolled over Bonanza Creek, a suitable place, we thought, for a mid-summer party and a respectable 50 miles from where we had started.

Leaving the Union Jack from the trailer waving idly on the roadside to indicate our presence to the other two in the truck, we rolled the bike down the embankment and parked up in the grass on the banks of the creek. Almost immediately, the bugs clocked us. A discordant whining chorus broke the calm, windless serenity. The sound, and the irritating little bites, caused us to swipe at our ears as we unpacked gear and busied ourselves with a small fire. With the tent up, I turned from laying out my sleeping mat to see Charlie with everything but his head obscured by thick billowing smoke caused by a fresh green spruce bough on the fire. Standing in the dense smoke was the only possible way to keep the mosquitoes at bay.

Keen to test the waters, I took out my fishing line and fly, lovingly tied by my grandfather some 40 years previously, and wandered over to the shadows of the bridge. Grayling swam lazily in the slight current, staying out of the sun. I carefully lowered the fly onto the water, barely causing a ripple, and drifted it past the fish. I tried it dozens of times, and each time they couldn't have shown less interest.

'Must be too hot,' I reasoned weakly and wandered back to the safety of the smoke with perhaps 30 more bloody bites on my arms and legs to show for my failed hunter-gatherer effort.

It had been easy-going with two pairs of legs and a lightened load, but sitting at Bonanza Creek at 6 p.m. with only a little food, no stove and nothing to do made me wish I'd at least brought my harmonica on this stretch.

Every so often we'd shut up suddenly, ears pricked, listening to the sound of an approaching vehicle.

'It's coming from the north,' we'd say optimistically, then, 'Hmmm, sounds like them!', only to hang our heads in disappointment when a white tourist van or pipeline truck rattled over the bridge and out of sight. Silence would fall again and we'd chat half-heartedly, each thinking about the tasty treats, liquid refreshments and the small bottle of barely diluted DEET in the Land Cruiser.

The sun was getting lower and shone directly through the flag still hanging, now limply, from the sign on the bridge. By 10 p.m., we'd walked a good way down the warm asphalt and back a few times, wondering why the boys were so late. Were they actually extracting the diesel themselves, we joked, trying to hide a growing hunger-fuelled frustration.

At 10:34 p.m. there was a growling and then the unmistakable sound of the Land Cruiser. By the time it rushed over the bridge we were up on our feet waving at the boys, who were be-goggled and scanning the road intently. Seconds later, dust climbed slowly in the sunlight then fell lazily to earth as we ran out onto the road, still waving frantically.

'They'll be back in a second,' said Charlie, whose face said something else entirely, mouth open, brow furrowed. Soon the noise had disappeared and we stood there like kids who'd just missed the bus but didn't want to admit it.

'Yeah, they'll be back in a bit,' I replied, staring in disbelief at the flag on the bridge. 'Fifty to seventy miles we said, so they'll realise and come back looking.' It dawned on me as as I said it that if they didn't, not only would we be lacking any Scotch – a very serious predicament to be in on such an occasion – but we wouldn't have any food either, other than a pathetically small bag of nuts.

As the blacktop remained silent under the deep yellow sun, Charlie and I kissed goodbye to hope of more food or a tipple that night and retreated into the mosquito-free confines of the tent. For the first time there were two in my tent. It was cozy, with no room for visitors or even bags. But despite this, the heavy snoring I'd heard that morning resumed within minutes.

The boys didn't greet us in the morning. No sign of one of Billy's fry-ups, only a fresh squadron of mosquitoes that darkened the fly mesh as I yawned and looked outside. There's little in this world that destroys my will to get out of bed more than the knowledge that, rather than spending a few semi-conscious minutes sleepily poking the remains of the campfire and watching fish jump in the creek, I will be scratching myself raw thanks to a bunch of whiny little bloodsuckers. Lying there contemplating my imminent fate, my right Achilles tendon throbbed. Feeling blindly into a tent pocket, I found my wash kit and crunched down some tablets from a small bottle of painkillers, too lazy to reach for my water. I'd forgotten the shooting pain I'd experienced three days before every time my foot slipped while pushing the bike up the pass, my heel punching against the rear pedals.

I crawled reluctantly out of the tent and let the mesh flap hang open, hoping the bugs would prefer the taste of Charlie as I hurriedly rolled up my mat and packed the few belongings I had taken out of my pack the evening before. Charlie emerged minutes later, scratching his puffy face, and after a small handful of peanuts each, we pedalled off, unsure how far that meagre breakfast would take us. We were both hungry and in a bad mood. My ankle hurt, and when I stopped to massage it I found it to be swollen and lumpy. But there was little I could do out here, and we carried on in the heat, pedalling more and more slowly, our bodies burning whatever they could to keep us moving. Charlie's arse saw to it that we were now resting twice as much as before, and on the fifth stop, Charlie lifted his tender rump off the saddle, groaning as he did so. A heat haze banded the gravel ahead of us and a slight breeze kept the mosquitoes at a safe distance as Charlie exhaled heavily. 'Maaann, I feel like an abused porn star!' he said as if he meant it. Finding enough energy to chuckle then cough dryly, I was grateful for the deadening effects that ten years in school and university rowing crews had had on my own arse. The leather saddles on the bike were hard, but not as hard as the thin, uncushioned wood laminate seats in those boats.

Running on nothing but fumes we cycled a never-ending 12 miles before arriving at a sign, obviously designed for those coming from the south.

WELCOME TO THE ARCTIC CIRCLE, it read, and off to our left the trees unveiled a collection of large buses and pristine tourists wandering around with sun hats and cameras. They were like carbon copies of the ones I'd seen in Patrick's van. There was no need to say anything; we both knew that begging was at this point a necessity and cycled with renewed hope in the direction of a small herd of snap-happy old-age pensioners. Charlie and I hung back on the outskirts of the gathering. Despite feeling faint, we paused, sensing something special was going to happen at any moment. I was surprised that our dishevelled appearance and even what must have been a fairly ripe odour went unnoticed, since the crowd's eyes were glued to their tour leader, who was rummaging around in the luggage compartment of the bus. With a triumphant look he emerged with some rolled-up material and walked round to the other side of the group next to a bigger sign that also welcomed them to the Arctic Circle.

He unrolled the cheap and faded rubber-backed red carpet with a small flourish and straightened it up. In the middle, running across it, was a cracked and creased strip of duct tape.

'Right,' he said, with an air of anticipation, 'I want you to line up and get ready, folks! One by one you're gonna walk across this white line.

'You might want to give your camera to a friend so they can snap you crossing the Arctic Circle,' he added, smiling like he was letting these aging sightseers into a state secret. There was a flood of activity as people lined up and hurriedly handed out cameras like munitions boxes in an unexpected bout of trench warfare. Sun hats repositioned, glasses put away, and they were off, one by one crossing the tape and pausing in mid stride for a photo, the rest of the tour group cheering good-naturedly.

Charlie and I looked on with dry mouths open. 'How are we gonna get out of the Arctic Circle?' I said. 'I never knew you had to bring a mat!' I had visions of being stuck *Truman Show* style inside the invisible yet impenetrable bubble of the Arctic without a faded red doormat – the only means of escape. But hunger quickly overrode my bullshit daydreaming and we leaned the bike against the sign and jostled in amongst the thronging tourists, smiling and hoping we didn't smell too much. As they lined up again, this time to re-board the bus, I sheepishly approached their leader, who was standing at the door ticking off names.

'Hi there, me and my friend here are a little short of food and we wondered whether you had a bit of trail mix or some cereal bars to spare perhaps?' I said in my best English accent.

'Say, you're the bikers!' an old man sang out, and suddenly tens of pairs of pensioners' eyes were on us. I tried again.

'Yup! We've cycled down from Deadhorse and we've run out of foo—'

Before I could even finish, old ladies were reaching into their handbags for the half-full bag of regulation trail mix they had been given by their guide. Lacking any kind of collection bucket, Charlie and I waited at the bus door stuffing food into our pockets as the tourists filed past and handed it to us. To an onlooker, it must have looked a little like a hold-up. We smiled at each other, both dehydrated and weak under the energy-sapping sun, but happy in the knowledge that this voluntary emptying of bags and pockets would see us right again, at least for a few more miles.

The nuts began to fill an edge of the gaping hole in our stomachs as we pushed the bike weakly up Beaver Slide, a gravelly hill stretching away from the tourists and their buses. I felt sick with hunger and exhausted, the sparse landscape offering no shade from the harsh sun as we trudged uphill, taking it in turns to push.

FOUR LEGS GOOD, TWO LEGS BAD

Four miles further and the boys came back.

After a short and intense outburst of exhausted anger and frustration when we found that they had travelled 170 miles before thinking they might have missed us, we ripped open the food bags in the truck and ate ham sandwiches smeared in pounds of mayonnaise to fill the hole that the nuts could not. The anger disappeared and a kind of engorged trance came over us as we sat heavily on the grass. One thing was for sure: Charlie had finished his bicycle journey. Doubtless the truck seat he'd spurned 24 hours earlier had never seemed so appealing.

After a few miles of experimental, amusing and highly dangerous towing experiments, with the Land Cruiser occasionally jerking my front wheel off the stony ground as the truck lurched through its gears, I cut loose and the boys bade me farewell for the last time. Their engine noise died away, and I soon lost sight of Charlie waving from the backward facing seat, their presence quickly no more than a dusty speck disappearing over a series of rollers in the distance. This was the first time company had left me on this journey, and the hole that the sudden loss created seemed to wind me, a totally different pain from the numb though predictable loneliness of before. But though the silence was quieter than before and the challenge ahead seemed bigger than ever, I had through Charlie's companionship proved one thing at least: it was, even here, possible to lure people onto the back seat, and surely further south, as the land became more populated, that task would only get easier.

I leaned away from the now fully loaded bike, lifting it off the dirt like a windsurfer lifts a sail, and pedalled slowly off, trying not to think too far ahead, grinning instead as I recalled Charlie's all-American image, only let down by a persistent and doubtless traumatic arse ache.

4

Fourth of July farewell

DAY 9: 440 MILES

I sat, irritated and bloody inside my saturated tent, coughing through a cloud of smoke produced by three toxic mosquito coils. The toxin that caused the winged intruders to drop – like flies – onto the floor of the tent also stung my lungs and made my nose stream and my eyes water.

I had camped on an old fire-scarred hillside, not managing to set up my tent before a huge thunderhead darkened the sky and rain briefly soaked the lush grass. Wet, tired and aching I wandered into the grass to set up the tent, and in doing so inadvertently rang the dinner bell for all bloodsuckers in the vicinity.

The next day was the eve of my birthday. The road had changed now. It was asphalt, softer-seeming, and there was a yellow dotted line dividing the road in two. I cycled through the trees late that day, only the whirring of my bike chain invading the stillness, until I heard a twig snap. Reflexively, I looked back over my shoulder. Behind me, maybe 30 feet away and lit up by the evening sun, was a huge cow moose, its spindly legged and slightly knocked-kneed calf standing by its side looking at me. I stopped to take a better look. They stood calm and still on the road staring me down, their droopy noses lazily sniffing the air. A couple of minutes went by before the mother dropped her head and walked slowly across the road, the calf following unsteadily into the bush and out of sight.

FOURTH OF JULY FAREWELL

I was a day away from Fairbanks, the second largest city in America's breakaway state (after Anchorage), but only a tiny increase in traffic and the well-maintained asphalt gave it away. An hour later I rolled over a bridge and stopped next to a creek where a fisherman was packing up his tackle in the back of his truck. It wasn't long before we were sitting on the tailgate sipping beers, but not a shitty Budweiser or Coors; it was something from a local microbrewery, fresh from the icy confines of his coolbox. He left me with another before heading back to town, but I held off drinking it until I'd cut a spindly old spruce bough, stripping it of dead branches and attaching a small length of fishing line to the end of it. To the end of that, I tied my grandfather's mosquito-like fly. Two minutes of scrambling along the edge of the tussocky bank took me to a deep stretch of water eddying powerfully beneath two boulders. I touched the fly delicately on the water a few feet out and almost immediately felt a bite, but then nothing. I tried again and within two minutes I had a small grayling twitching next to me. Still with half a beer left, I'd lit a small smoky fire and sat next to it fashioning a small grid out of a length of wire, on which to cook my dinner. I had brought two wire coat-hangers with me for just such an occasion. Coat-hanger wire proves useful for lots of things, as I'd guessed it might before setting out, not least fashioning spare fasteners to fix my trailer to the bike, two of which had bounced and vibrated off already during my ride on the rough-haul road.

The fish cooked quickly, the scales blackening and curling off in the smoke of the fire. I set the camera up on the far side of the flames and sat down, my food in front of me and the dregs of my beer within reach. It was past midnight as I cut into the skin of my first birthday meal on the road. It was silent other than the welcome company of a family of ravens and the occasional hiss from the dying flames. I would have liked to have shared this tranquillity with a companion, but I tried to absorb the rare silence before washing in the creek and falling asleep. I was 26. Tomorrow I would arrive in a city. Tomorrow the silence would disappear.

I covered the 15 miles to Fairbanks quickly the following morning, only pausing to treat myself to a greasy birthday omelette and hash browns at a diner on the edge of town. The thin mantle of loneliness from the night before had slipped off my shoulders, and I sat happily listening to the confusion of voices of truckers and hunters eating their meals and the hasty clatter of waitresses tap-tapping from table to table.

Fairbanks reinforced a feeling that had been growing inside me each time I brushed shoulders with a local on the Dalton Highway: Alaskans are nothing if not hospitable. Craig Hughes, a resident of Fairbanks and a friend of a friend back home, had extended his welcome to me via an email weeks before I started the journey, but it was a trucker colleague of his who, on seeing me on the road, had warned him of my impending arrival. Minutes after I rolled into the small city center Craig arrived in a pick-up, lifted my rig into the back and propelled me to the shelter of his family home.

Relaxing in their house, running errands with the family and eating was the perfect antidote to the very physical and transient nature of my journey. A lifestyle that would have driven me mad back home had suddenly become a blissful experience. But like all blissful experiences it didn't last long. The family had to leave for lower 48 the next morning, so I cycled into town to explore other options; I wanted to stay and lap up normality for a little longer. When I asked a girl working in a coffee shack for directions to a phone box, I stumbled upon a solution. She introduced herself as Katy and an hour later, I was sitting with her and her family in their kitchen eating Alaskan halibut. Katy's mother, Polly, on hearing I was currently homeless, took me to one side. Looking into my eyes, she levelled with me – I could stay with them, but if I tried it on with her daughter she would, she said, 'rip my balls off' herself. Barely managing to meet her piercing stare, I nodded weakly, nothing in me wanting to put the authenticity of this statement to the test. And so it was that Polly Kadel not only became my Fairbanks mother but also companion number two. She casually mentioned the night before I left that an hour or two on the tandem could substitute for one of her twice-weekly spinning classes.

FOURTH OF JULY FAREWELL

I had spent a lazy three days in the city, resting and trying to fill the hole my pathetic rations had left in my belly, but my ankle had not improved, reducing my walk to a hobble and causing me to knock back anti-inflammatory tablets like peanuts. I needed to leave, though, since not only might I outstay my welcome, but getting comfortable so early on in the journey might stop me indefinitely.

Backing the bike loaded down with fresh supplies out of Polly's garage, she asked me if it had a name. Were bikes supposed to be female, like boats, I wondered? Or male, like cleaning fluids? During the seconds it took to think about this, the back of my ankle twinged with fresh pain as I rolled onto the ball of my right foot. 'Achilles,' I said, sounding official. 'He's called Achilles.'

The road Polly and I cycled down was straight, uninspiring and the busiest I had seen on my journey so far, but we chatted and the 20 miles to the city of North Pole passed quickly. I hadn't known that this town is the residence of Santa and his apparently alcoholic wife, nearly toothless and a little more rotund than her festive husband, Polly informed me confidently. We leaned Achilles against a grotesque red fibreglass Santa and wandered over to the animal enclosure. Looking at the moth-eaten state of Donner or Dancer or Rudolf or whichever two of the famous beasts these sorry-looking animals were, I guessed that this Father Christmas had given up handing out presents a long, long time ago.

As Polly waved and got into a truck with her dad, who'd driven over to pick her up, an old man I'd seen sitting on a bench across the road sidled over. Without offering a word of introduction he leaned close enough to my ear for me to hear his rasping breath and pressed something into my hand. 'Somethin' for the road,' he said huskily, smiling broadly as I looked down to find three neatly rolled spliffs laid across my palm.

Roadside meetings were becoming more frequent this side of Fairbanks. I saw motorbikers on journeys of their own. I passed silently through almost deserted villages, saw a tough-skinned old man hacking at an animal carcass near the roadside. I met jovial and often slightly drunk native guys hanging about outside little stores, who might ride round the parking lot with me before I sucked down a litre of life-giving chocolate milk and continued. Near Delta Junction, a store at a faint crossroads, I looked up to see, for the first time, two other cyclists heading towards me. They introduced themselves as Miriam and Philip, a Swiss couple. They told me when I asked that they'd cycled up from my planned destination, Ushuaia, in Tierra del Fuego. Keen to hear their stories, and to take advantage of the cafetiere poking out of one of Philip's panniers, I suggested we camp that night together in a nearby clearing, and, only pausing to purchase beer and doughnuts, we cycled off in convoy, the couple flanking me like escorts for a lumbering and overloaded freighter.

Sitting comfortably on a carpet of pine needles next to my roaring stove, I learned more about where they'd come from and where I was headed – a place so far away I didn't dare think about it. It had taken them two and a half years to cycle from Ushuaia. TWO AND A HALF YEARS! I thought . . . that's too long, too lonely, too transient. I'd have to do it quicker than that to stay sane, I thought. But I guessed it was different when there were always two of you.

It was late enough in the summer now for the sun to dip below the horizon and create a night-time half-light, almost darkness, under the trees where we were camped, and as I crawled into my sleeping bag, not bothering to pitch my tent, I was envious of the Swiss couple's constant companionship.

Early the next morning we parted company in the crisp air, bikes covered in a film of condensation under the clear sky. In a few weeks, Philip and Miriam should have reached the end of their journey, I thought. I couldn't really process what they must be feeling. Excitement? Relief? Impatience? I had no hope of understanding . . . unable to compute.

While Patagonia was still on the other side of the world, the Canadian border was now on my radar. The wilderness frontier, about 120 miles south and at least a couple of thousand feet higher than where I was, was guarded by a small village called Chicken.

The reputation of this diminutive community preceded it. It was tiny, but it fought well above its weight, I was told, with life there revolving around one tiny room, the Chicken Creek Saloon, practically the last building before the Top of the World Highway climbed over nearly treeless hills into Canada. Legend has it that the village was named after the birds found in the hills of that area. They weren't chickens, but for the villagers the name ptarmigan apparently proved to be an insurmountable spelling obstacle.

I was tired after the lengthy climb, and liquid refreshment was a priority when we rolled into the one-horse village. Colleen, a lady who'd registered an interest to ride with me when we'd met briefly in Anchorage during my journey up to Prudhoe Bay, had met up with me the day before and now rode in tandem with me, but at the wheel of her old Volvo estate.

I didn't feel like Colleen had got the best deal out of the 'Take a Seat' experience. I had cycled into her campsite at Tok (where we'd arranged by email to meet) as she was packing up her airbed. She was brandishing an intimidating-looking 'she-wee', obviously designed to level the playing field between the sexes with regards to wilderness peeing. The first morning we cycled together also proved to be the last. I was stronger than I had been three weeks before, my legs had become accustomed to the heavier than average bike, but that day there was a headwind, which, together with my still swollen ankle and the steepening hills, meant the bike slowed nearly to a stop after each pedal stroke. A few miles into the gradual climb, still 60 miles from Chicken, my lungs burned and my temper frayed as Colleen gamely pedalled on, occasionally bursting into song behind me. But I couldn't keep it up; we were going too slowly for the bike not to prove a gargantuan effort to balance, and while my legs were suffering, my arms were cramping with the exertion of constantly balancing nearly 500 pounds of bike, bags and riders.

This was the first negative milestone in my journey with company, and for the first time I secretly begrudged someone's presence on the back seat. The more exhausted I became, the more Colleen would have to suffer my barbed comments about excess weight or lack of effort. I transformed from Me to Mr. Hyde, going from fairly tolerant and flexible to irritated and stubborn, clenching my jaw and muttering forcefully under my breath about pedalling properly or using your breath to cycle not sing. It was only thanks to Colleen's incredible ability to ignore me during my outbursts and the fortuitous passing of a friend of hers in a truck that our working relationship blossomed into a different animal. The rest of the day saw us travelling a little distance apart, Colleen leap-frogging me in her Volvo (which she'd retrieved from Tok, taking advantage of her friend's truck for a lift), stopping to brandish my video camera as I passed, then speeding off again with a good chunk of my equipment in the back. We made much quicker progress this way, arriving that night at a small trapper's cabin, then on the following morning to Chicken.

It wasn't hard to find the watering hole, its tiny porch plastered with US flags in preparation for the next day, the 4th of July, when in true British fashion I'd be getting the hell out of the States.

The man behind the bar, who introduced himself as Randy, was wearing what I understood to be standard-issue Alaskan uniform – jeans, T-shirt and a well-worn baseball cap. The ceiling was festooned with tatty-looking material – hard to make out exactly what it was without a close look. It was underwear, all female, and all in ruins, as if each pair had been on the wrong end of a shotgun. Now, I'd learned over the last three weeks that most of what you see in Alaska is exactly what you get, no more, no less. The decor of the Chicken Creek Saloon was no exception. The log beams of the ceiling were completely obscured by panties of all styles, colours and sizes that had been fired from a cannon in the parking lot outside with, Randy informed me, the entire village – all eight of them – watching the spectacle.

It wasn't long before Colleen had parked up behind the small cabin-cum-pub and we'd wedged ourselves between the pool table and the bar, doubling the number of occupants in the room.

Sitting there, allowing a smile to creep onto my face, I began to feel that this was the place for an Alaskan send-off, the last-chance saloon. A couple of bar stools down sat an old man in leather trousers and a denim waistcoat, one eye twitching slightly as he stared at his Rolling Rock. I was sure he'd be up for a party, too – he'd probably been partying every night in this tiny place since Vietnam.

FOURTH OF JULY FAREWELL

The place slowly filled up as the light outside became twilight, giving the cabin a cozy glow, a few strings of lights shining through the flags. A handful of Americans from lower 48 mixed with the locals and cheeks got slowly rosier. Randy made it clear to me that if I wanted a demonstration of the fabled cannon I would have to source suitable wadding. I didn't have any suitable underwear myself, and, looking around, there were perhaps four girls to choose from. Naturally, I approached the one I knew best to explain the situation.

After some gentle coercion from Randy, Colleen wandered off to the car, next to which we had pitched our tents. She reappeared moments later brandishing a large pair of brilliantly glinting golden panties, bunching them up in her fist, hiding their size and thumping them down on the bar, grinning. Randy the powder monkey grinned too, pleased to have the opportunity to demonstrate the might of the Chicken Creek Saloon firepower. The stony-faced old-timer still sitting on his stool turned his head slowly and looked sideways down the bar at the glinting undies. Eye still twitching and sitting stock-still, his mouth widened and his cheeks creased into a sly smile.

Randy – now carrying a hefty cylinder of iron – walked out onto the porch. Cigarette smouldering and drooping from his bottom lip, he proceeded to empty two shot glasses of gunpowder into the barrel of the stocky cannon. Frowning at the undies for a second, he added a third shot of powder. 'We better make this a big one,' he murmured, cigarette still wobbling from his lower lip. With a rubber mallet and a stick, he pounded the underwear down into the small hole, getting all but a few silky inches of material wedged in tight. The crowd ambled happily out into the dust as Randy carried the charged weapon perhaps 50 feet from the porch, laying it at an angle in the dirt. The old-timer was standing in front of the bar now, readjusting his bandanna and muttering happily, 'C'mon, boys, let's blow some shit up.'

Then the fuse fizzed sharply, allowing Randy time to backtrack a few feet before the wilderness tranquillity was split by the report of the cannon as it spat three, maybe four, bits of material high above the dusty clearing. Blackened nylon and shredded knicker elastic punched holes through clouds of mosquitoes in the still air, before they floated harmlessly to the ground. As Randy had assured me they would, men whooped and the cannon's echo bounced back to the parking lot off some distant hill. I switched off the camera, finding myself whooping along with others, and stumbled drunkenly on the step as I wandered back into the bar to retrieve my drink. The old-timer had been recharged – as a statue-like mime artist magically comes to life when a coin is dropped in his hat – jigging around in front of the jukebox with anyone who cared to join him. I sat heavily though happily in a corner, and with my brain addled by cheap beer, imagined this man being kept alive not by the recommended five a day but by the sporadic and dramatic marriage of cordite and lingerie.

I rose the next morning aching, to find Colleen snoring loudly in her tent, which had collapsed on her during the night. I had found a new partner during the revelry in the saloon sometime after the panty firing. Josh was a tall man who I vaguely remembered smiling maniacally when I suggested he join me the following day. He was on a road trip around Alaska with his girlfriend Jimael but seemed keen to blow some cobwebs out on the bike. That suited me; I was keen for some muscle to help me up the long climb to the border.

After we'd fought off the worst of our hangovers and eaten breakfast at the picnic tables outside the bar, we saddled up with half mesh camo-caps we'd bought to fit in with the locals and pedalled rapidly out of the parking lot.

Josh didn't suffer from the normal problem of having his view obscured by me as we rode. He towered above me, his knees only just clearing his bars as he pedalled, providing a healthy chunk of power beneath the strong morning sun. This was as much fun as I'd had on Achilles. The hills were beautiful, layers of greens and blues like a layered theatre set fading into the distance. Our heavy gear was with Colleen and Jimael in Colleen's Volvo, and I was cycling with Josh the carpenter, making good progress. But the partnership was short-lived. Josh badly wanted to carry on into northern Canada, but his lack of passport meant that this isolated and lofty border crossing spelled the end of his bicycle adventure.

One small, rolling hill before the tiny white checkpoint, we pulled up next to the car. Josh hung the sweaty cycling shorts I'd loaned him on the Volvo's aerial, then removed a coolbox, a stove and some brightly coloured plastic glasses from the trunk. Generous measures of cocktails were poured while the beef and cream cheese we'd stocked up on sizzled, and the four of us toasted our brief companionship on the warm, treeless hilltop.

Half an hour later, I crossed into Canada heavy, sluggish and alone once more, with three friends standing at the red-and-white striped barrier waving. I waved back until I coasted over a small rise and I was alone again, all evidence of my first border crossing wiped from view by this, the Top of the World Highway.

I felt a little like a box that had just had half its valuable contents removed, the remaining items rattling about, allowing my mind too much room to wander. And I knew as my waving friends appeared again, smaller this time as I climbed the next rise, that it would invariably wander into a melancholic place as the evening drew on and I found myself camped for the first time on the majestic hills of Yukon Territory, northern Canada.

Alaska had treated me well and allowed me to find my feet on this journey. When the bush hadn't provided its own hospitality, I'd been taken in. My fears about being a stranger and staying that way had disappeared. I no longer thought friendly faces were way out of reach on this side of the Atlantic. A couple of weeks in the saddle had taught me that, if I looked at them, the faces of strangers were just as friendly.

As I'd crossed the border, I panicked for a second, a whiskery old face and the words 'somethin' for the road' flooding into my brain. There was a German Shepherd at the checkpoint, a sniffer dog who must have busted countless stoners here. Hesitating for a second, I relaxed again, remembering I'd thought about this ahead of time and offloaded the three spliffs on a surprised-looking local loitering outside the grocery store in Tok.

'Are you shittin' me?' he said, looking down at what I'd put in his hands.

TAKE A SEAT

'Nope, I'm not shitting you,' I replied, the 'shitting' sounding clipped and incongruous.

I saw him half an hour later, walking a wavering line down the sidewalk and smiling dreamily, presumably having smoked all three spliffs back to back.

5

A Canadian homecoming

DAY 21: 969 MILES

I could see a lake through the lightly fluttering aspen leaves over to my left. I rolled off the dirt highway onto a track that took me after a couple of hundred yards down to the water's edge. Three days before, I'd left Colleen, Josh and Jimael in Colleen's trusty green tank of a Volvo at the border, and this morning I'd left more friends behind in the Western-style city of Dawson, complete with a picnic table I had made by way of payment for their hospitality.

There wasn't a whisper of wind and the lake was mirror-like, only disturbed by the gentle ripples of two beavers playing out beyond the lilies. In the distance, the lake ended abruptly, cut by a drab, thin seam of scrubby land, the only thing preventing the reflection merging seamlessly with the sky, filled with enormous, almost majestic, thunderheads inching their way towards me. I pitched my tent and assembled my trusty little stove, putting two packets of anemic noodles on to boil as I sat back and took in this new theatre of beautiful emptiness. Even the bugs seemed more relaxed here, and the only noise was that of beaver tails slapping on the water. I crawled into my tent at ten, and I must have drifted off quickly after admiring my growing collection of squashed fly specimens on the nylon ceiling. At nearly midnight, I jolted awake to hear the low growl of a sturdy pick-up bouncing along the rutted track towards the lake in the half light. I was naked, as I often was, enjoying the airing my manhood got after removing my cycling shorts. Hurriedly putting on trousers, I unzipped the fly screen and crawled out to see who was joining me.

A man and a woman, friendly but tough-looking natives who didn't look like they'd driven out here to 'make out', climbed down from the cab.

Robert and Christine Hager, whose truck had bumped to a stop only a few feet from my tent, which was well camouflaged in the grass, told me they'd come to hunt moose that often come to the lake to drink. They lived at their summer fish camp only a few miles downstream along the Stewart River, and in the winter they returned to Mayo, a village not far from here. While we talked, Christine scanned the shoreline looking for animals in the lush grass and aspen saplings. Robert looked up at the sky.

'You're gonna get some rain out here,' he remarked casually, the thunderheads now more sizeable and starting to steel the light above us. 'Best come back with us to the fish camp, there's room for your bike in the truck,' he added in the same matter-of-fact tone.

I looked at Christine questioningly, and she nodded and said by way of encouragement, 'Yup, you'll sure get pretty wet here.'

Within minutes, Achilles and the trailer were packed up in the back of the scratched-up Chevy as we bumped over tree roots, reversing up the track. I sat snugly between the married couple, both in their 50s or 60s I guessed, as we cruised along the gravel for about 6 miles until we reached a faint grassy side road which led down to some wooden tent frames and a couple of ramshackle cabins. This was the Hagers' fish camp, where many a troubled local youth had passed, Robert taking time to teach them about the old ways – fishing, drying and smoking the catch and other Tutchone native traditions that he said were disappearing all too quickly in the small northern towns.

He enlarged on these stories from the comfort of a worn-out sofa under a corrugated iron roof where we ate bannock, the native homemade bread a little like scones, with Spam or jam spooned onto it. It was almost hypnotic to sit and just listen to his stories. His skin shared the characteristics of the old lady I'd seen on the plane. He looked tough but somehow soft, and yet his body hadn't let go of the strength of his youth. This man was special, that I recognised, but one thing struck me in particular as he recounted small snippets of his life. Robert was utterly impartial, with a wealth of experience and a heart big enough to share amongst his community as if each and every one was his own child. He had been instrumental in settling land claims of the local Tutchone, a problem that will plague a number of native North American communities for years to come. I could see sadness in his eyes when he described his efforts to encourage the current generation of teenagers to come and help him at the fish camp – it became more difficult each year, he said.

There was one other man silently going about his business at 2 a.m. while we sat there, chopping a bit of wood or filling a huge kettle and replacing it on the fire. That was Frank, Christine's brother, Robert said. A few months ago, he'd been an alcoholic who'd lived mostly on the street and had become unable to help himself. Robert got him out here, where the bush provided ample therapy. Just the effort of living out here takes time enough to forget about your vices, Robert explained. He talked sometimes looking up at me with a sad smile on his face and sometimes looking out into the trees. I tried to imagine what it was to see your community slowly changing with the times, moving away from much-loved practices and traditions that seemed to make more sense than what was overtaking them.

I slept badly that night, sweaty and irritated from the effort of trying to swat at mosquitoes from the spongy depths of an old sofa in the moth-eaten living area. I'd got used to deftly eradicating a small force of winged intruders in my little tent within about five minutes of zipping the door closed. In a large room, that task would last all night and still be unfinished due to cracks in the flimsy door or rips in the mosquito netting over the windows.

By the time I got up, eyes puffy and fresh welts on my cheeks from the night's battle, Christine was already lifting the huge iron kettle, freshly boiled, off the fire to pour three sweet cups of tea for us.

An hour later I'd left these people and I cycled back past the lake and towards Pelly Crossing, one of tens of tiny nondescript villages along the road. I met more Tutchones, some drunk and matching the stereotype of life up here and others keen to talk as I cycled by. I stopped for soup when invited by Kenny, Jerry and Thomas, three more Tutchones sitting outside the small general store surrounded by government-funded housing – cheap, single-skinned prefabricated boxes. Jerry told me of his experiences in Residential School, the institutions aboriginal children were sent to, to be 'civilised' – taken from their family home and 'persuaded' to forget their native tongue in favour of English. They still had the scars, he said, from plentiful beatings they received every time they tried running away from school.

These often depressing places were split up by nothing but miles of spruce trees that slowly increased in size. I continued to meet people along the road, making fleeting friendships, perhaps through the rolled-down window of a truck or round a small campfire for a night. Pedalling was now what I did. I'd settled into an often detached work mode, drifting off, letting the songs from my little MP3 player take me somewhere else as my legs continued to revolve. Each tune was beginning to own a portion of the landscapes I'd seen. A simple guitar riff might take me back to Gravel Lake or a freeze-frame of a grizzly with cubs sitting in the grass hundreds of miles back. Often, though, they'd take me back across the Atlantic to the solidarity of long-standing friends. The transient nature of my friendships out here was frustrating. I'd leave a recent acquaintance knowing nothing of their habits, gripes, twitches, passions, loved ones or family. I craved that intimacy, but on the other hand I knew the grass was always greener on the other side of whichever fence I was on. These fleeting acquaintances left no room for boredom.

Since Dawson a northerly wind had grown in strength, doing its best to keep me from my next milestone that, thanks to Sarah, an email contact, offered guaranteed hospitality. The road was straight, and lacked visual incentives until, in the distance, I saw the telltale square of a road sign. Making it painfully to the end of the aptly named Ten Mile Road, swearing for the millionth time at the wind, I arrived at the sign welcoming me to the city of Whitehorse. I was close to being able to put Achilles out of sight for a few days and pretend I wasn't moving on.

A CANADIAN HOMECOMING

Whitehorse was a small bastion of eclectic culture deep in the bush – it had everything that was missing elsewhere in the north, yet retained the limitless beauty of the wilderness. Sarah and her friends looked after me extremely well – so well, in fact, that I sank into Whitehorse life all too comfortably overnight. I was interviewed by the local radio station, I went out at night with Sarah and her friend Danielle and I even had the local MP join me for a ride on the back of Achilles.

Four days after arriving in the city, I was still doing my best to force thoughts of leaving out of my mind. Sarah, Danielle and I had travelled out to their cabin on the shores of the nearby Tagish Lake for the weekend, after which they would return to Whitehorse and I would disappear south. That was the plan, anyway. Early on the Saturday morning I lay awake, staring at the wooden ceiling, close enough to the girls to hear their regular breathing. They were both still asleep. Craning my neck to look out of the window from my small bed, I could see the spruce trees waving in unison; there would be white caps on the lake for sure. One more day to enjoy here, then I would go. I was warm under the goose-down duvet and had no reason to stir.

The previous evening, after having arrived at the lake, I had, after a few drinks, left the cabin and sat on the small deck, shadowy and almost dark under the trees. It wasn't the first time on my journey that I had cried, quietly, like a child trying his best not to. My eyes welled up and fat tears rolled down my cheek as I thought about how happy I was here with friends I had, over only a few short days, become attached to. For the first time I seriously considered hanging up my cycling shoes. I could be happy here, and it seemed obvious I wasn't cut out for solo travel. It wasn't the physical discomfort – I lapped that up – it was the psychological struggle. But as I let these inviting thoughts wash over me, two ugly words floated to the surface causing me to wipe the tears roughly from my cheeks. Giving Up.

Was that what it would be? I hung my head between my knees, confused and bathing in this new wave of self-pity and confusion. Out of the corner of my tear-blurred vision, I could see the dull glint of Achilles leaning next to the cabin. I turned my head the other way before hearing the heavy wooden door creak open and looking up to see Sarah sitting down next to me, feet dangling like mine over the edge of the decking, not quite touching the forest floor. She told me what I guess I knew deep down. I had to continue.

'Imagine the adventures you'll have, the people you'll meet – you can't stop now!' she said, talking with the objective clarity I didn't possess. 'This is just one of a million good times you'll have!' she continued.

Shit, I thought, wondering whether this was true. If it was possible to have repeat occurrences of happiness and heartbreak with this potency, I'd have a full-blown mental breakdown.

I left on the Sunday as planned, but I felt like a domesticated animal being re-introduced to the wild against its will. I had an hour of the girls' company as they took turns on the back seat before I cycled on alone, trying to concentrate on the positives, the good times. 'Imagine the adventures you'll have,' I repeated to myself out loud as I weaved slightly on the hard shoulder, taking a minute to become accustomed again to Achilles with an empty back seat.

Only the odd smudge between the road and the forest ahead interrupted the sometimes pleasant, sometimes wearing monotony of these roads. Occasionally the smudge turned out to be a bear grazing on the lush grass, and other times it was a herd of bison, their huge prehistoric bodies lumbering across the road.

Hineck, a Czech tourist, was on the back of Achilles for my first bison encounter, 150 miles south of Whitehorse and a little way before the therapeutic and muddy soak-hole of Liard Hot Springs. We stopped about 25 feet from a huge beast that wasn't in any hurry to move from the gravel shoulder where he stood surveying us. I looked over to see Hineck – the Eastern bloc's answer to Rambo, complete with bandanna – standing by the bike snapping away with his camera. These animals could crush a car, let alone Achilles, so I hung back until the bison, snorting lazily, turned away, lowering his sofa-sized head back to the grass.

Sometimes, more rarely than a grizzly or a bison, the smudge would turn out to be a person, and one day, as I drew nearer, I could make out the spindly limbs of a human, who looked up when the whirring of the bike was close enough to be heard. The man was young, my age or younger, with a bandanna and a hooded top sporting a large marijuana leaf on the front. The lump I'd seen a way off was too large to be just one man though, and as I rolled to a stop and he stood up, I found most of the bulk consisted of a large backpack and a shapeless sack. He introduced himself as Pierre in a thick Quebecois accent, and told me he was hitchhiking south, having been up north meditating and living in the bush with his girlfriend. Trying to ignore any useless hippy preconceptions I had, I invited him to jump aboard, and he accepted casually as if this were an everyday occurrence, confidently informing me that he was 'a verree goood seeclist'. 'You weell zee,' he added, smiling his confident 18-year-old smile.

The backpack was heavy, which worried me, but not nearly as heavy as the other sack, apparently full of about 40 pounds of fresh vegetables. My heart sank slightly at the depressing thought of carrying 70 pounds of extra gubbins, and, not having tested Achilles with such a heavy payload before, I became anxious. 'Don't worreee,' Pierre said, reminding me that despite his small stature he was apparently as strong as an ox.

We cycled off tentatively, the tires spongy under the weight but managing just to keep us off the rims. Painstakingly slowly, we pedalled forward, as Pierre talked at me about life, the universe and everything. I would interject with the occasional 'oh' and 'uh huh' as he told me about the purity with which he lived. He meditated often, travelled extensively in South America and smoked copious amounts of weed, since it allowed him to think clearly. I passed no comment, deciding it was safer just to listen. Our speed slowed further as I felt Pierre fidget and flag after 15 miles. Thankfully, after a further 10 we rolled into Teslin, stopping at the grocery store for a well-earned beer before vibrating over the steel plate bridge and onto a dirt slipway on the far side of the river, just managing to put up our respective tents before raindrops the size of pennies poured down, bouncing a foot up off the soil. I hurriedly stashed my panniers under cover before Pierre shouted over, inviting me to hang out in his spacious tent. With the rain drumming on the nylon, I unzipped the flysheet, crawled in and was hit instantly by a thick fog of marijuana haze. He pointed the pipe in my direction, offering me a toke. I declined – I didn't much like it anyway, but the fact that I was carrying kilos of herbs and vegetables without much help from him grated on my nerves. The rain let up as my eyes started to water in the smoky capsule, so I escaped to watch the emerging sun strengthening the reflection in the calm but eddying water on the shore. Pierre, having finished his pipe and followed me out of the tent, called over on seeing me taking photos. 'Can I take some photos? You'll see, I'm a good photographer.' I'd heard that kind of talk from him before, but I passed my small camera over before stamping on a few tent pegs that had come loose in the now soaking earth.

'*Merde*!' I heard behind me and turned around in time to see my camera being thrown in a graceful arc across the gravel near the water's edge, landing with a tinny thud in the dirt. My blood, until that time only simmering slightly, began to boil.

'Why the FUCK did you do that?' I said, nearly shouting, walking over to the camera and inspecting a large dent in its body but finding it still worked. '*Merde*!' Pierre repeated. 'A mosquito bit me in zee face!' he said by way of explanation. I bit my tongue and stayed a safe distance from him lest I was tempted to lash out at the little shit.

We said little for the rest of the evening, despite sharing food outside my tent. By the following morning, little that came out of that guy's mouth would have surprised me, so when he told me he could not carry on because he was an insomniac and hadn't slept even for a minute, I was just mildly pleased. I'd be relieved of the 15 cabbages or whatever was in the sack, as well as Pierre's watery pedalling efforts, and I looked forward to a morning of cycling not punctuated by theories about the benefits of marijuana.

The remedy for the small mental wounds left by the French Canadian came that same day in the form of Ralf, the perfect antidote in every way. Ralf and Gabbi were travelling by car, a couple of youth workers from Germany taking a road trip in the north. At 6 ft. 3 in., with long blond hair, he was a pedalling force to be reckoned with and helped to get Achilles and me 25 miles further south in a heartbeat.

* * *

A CANADIAN HOMECOMING

Sometimes it seemed like days before I would see changes in the land-scape. The dirt of the highways further north was more often tarmac now, light grey with a pale yellow line dividing it in two. The bush had been cleared on either side of the road for about 20 yards, and in these treeless areas there were often berry patches. When the bears hadn't found them first, I would occasionally stop and feed on tiny ripe blueberries, the only trade-off being the persistent bite of bugs hiding in the tall, moist grass. Then there was the bush, with birch or aspen poking through the spruce making it in places impenetrable.

Late afternoons and evenings were the nicest time to ride. A silence fell and the slightest rustling in the bush could be heard. I'd see animals: bears, maybe a lone wolf or a skunk usually feeding or moving slowly in the grass. Once, though, a moose, spooked by something, barrelled through the dense wall of trees and onto the stony ground a few paces in front of me, leaving a hole in the young sturdy birches as if they were made of crêpe paper. On seeing me, its eyes widened, and in a show of impossible agility it turned 45 degrees without tripping on its flailing limbs and punched another cartoon-like hole in the trees to disappear instantly 15 yards from where it had materialised. The whole commotion lasted perhaps seven seconds, then silence descended again, allowing me to hear the blood pumping in my head.

Less than a week went by before I met another transient sitting on his pack, just outside Watson Lake. I'd been riding only 15 minutes that morning before squeezing gently on the levers and stopping Achilles with all the braking characteristics of an oil tanker. A bearded man wearing black dungarees, a baggy turquoise T-shirt and a red bandanna brightly returned my greeting, revealing a broad, gap-toothed smile. He didn't look much like someone who'd want to pedal anywhere, and introduced himself as Steve Spratt as I brandished my video camera at him. Stepping sideways to take in the full length of my bike, he suddenly looked up.

'Man, I heard about you on the radio!' he exclaimed in a strong Canadian accent – he'd heard the interview I'd had back in Whitehorse.

'So, umm, d'you wanna ride?' I said, half-joking.

'Well, suuure!' Steve said, evidently delighted. 'My friends won't believe me when I tell them I met you,' he added, picking up his pack and walking over towards me. We shook hands and I secured his pack on top of the trailer's load, then gave Steve a hasty tandem-riding lesson. 'You can keep your feet on the pedal – yes all the ti . . . – yup, even when we stop, like a passenger on a motorbike. Brakes? Nope, I've got those on my handlebars. Good, OK, you ready to go?'

Steve hitched his dungarees out of his arse crack and pulled one strap back up over his scrawny shoulders. 'Yup, I reckon,' he said, still smiling.

In fact, we both wore broad grins as we moved off: me for having snagged such an unlikely stoker, and Steve for the novelty of it all. 'I hitch up north and stay for three, four, maybe five months, then I head down south, but I hate it down there, so after a few weeks I head back up north,' he explained as we went. Steve had been leading this happy hand-to-mouth existence since before I was born. He added, though I'd suspected as much, that during that whole time he'd never been picked up by a bicycle.

The road rolled gently, but not enough to piss me off. Big rollers are the worst, not allowing you to get into a rhythm and tiring you all the quicker. Steve was not a strong cyclist, but neither was he heavy. He cut a kind of modern-day Dick Whittington character, travelling seemingly carefree and with little weighing him down. Half an hour into our ride and after one readjustment stop, I felt Achilles wobble. I turned to see Steve retrieving a cigarette from behind his ear and trying to spark it up, cupping the lighter in front of his face in an effort to protect it from the light breeze. He gave up after a minute and smoked the cigarette on the next break, the smoke keeping at least some of the bugs at bay.

We shared our campsite that night, next to a concrete bridge, with an unnaturally tame moth-eaten fox that licked my hand and perched on my saddle, sniffing the air as Steve scooped pasta out of an old yogurt pot, flecks of sauce sticking in his beard.

After chasing the fox back into the bush and clearing my stove away, we retired to our tents, retreating from the advancing mosquito hordes.

From a few feet away, Steve carried on regaling me with stories from the road, ranching down on the prairies near Calgary, his days of gold prospecting up in the north, the countless times he'd travelled this highway and how it had changed. When my eyes eventually rolled and I drifted off to sleep in the half-light, Steve was still talking.

The next day, after only a few miles, he sat back down at the side of the road. He was, he said, lucky to have been able to experience life on Achilles, but his corduroy dungarees were beginning to chafe his scrawny thighs. So, I left him as I had found him, sitting contentedly and silently on his backpack in the wilderness.

If nothing else, I was learning to appreciate the little things. Hanging out at cafés just sitting, watching and talking to anyone unfortunate enough to sit nearby was all I wanted, whenever picking flies out of my tainted plastic cup on the side of a silent road became routine.

After riding wind-harried miles on a road nudging up against the northern Rockies, past turquoise lakes and dry river beds that had long since shed the snow melt, I arrived in Fort Nelson, a town that provided washing facilities, a store that sold chocolate milk, and plenty of people whose ears I could chew off. I sat for a while in the Laundromat, letting the now alien smell of laundry soap waft pleasantly around my nostrils before wandering over to Cappalu's, a café I'd heard about from Mairin, a passing lady in a truck, who'd told me to swing by when I arrived. These days the grapevine of the one main north–south road in this part of the world was making friends for me ahead of time. Within seconds of entering, a hot chocolate and a flexing plate dangerously overloaded with food were thrust into my hands. I sat down quickly next to a friendly bunch of 18-year-old girls and began to eat, courtesy of one of their mothers. Struggling to cram in the last mouthful of beautifully stodgy cake, Mairin came over from behind the counter with good news: she'd found somewhere I could stay in town. She ushered me outside to meet a nurse called Alicia, who was backing her car out of the space in front of the café. Alicia casually gave me her number and told me to give her a call and arrange hooking up later that evening.

Full to bursting, clean clothes, an invitation to stay in a house full of nurses and still a couple of hours in hand to find a beer – Nelson had within some time of my arrival proved itself to be everything a road-weary, lonely, stinking limey cyclist could possibly want.

I was nervous though, of one thing. I was only seven hours' drive from Fort Simpson, the home of Tiiu, my ex-girlfriend, and since I wouldn't any longer be cycling down the 250-mile dead-end road to her house, she had decided to drive over with her children and visit for the weekend. As much fun as I was having that evening, drinking with Alicia, the other nurses and a young Frenchman we'd met, I couldn't quite push a complicated set of emotions from my mind. I knew Tiiu was trying to be pragmatic about her life, and she desperately needed a partner who could provide a role model for her children, someone who was physically there for them. But a month and a half on the road had given me way too much time to think about things. Loneliness had made the yearning for the stability of life with her stronger, or was it as much my love of the north that made me feel this way? It was difficult to separate the two. The last time I had seen her was during Easter, four months previously – before I'd even begun my journey – in her town, with two feet of snow carpeting the small streets surrounded by the sea of spruce that separates Fort Simpson from other villages hundreds of miles away. I'd burrowed small tunnels in the snow in their yard, making an Easter egg hunt for the kids. I'd walked them to school and made lunch while Tiiu worked. It had been so 'normal', and the more I thought about it while rolling down the road, the more attractive that family life seemed. Forcing myself to look at it objectively, I knew this was a common illness, a never-ending epidemic that affected nearly everyone. Heartache. One of the most troublesome symptoms of this particular disorder seems to be the belief that this feeling is terminal.

The next day I sat uneasily, trying to read in the parking lot of the motel where Tiiu would be arriving. Twenty minutes passed before I heard a car horn and looked round to see her behind the wheel of a new-looking truck, her jet-black hair and dark eyes making her smile all the whiter. All the pragmatism I had tried to muster disappeared instantly. I spent the weekend taking the kids for hot chocolate or swimming in the hotel pool – the novelty of swimming in warm water doesn't wear off if you live somewhere that's frozen for most of the year. I talked with Tiiu, wandering from café to store to pool and even the local bowling alley, trying not to collapse in floods of tears and beg her to have me back.

After 48 hours and a tearful hug goodbye, I watched as the truck drove slowly out of town, Tiiu and the kids waving out of the back window, until dust obscured it.

Returning to my new residence and cleaning Achilles in the afternoon sun with beer in hand, I wondered what I would have done if, after begging Tiiu to take me back, she had done so and asked me to cycle to Simpson to stay. Would I have risked losing the possibility to experience a journey like this ever again? Sarah's wise words rang clear in my head, 'Imagine the adventures you'll have, the people you'll meet – you can't stop now!'

Later, I took out my map and traced the long road south as it edged its way towards the Pacific Coast Range, then over the mountains to the sea.

That evening, after doing a grocery run with Alicia on the back of the now shiny Achilles, we had a party. Friends of Alicia began to trickle in as the aroma of a chicken being cooked with a can of beer wedged inside it began to waft round the house. They were mostly medics or paramedics, and before long there was a full house, with beer flowing and chicken bones littering the table outside. At nearly midnight, when the majority had left and only the three girls remained, I discovered the cost of living in such style for a few days. Out of the airing cupboard a furry suit was fetched and brandished in front of me. It was hard to identify, but whatever it was, it was obviously meant for a five year old and they wanted me to put it on. Sobering up rapidly I tentatively put a leg where I thought it should go, and then the other one, heaving the costume up round my waist with difficulty, expecting to hear a rip somewhere around my groin. I looked down to find the suit ended just below my knees where a pair of fluffy feet flopped. I had to hunch over to get the top half on, and even then the front zipper only did up halfway and the hood, a fluffy rat-like head, bit into my hairline. It was a kangaroo suit for a toddler. Alicia, Lorraine and Kerry sat on the sofa ordering me to adopt a number of poses while they took photos and collapsed in giggles. The stitching around the shoulders and groin of the outfit began to numb my limbs and with every minute a little more sweat soaked into the nylon fur. After mumbling something about nurses playing sick games with guests and doubled up like a contortionist in order to escape the choke hold of the kangaroo, I twisted my way out of the costume and stumbled off to bed.

The next morning, with sore heads, the girls went to work, not one of them able to escape and accompany me south. I'd learned the previous day that a local 18-year-old boy who'd been keen to join me had been refused permission by his parents. Reading between the lines as he made his excuses over the phone, I understood that it was because his protective father considered there was a significant risk that I was a kiddie-fiddler, that I'd dreamt up this evil adventure simply to take advantage of young boys and girls en route. That would have made me the most imaginative pedophile that ever lived, I thought, while trying not to take this unfortunate and distrusting viewpoint personally.

As I pushed on alone and reflective, it rained. It rained hard and hailed for three days, stinging my arms and legs while I shielded my eyes from the water bouncing off the road. Within a minute I'd be soaked. Stopping would just make it worse, so I'd slug it out leaving a wake behind me in the road awash with run-off. With all electrical equipment stashed safely in dry-bags, I had no music to distract me, and when trucks thundered passed, a wall of spray would knock me sideways and fill my left ear with gritty water.

When the rain let up enough to look up, I saw the prairies that surrounded Fort Nelson change slowly into lakes and mountains and then back again to prairies as I neared Dawson Creek and Fort St John. The lakes I camped by got warmer, and sometimes I'd meet others camping in the isolated provincial parks. At Hart Lake, arriving tired after an undulating day through the foothills of the Rockies, I heard the echoes of children in the forest. Moments later, kids surrounded me like Ewoks and I had my work cut out, with two, three, four kids at a time draped over Achilles while I weaved figures of eight through the trees.

I continued to meet stokers in all shapes and sizes who helped me south for an hour, or a day or two if I was lucky. One hitchhiker was so enamoured by my journey that he chose to pedal 5 miles in the wrong direction just to take part. Eli and Mike, summoned by a family I met on the road, helped me pedal to their home in Fort St. John. Bulky and powerful Canadians, they switched regularly on the back, keeping the propulsion unit fresh and meaning we never dropped below 25 mph, covering the 50 miles to their home in well under two hours.

With exceptions dotted along the way, I began to notice a trend as I ventured south. The further I went, the more diversity there was. Northern British Colombia was dominated by those working the oil-fields. Even Eli and Mike worked in the oil industry, X-raying sections of pipeline, checking for weaknesses and cracks. But in Prince George, another 120 miles or so further south, I sat in a coffee shop surrounded by an eclectic bunch of chess players, hippies and businessmen. That same evening I was taken in by a household consisting of a tree planter, a folk musician and someone who made jam for a living. It was one of their friends, Cassie, stopping over on a visit from Montreal, who succumbed to the lure of bicycle travel. She opted out of a wilderness berry-gathering trip for the jam man to head south on the back of Achilles.

After a night of rain that saw us huddled together avoiding the tent's damp nylon walls on the banks of the sprawling Fraser River, the rain stopped. In fact the weather changed completely as we rolled from one beautiful camping spot to the next, always in the shade of pines near the banks of the river. It heated up, and the lush irrigated fields on the flood plains were in stark contrast to the dry earthy browns of the grassland above. We followed the Fraser Valley on the tough gravel back roads avoiding the now ever-present traffic on the highways, cycling without the threat of getting run over by some gashead in a super-charged Dodge. Those roads were beautiful, and with only the crunching gravel to talk over, we chatted as we pedalled through cowboy farmland, sometimes stopping to fill up with water at dilapidated homesteads, paint peeling off the timber decks, fly screens always squeaking as we were beckoned in.

In gaps between the fields, there was scrub and small pine forests. We saw a black bear lumbering off into the bushes, the odd snake and skunks, many flattened in the dust. In the evenings or during the day if we crossed a bridge, we'd strip off and swim in the Fraser, washing and enjoying the refreshing water. Once, as I waded out into the turbulent waters, I noticed a baby toad valiantly but ineffectively kicking out, trying to combat the current sweeping him south.

Cassie seemed to enjoy life on Achilles. During the day, the heat and the beauty of our surroundings encouraged a sedate pace and regular rests. Sometimes she'd break out a tune on the miniature harmonica that she had close to hand on her necklace. She had no aspirations as to how far she would travel with me. All she knew was she would have to get back to where we'd started at some stage to pick up her belongings before returning to the east coast. It was a week before Cassie decided that she'd had enough, she was tired, the continual vibration of the gravel roads taking its toll. It was difficult saying goodbye. She'd spent a week at close quarters with me, longer than anyone else on this journey, and we'd really got to know each other. She was brilliantly liberal and relaxed, making travelling with her easy. As was often the case with company, we covered less ground than I might have done solo, but only because chatting on longer breaks was preferable to sweating forward, and as I knew well by now, an unaccustomed bottom needs regular rests.

Cassie's farewell took place after an alcoholic picnic camped next to a small river running through a forest outside the small town of Hundred Mile House, and I watched as she turned away and boarded a silver Greyhound bus to head back up north.

She was unaware that she'd escaped only 20 miles short of the biggest hills of the journey so far, I'd only noticed them when I laid the map out on the ground where the bus had been. My Achilles tendon ached just looking at the scrubby hillside where the road zigzagged up beneath the pine trees. The roads here were unpaved, and there was every reason to believe they'd treat me as the Atigun Pass had done only three days into this adventure. But as it happened, more than 2,000 miles of cycling had made me stronger than I'd realised. Despite barely going fast enough to balance, and toiling up 15 per cent gradients only just guiding all 14 feet of Achilles and trailer round the tight hairpins, I reached the top without having to put a foot down. I already knew that attempting to push a 200-pound bicycle uphill was a waste of time and that made me strain all the harder, with sweat almost bubbling through my skin and dripping off the base of my holed and faded shirt.

Leaning the bike against a tree, I wiped my face with my shirt and looked south. The road disappeared in the hazy air surrounded by cornfields beneath me. Beyond them was the largely indigenous town of Lillooet, and beyond that the ski resort of Whistler where the kindly Mr. and Mrs. Dannhauer took pity on me and treated me to their luxury ski chalet, complete with clean sheets and an en-suite bathroom. From there, the tarmac of the Sea to Sky Highway took me through Squamish to meet the sparkling Pacific, where myriad dark, tree-covered rocks crowded the ocean in front of Vancouver Island, whose mountain ridges were visible on the horizon. I stopped short of Horseshoe Bay and sat on the low concrete wall looking out to sea, weak and tired, but so close to what I thought of as home, having lived in Vancouver a few years before.

So much had happened. I'd travelled 2,700 miles since cycling out of the Arctic wasteland parking lot of Deadhorse two months before. I'd had 14 companions since then. Or was it 15? I couldn't remember.

My 'home-coming' wasn't a disappointment. I was absorbed instantly back into a family atmosphere beneath the majestic coastal range that surrounds the city. I was pleased to have my first mail waiting for me with my friends there. Hungry for knowledge of home, I read emails telling me all was well back in England and read a newspaper article my father had kindly sent me. For years he'd sent me snippets he thought might interest me, but this one had a title that read 'Not every woman finds premature baldness a turn-off . . .'

I began to wonder whether it was two months or two years since I'd last seen my family, before turning the page over and finding the lengthy obituary of Edmund Hillary on the back.

6

A spiritual journey

DAY 84: 3,592 MILES

Achilles leaned loaded against the swings with handlebars newly taped
after his rest. I took a last look around the yard and picked up a luggage
strap I'd forgotten in the grass. The usual pair of tiny wellington boots
lay kicked off on the deck by the door, Kate having galloped outside
without them. She and her sister Mary Jane now stood prim and
proper, observing from the porch of their new playhouse, raised above
the ground beneath the yew tree in the far corner of the yard. I'd been
resting up in Vancouver for more than two weeks, and I'd wanted to
give a little something back by building it for them. Further north in
Dawson it had been a pub-style picnic table for Greg and Crystal.
For the Lynches it was a playhouse, complete with tin roof, weather-
boarding and a child-sized deck. As a little boy, hours spent sitting in
the garage while my father worked on carpentry projects had given me
a skill with which I could at least attempt to repay my hosts for their
hospitality.

The night before I left Vancouver I returned late and tiptoed through
the gate and round the house to the open back door. Halfway up the
steps the glow of a night light in the playhouse caught my eye. I'd
finished it that afternoon and, walking over the grass, I saw that the
girls hadn't wasted any time in moving in. Kate's boots stood neatly
next to the little door and, peering through the window, I saw the
two of them wrapped up in sleeping bags together, fast asleep in their

new home. Smiling, I went inside and rested up for the last time on mainland Canada. Dagmar, the girls' mother, had found me a work colleague for company the following day, and I'd bought a garish but practical Hawaiian shirt from a charity shop. Everything was set for departure.

Lisa Webster arrived kitted out the next morning with her partner Jack. I'd only met her once briefly months before, and that was before she'd completed an Iron Man and got sick. Every time she spoke, I could hear the thick rasping of what sounded like pleurisy. Lisa gurgled when she talked and occasionally turned away, trying to stifle a lung-ripping cough. It didn't sound promising, but Jack provided the solution – the two of them would swap over whenever necessary, with the other driving the sag wagon (in this case, their old Volvo). This arrangement not only meant I could dump my heavier stuff but it came with the luxury of a driver-cum-cameraman. I never relished the 100-yard sprint I was used to in order to set up the wide shots. Every day or two I'd identify a pretty spot, dismount and run off, my bike lying in the road or in the hands of a stoker. Leaving the camera running, propped on a rock or fence post or in the crook of a tree, I'd sprint back, mount up and cycle past, before dismounting again and running, slower this time, back down the road to retrieve it. The wearier, angrier or more depressed I was, the harder it was to galvanise myself into carrying out this necessary task. With Jack and their car accompanying us across the bay and south down Vancouver Island, my running legs were saved the trouble.

Despite her rasping lungs, for two days Lisa did the lion's share of pedalling, Jack taking her place only on the longest of the island's hill climbs. The highway was larger than most of those I'd travelled so far but not without its beauty. The Malahat summit unlocked a view of the sinuous coastline surrounding Victoria, small ferries like water-boatmen skating in slow motion across the surface of the sea connecting the archipelago's communities that crowded the wide straights between the Island and the mainland. Fluffy clouds came and went in the blue, only occasionally wetting us as we covered the remaining distance to Victoria. Lisa, both on and off the bike, kept me entertained. She was brash and feisty and prone to garbling comical nonsense stories between bubbly coughing fits that caused Achilles to convulse in time with her spasms. I'd stop pedalling during these painful-sounding interludes, expecting at any second to feel the warm jelly-like spatter of a lung fragment hitting my shoulder.

Late in the day, as it got dark, the three of us arrived on the outskirts of Victoria. Lisa's cough was no better, her dark skin was pallid but she was still alive, and the three of us parked up outside a restaurant having not eaten properly since breakfast.

Eleven hours later I woke, my brain fogged and clouded by the evening's alcoholic celebration, in a cheap hotel room. Jack and Lisa had left. What time was it? I stretched across the plastic double bed, my eyes half closed as if trying to hide from a headache. Just managing to focus on my watch my brain suddenly threw off its bogginess as I flew into a panic. 'TEN O'CLOCK!!' I shouted out loud . . . I had to be on a ferry at 10:30, having filtered through immigration. I started to sweat again, hurrying into the same sweaty and now crusty cycling clothes that I'd worn the day before and running down the corridor with four pannier bags bashing regularly into door knobs. I made it to the dock, and shoved an elderly tourist out of the way to get to the immigration desk.

While I'd been resting in Vancouver, a friend of Josh way back in Chicken had got in touch. Heather and her daughter Skye were due to meet me off the boat in Seattle, and as the boat slid slowly past old marine timbers in the harbour entrance I wondered what my new friends would look like. After successfully passing into the US under the watchful eye of American cops, I found them happily ambling along the pier.

For two days we wandered through the streets of this cosmopolitan city, finding a fairground for Skye and cheap food for me to satisfy my cravings. It was a vibrant and beautiful cycle-free introduction to the United States, and I only jumped on Achilles briefly to cycle Skye round an underground parking lot. But when they left I was in no mood to leave Seattle and I knew someone else I'd met up in Chicken lived here, somewhere near the edge of town. Two days after finding my way to her house, I was setting off with the bubbly Samantha sitting on the back, quietly squealing with muffled laughter each time I twitched the handlebars to keep us heading straight. With not much convincing, she and her friends Lindsay and Diana decided to accompany me from Kenmore south towards Centralia. As we cycled that first day, Sam and I talked about most things. She told me her boyfriend, a German, did bicycle acrobatics, and that she very much wanted children. Bicycle acrobatics sounded painful to me, and a possible risk to fertility, but I said nothing.

For two more days the girls took it in turns on Achilles as we headed back to the main highway, with Mount Rainier out to the east and visible when the cloud lifted above the trees. Nights saw us sitting round a campfire, laughing and learning a little of each other's lives as flames danced on our faces. They dropped me a day away from Portland where the kindly employees of The Bike Gallery were ready to catch me before loneliness had a chance to take hold.

It had been less than a week since I'd rested up in Vancouver, but I stopped again, enjoying this city of good coffee, amazing bookshops, bicycles and biodiesel. The first touch of autumn was in the air and it reminded me of home.

On my last day in Portland I came across a bunch of other travellers also on their way south. Seated on a grassy embankment with a small crowd of others, as the sun started to creep towards Portland's skyline, birds began to fill the sky, and soon thousands of swifts were ducking and diving as one fluid circling mechanism high above an old furnace chimney in front of us. All of a sudden, as if a plug within the chimney had been removed, the birds spiralled into a vortex, a tornado reaching up and up until my eyes couldn't focus in the dusk. The swarm coiled down in slow motion, disappearing into a small black hole. For minutes a stream of swifts disappeared, the chimney apparently bottomless, until what little was left of the pattern faltered and began to break up. The sky was nearly empty, but for the last handful of swifts there was no more room. After a few abortive attempts, they flew south to escape lurking hawks on the lip of the smoke stack and roost in the nearby forest. This chimney was an age-old road house on the birds' long flight south for the winter. They'd be there well before me, I thought, but I wondered whether I'd see the swifts again sometime in Mexico.

Joel, a Bike Gallery employee, my host in Portland, and for a few miles a companion on Achilles, left me riding south with a string of equally hospitable contacts. His successor, Kendan, was small, nearly a toddler in fact. The four year old's father, Geoff, had insisted in an email (my website was beginning to get a lot of traffic) I pick his son up from school, so I did. I'd never given my autograph before, but with Kendan straddling my trailer, I was confronted at the school gates by a gaggle of small children brandishing notebooks and T-shirts. Once we got back to their house Geoff relieved his son and helped me pedal to McMinnville, beer incentivising us to travel quickly to the Golden Valley brew-pub, where the brew master – another of Joel's contacts – was waiting to receive us. In return for many pints of his award-winning elixir, I washed kegs for a day with pressure hoses and carbolic.

From there, before I stalled yet again, I fled through huge corridors of trees to Lincoln City and on to the vast, wave-swept beaches of the Oregon Coast. I'd visited this stretch of road once seven years before, and sights and sounds unchanged triggered memories. The same ghostly stacks of rock lazily drew back curtains of sea mist to spy on the mainland, but I skirted the campsites I had used in the past to camp for free elsewhere.

One evening, however, rather than camping out of sight in the tall trees, I sat with a couple on the sea cliffs not far from their home watching grey whales gliding through the kelp beds below us. Then, having been cycling the coastal road for only a couple of days I turned left, through forests to hot plains of dry, dusty earth at the foot of the Cascade Mountains.

Leaving the coast coincided with an event that had been a long time in coming. It had taken well over 3,000 miles for the tough, steel-laced rubber of my first pair of tires to be breached. I had two punctures in quick succession, whilst rolling through ever steepening avenues of trees which unlocked views of jagged peaks ahead. Then, having fixed the tube and cycling through an apocalyptic fire scar, the blackened trunks doing little to shade the road from the hot late summer sun, another problem arrived. The chain had adopted a soft rubbing noise since the fixing stop, then suddenly something jammed. I stamped on the pedals harder, but whatever it was – a twig maybe or a bent chain link – didn't budge. The bike slowed to a stop within a couple of yards and, fishing around with my knife between the chain links, I hooked something soft and flexible. Leaning the bike against the barrier to take a closer look I untangled the remnants of a small snake, now mangled and most definitely dead.

Reptile removed, I passed through the monotone of the fire scar and swept quickly back into the woods while the evening sun enriched the reds, yellows and browns of autumn in the Cascades. The road led me up again on the far side of the agricultural plains that surrounded the city of Bend, and the temperature dropped sufficiently for me to sit close to my stove in the evenings, playing the harmonica in gloved hands. The highway here was cold and quiet, climbing first through trees then a pumice desert towards Crater Lake and on to the jagged rim of the crater. After over a week of clear skies, it was then, up there in the cold air, higher than I'd yet been on Achilles, that the weather chose to break. But before it did, I stood on the edge of the steep sweep of volcanic scree, looking down into the lake 500 feet below. The water was perfectly blue, so much so that I lost almost all sense of depth or perspective. It was the same as the limitless blue of a cloudless sky, making me dizzy as I looked down, before the thunderheads encroached and dropped curtains of rain on its surface, turning it gunmetal grey and earthly once more.

Two days later I could still see the crater. The city of Medford and the forest were behind me and I was above wine country in the Applegate Valley. I sat at a lookout on Tallowbox Mountain, watching the new moon rise with a couple who rescued me from exhaustion outside an overpriced food store.

Medford, Oregon, isn't a pretty place, especially in comparison to the prehistoric landscape surrounding the crater. But there I had been on a mission to find a street stand where I'd been ordered by a waitress at a now distant café to taste my first chili dog free of charge courtesy of the vendor, her husband.

There were few landmarks by which to orientate myself in those grids of grey cement, and after an exploratory foray around the streets, I came to a halt in a mall car park, none the wiser as to the whereabouts of the hot dog man, who was supposedly based outside a sport-fishing department store. The car park was empty, so I cycled to a drab office building where a lady loitered next to a car.

'Excuse me, do you know this area well?' I asked, trying to get her attention – she had her back to me, fiddling around in a bottomless handbag. On hearing my voice, she turned and I knew instantly, though I don't know how, that she wouldn't be able to help. I put my left foot back on the pedal.

'Oh hello!' she said, her eyes wide and magnified further by huge glasses topped off with thick white hair roughly bunched into a bun on top of her head.

'Can I help you with something honey?' she said like a helpful fairy godmother. I was looking for a shop called Fishing Mart, or Sport-fishing Mart or something like that, I said. The lady looked at me intently, before offering up what she must have assumed was helpful advice.

'Well, mmmm, it could be down there,' she said raising her eyebrows and pointing down the road. Yes, I thought, it could, but equally it might not be, and as if reading my thoughts, she added wisely, 'or maybe up there?' pointing in the opposite direction.

Then it was too late, I'd lost my chance to bow out of this cretinous exchange, as her eyes dropped to Achilles, taking in the baggage, dust and dents. She began again, 'Boy, you're on some journey,' seeming a little surer of herself this time. I agreed with her and told her a little of my travels, but she wasn't listening. Instead she'd raised her head, fixing her gaze somewhere in the center of my head as a serene, glazed look came over her. Before I'd finished she cut me off as if she were deaf.

'Tell me, honey, is God travelling with you on your bicycle?' she asked, the words flowing out in a heavy, self-righteous mush.

I remembered then that this side of the Cascades was different from the coast. As well as selling guns and alcohol at gas stations, it was an 'evangelical' zone. I smiled my most sickly smile and glanced briefly over my shoulder theatrically at my back seat to double-check nothing had changed. I explained that while God didn't appear to be travelling with me at the moment, he was welcome to jump on any time he wanted, providing the seat wasn't taken. I was pleased with my little joke but it had obviously fallen on dead ground.

'You *must* take God on your bicycle,' she said.

I sighed, my smile becoming apologetic, then fading. 'Why *must* I?' I asked, feeling myself rising to the bait.

'You simply *must* because God *loves* you,' she said, her words still coming out overly compassionate.

'Will he only love me if I invite him to ride a ways with me?' I continued, spoiling for a fight.

This increasingly irritating conversation continued until a younger lady wandered out of the office building. She saved me, cutting her mother off and quickly giving me directions to the sport-fishing shop. I found it and ate my chili dog while chatting to the shy, rosy-cheeked Greg, then got the hell out of Medford, hightailing it to the quieter, beautiful and altogether more exclusive Applegate Valley, where the full moon now lit row upon row of hills with small orchards in valleys nestled 1,000 feet below.

I reached the coast again a few days later, but was now in northern California. There, the air was as damp as it had been in Oregon on this side of the Cascades, but the forests were bigger, much bigger. I was, after all, entering the Redwood National Park, home to the bulkiest trees on Earth, whose canopies made the black of night seem almost solid as I camped under them.

One morning, after crawling out from the shelter of a giant upturned root system, I found the air still damp, drops of dew silvery on the dark trees. The ocean was less than half a mile away but the thick pines blocked any sight or sound of it. Only the air gave it away, thick with banks of sea mist rolling through the forest as I pedalled stiffly up a gradual hill. There was no traffic this early and the only movement was someone up ahead, walking in the same direction and pushing a bike.

I gained on this person steadily until I could make out the fairly standard uniform of a homeless guy. Baggy and over-insulated trousers rubbed as he walked, and an equally baggy and holey jacket was topped off with a black woolly hat. His bike was festooned with garbage bags and an old, heavy and broken-looking radio. A cursory glance told me the bike was inoperable – it might at best coast down hills, but the chain was thick with rust and one wheel heavily buckled. He stopped when I greeted him, and leaned heavily on his handlebars, steam rising from his face into the cold air. His name was Scott. His black skin was streaked with lines of sweat and his nose was streaming, snot welling up on his upper lip. He told me reluctantly, as I pried his story out of him, that he'd cycled from Georgia to Seattle in the hope that he might be more happy there. Having found it wasn't what he expected, he'd decided it was time to go home. Back to Georgia. On the hazy map of the States in my brain I could visualise his trajectory, the longest diagonal across the land mass, 4,000 or 5,000 miles I guessed, then back again. I looked again at his bike and suddenly felt small. I offered to help but Scott politely refused food, water or anything else.

'I'll be all right,' he told me, his sad, calm eyes staring into the middle distance. The whites of his eyes were unblemished but he looked exhausted. 'Once I get to the top of this hill, I'll be all right,' he murmured calmly, more to himself than to me. I gave him the vitamin tablets I had to help him fight his cold and left him at the brow of the hill, where he was able to coast a short while before I lost sight of him as I sped on into the redwoods.

Those eyes branded themselves on my memory in the damp morning air. Suddenly the ego in me that had been fertilised by people's enthusiasm and admiration for my adventure was stamped out by this chance encounter. Scott wasn't a traveller, yet he had upped and left on a 5,000-mile journey fuelled by the simple hope of a better life at the other end. No guarantees, no loved ones. No safety net. But there was something else, something I've never seen in recreational travellers like me. He didn't moan, not even for fun, about the hills or traffic, such as it was. Perhaps the energy to moan was a luxury he couldn't afford. He just took each hill as it came. Hill, after hill, after hill, until he reached a place he could call home.

The calm, inviting redwoods remained quiet for an hour or two, but my brain now clamoured with thoughts about home, and the security of friends and family I'd valued so little when it surrounded me. I thought about the pragmatism with which Scott tackled his journey. 'It's only a hill . . .' I silently practised the words not far from the world's largest tree.

'It's only a hill, once I'm at the top I'll be fine.' I knew I'd have trouble putting this philosophy into practice when the next sizeable incline appeared.

Before I reached the south end of the redwoods, this mood of philosophical melancholy had been destroyed by the boisterous company of four Jehovah's Witnesses who interrupted the silence of the redwoods telling jokes as they wandered beneath the primeval canopy of trees before joining me. Their companion, a Kermit the Frog, spent some time with his limbs tied round my handlebars.

Not long after that, I arrived in San Francisco with Todd, the first person who, on hearing about my journey via the website, had taken the trouble to take a painfully slow bus 200 miles north to Fort Bragg to do a stint with me. Having camped in long-since closed state parks, tasted oysters for the first time and rolled gratefully across the Golden Gate Bridge in the last horizontal shreds of autumn sunlight, we arrived in the city in time for Halloween.

By ten that evening I was mingling with Egyptians, vampires and an intimidating bunch of transvestite policewomen. The gay Brazilian whose party it was was very polite, but obviously didn't think much of my hurried attempt at being a zombiefied Captain Jack Sparrow. It was the best I could do with what Todd could muster from his own dressing-up box.

For days I'd relax in Dolores Park surrounded by men, many of whom wore little more than a banana hammock while sunning themselves propped like Greek sculptures on one elbow scanning the surroundings for talent.

San Francisco, like a handful of places before it, nearly trapped me, but before this magnetic and hilly city could get its claws in, I fled south again to keep an appointment with a cycling coach who held off from criticising my technique as she helped me nudge my mileage over the 4,000 marker. Then in the boringly cool town of Santa Cruz I taunted a skateboarding kid at a pedestrian crossing until he joined me to do some pedalling. That was the price he paid for shooting Achilles a sideways glance. After saying he 'didn't want to miss this opportunity of a lifetime' (to ride with me or skip class? I wondered) he told me I was lucky. If the surf had been worth a damn he'd have been rippin' it up rather than pedlin' with me. A couple of hours later he cruised back to town on the skateboard he'd strapped to the top of my trailer.

Every day as I pushed deeper into California I continued to come across passers-by interested in Achilles and his cargo. There was a variety of reactions, but one in particular seemed to increase in frequency as I approached the showbiz glamour of southern California.

Pulling up outside a store, bystanders would often be treated to the sight of me grappling with Achilles, trying to balance the rolling 200 pounds against a delicate shop front, dropping him, swearing and then struggling to raise him from the pavement and try again. It was not uncommon that after ample time to study the Union Jack, tightly packed spare tires and filthy lycras strung across the trailer, someone would saunter over.

'So, where'bouts in Australia are you from?' they'd say without introduction.

'I'm not, I'm English.'

'Oh really?' they might say as if I might be mistaken.

'Yes.'

'So, where've you come from?'

'I started in Prudhoe Bay, Alaska.'

'Where you headed?'

'I'm hoping to reach the southerly tip of South America.'

'Oh right, yeah, I know a guy that drove a Dodge down from LA to Mexico City one time . . .'

That's about as far as the line of questioning went, almost as if they were just looking for a polite way to start talking. Sometimes they'd throw in a bit more though, some second-hand story about how they'd known a guy who'd been shot in Guatemala.

Of course, there were others that would pin me down for an hour, quizzing me on every aspect of my journey. Mostly kids. One child outside a school in northern California asked if I was travelling through Mexico. On finding that I was, he asked in a quiet, humble voice if I might be able to come back soon and tell him what it was like. I'd like to have asked him to jump on, but his mother whisked him home for tea.

When I sat outside supermarkets drinking chocolate milk or out on the sidewalk just resting, it was always kids who asked the most interesting questions if they were given the chance. Often though, their parents, after a quick sideways glance at the filthy traveller, wouldn't break step, dragging the curious child along the pavement after them.

South of the soul-sapping, rolling cliff-top roads of Big Sur National Park, I stayed one night in a lighthouse where seals jumped like dolphins just off the rocky shoreline. Then, further south still, the road took me inland where the damp coastal air was replaced by dry heat, and the sea with fields. After a day of perfectly straight rows of young green crops that seemed to go on forever, I cycled into Lompoc, a city dominated by farmers rather than the nearby tourists, surfers or too-cool-for-school type of Californian.

7

Old man Ernie

DAY 135: 5,185 MILES

It was late in the day and a flat road surrounded by large arable fields led me into the small concrete city. I'd seen so much of the beautiful coast though, that a bit of drabness didn't matter – I looked forward to seeing what Lompoc would bring in the way of new people to talk to. The streets were the kind you find in most nondescript small North American cities, grey and square, large blocks of squat buildings making up one of ten malls, each to my untrained eye indistinguishable from the next. It didn't look to me like a place that was brimming over with camping opportunities. It might be another 'camping in a city park hedge' night, I thought. In an effort to safeguard against an uncomfortable curbside camp I pulled up on the pavement outside an ice-cream parlour, the best thing the city's mall had to offer.

Leaning Achilles gently on a rear pannier against a fake stone pillar, I wandered inside, wiping the grimy sweat off my face and wearing my best smile. Two girls worked the counter, both young, younger than me I guessed. A handful of people sat dotted around the small, round tables and on the cushioned bench running the length of the café.

I knew what I wanted without looking at the list of complicated-sounding ice-cream options. Still beaming, I ordered a chocolate milkshake from the dark-haired girl, and we began to chat as she prepared my favourite recovery drink. Always on these occasions there was a tinge of an ulterior motive. It wasn't to get lucky with a waitress, just maybe get invited to sleep on a patch of floor or in a garage. It had happened a few times so far on my journey south, and in these concrete jungles it was nicer to be on someone's property than the pavement.

While I sat trying to conserve my milkshake for at least a minute or two, I noticed someone stooped down, apparently examining the gearing of Achilles at close quarters. Every interested party represented to me a potential host or better still a companion. I got up and wandered outside to investigate.

Ernie introduced himself. He was old, 70 or more, and seemed a little anxious, rolling his tongue and biting it nervously between sentences. He was well-spoken and sounded educated, but his scrawny frame and scraggly beard gave him the appearance of a guy down on his luck. He was confused as to why the rear pedals of the tandem had been detached he said – I'd done it a day or two before, swapping my front pedals for the newer, less grinding rear ones and not bothering to replace them. He told me he'd been a keen cyclist 40 years ago, but had barely ridden since.

After quickly and silently estimating his ability to suffer some time in the saddle I told him he should jump on the following day, get 'back in the saddle'. The next minute or so provided a textbook example of the struggle people go through when an opportunity springs up without warning. I could almost see his brain wrestling with all those mundane day-to-day excuses . . . feeding the dog, doing the laundry, and then he dropped in the heavyweight excuse that his wife was sick and needed looking after. There was no reason for me to beg the old man, and Ernie wandered off back to his car with a small bag of shopping. I settled back down in my seat, the ice cream in the top of my shake now melted. I felt like the girls might just invite me to stay, so I made no effort to leave as they slowly began cleaning the place up and sweeping the debris of crumbled wafers and paper napkins into the corner. Twenty minutes later I was staggered to see Ernie peering around outside, apparently searching for me. He looked pleased when I appeared from behind the tinted glass doors and explained to me courteously that he felt that he'd be a fool not to at least try to accompany me on the day's ride to Santa Barbara

– he tentatively admitted having covered that distance before, though many moons ago. Ernie then uttered exactly the same words that the schoolkid surfer had let fly after I'd challenged him to jump on at the crossing in Santa Cruz. He 'didn't want to miss the opportunity of a lifetime'. I gulped, slightly shocked and humbled to hear that that was what I was offering. I doubted that Ernie, if he turned up the following morning, would be anything like the surfer in any other respect. I thought Ernie was a little humbler, and I was almost certain, too, that once Ernie had had enough, he would not scoot back home on a bendy-looking skateboard.

I did stay with the girls from the ice-cream parlour that night, and after trawling the grid-like streets eating fast food then watching a movie, fell asleep on a deep pile carpet in the living room of their small apartment. This was high living.

Ernie didn't disappoint. At 9 a.m. sharp he arrived back at the ice-cream parlour in crisp, clean but antique-looking cycle wear. The tight-fitting clothes revealed Ernie's modest frame in all its glory. I thought he might have trouble cycling the 60 miles to Santa Barbara, but standing there I gauged him to be about 135 pounds soaking wet – I could pull that if necessary.

It was, however, not necessary. Ernie delivered as much power as his sinews allowed. He sat on the back of Achilles and gave his all, the unseasonably hot sun beating down on us as we left the wide agricultural valley and rolled over the sprawling desert hills and down along the coast. I asked him, once we'd topped out on a particularly debilitating hill, what his wife had thought of his crazy decision to make this ride. His response caught me off-balance.

'Well, Dominic,' he began slowly with the air of a guilty man, 'I'm afraid I lied to you yesterday when I said my wife was sick. She died six months ago today.'

I offered my condolences, confused but keen to hear more.

'I knew today would be difficult, but decided I could either sit at home being miserable or come on this bicycle ride with you. And right now I cannot begin to tell you how pleased I am that I made this choice ...'

Ernie's wife had died after a long, painful period of battling illness. Money earned by Ernie in a long-standing job as a high-flying engineer had paid for the things necessary to make her comfortable for the last years of her life, but little remained for him. He didn't care. His life had stopped as if it had had the battery taken out. He'd let everything around him fall into disrepair. He explained that that was the reason he hadn't invited me to stay, he was too ashamed to let me see the state he'd let himself fall into.

I sat pedalling silently for a minute or two taking this in, and regarded Ernie in a new light, with more respect and more curiosity than before. I looked over my shoulder and smiled at him, his black helmet sitting at a jaunty angle revealing a clump of white hair. He smiled lopsidedly back at me. His face had relaxed, the furrowed brow and anxiety of the day before had fallen away. What struck me most was how much fun he was having. He hurt, doubtless his limbs were burning, but for that he seemed ecstatically grateful – it was a sure-fire sign that he was alive. It made me grateful too and served to wash away the slight film of indifference to life in the saddle that had begun to grow over my eyes since it had become the norm.

Ernie had helped me see what I was doing for what it really was – an adventure that others could, in some small way, benefit from. I liked that. It made everything seem a little more worthwhile.

We arrived in Santa Barbara as Ernie's energy reserves fell deep into the red, just enough power remaining to sustain his wide, white-toothed smile. 'I cannot begin to describe the pleasure and pain I've been feeling today,' he said outside the restaurant where he'd bought me lunch.

A month later I received an email from Ernie, back at home and cycling again. A local newspaper article about our ride together had been published online, he told me, and as a result he'd heard from his son, who'd read the story. He hadn't spoken to his children for years due to family complications that he didn't enlarge upon. But now, due to this little piece of editorial, he was in touch with both children, and two grandchildren he never knew he had. My pleasure was only equalled by the gratitude Ernie poured out to me for that modest sunny day in the saddle. I wanted to contest it, saying that the truth of the matter was I'd done very little, but I let it go, basking in the heart-warming progression of events following his ride. It had changed us both more than we could have guessed was possible, and given our respective journeys a new set of wheels.

I spoke to Ernie on the phone two years later, having maintained contact. He sounded like the same smiling man I'd left in Santa Barbara. Still curious about his long and varied life, I asked him again about his job. 'I remember you telling me you were some kind of flight or electrical engineer, you were working on defence projects or something . . .?'

'Well, Dominic,' he replied, reminding me of the last time he'd caught me unawares, 'I wish I could tell ya.'

I could hear in his voice that he was smiling. I laughed, wondering what else this skinny gentleman had up his sleeve.

The day after my ride with Ernie I sat in a café on State Street in Santa Barbara. Everything here was manicured: the people, the small shrubs outside the coffee shops, even the car parks were made to look like Spanish palaces. But Santa Barbara lacked the charisma I'd found in less notable towns further north. For once I had no yearning to stay. Instead I had the pleasant sensation of looking forward to seeing what was round the corner. The fact that Mexico wasn't far away filled me with an addictive anxiety. With about seven words of Spanish but fluent in the dozens of scare stories I'd heard about Latin America, I felt like a small child who had an urge to climb over the fence and stroke a tiger at the zoo.

8

Into the unknown

DAY 145: 5,255 MILES

From where I stood, I could see a boy gliding along the cycle path like a modern-day Mary Poppins. With an umbrella held up in one hand to catch the keen wind, he appeared to float along the cycle path at the seafront on a skateboard hidden from view by the low sandy scrub.

The long straight beach seemed to stretch all the way to Los Angeles as I cycled past a line of trucks and campers, mostly the rolling homes of surfers taking advantage of long lines of uninterrupted waves. Misha, a photographer, helped me pedal for a day on Achilles out of her college town. She was a student in Santa Barbara but didn't fit in on the main street there, her dreadlocks and timid smile at odds with the monopolising sheen of blonde, manicured 'perfection'.

Not long after camping on a deserted football field outside Ventura, a press article kept me lucky, fortunate you might say. Richard Fortune turned up on the doorstep of a family who'd taken me in for the night, with shaved legs and a yellow jersey to provide the driving force that propelled Achilles to Santa Monica. That 65-mile stretch was very definitely powered from the back seat while I merely kept time, steered and admired the arid hills speckled with cacti and the spreading whitewash of cresting waves. We arrived on the LA Beachfront as the sun set blood-red over the famous pier, Ferris wheel and lifeguard huts, while I half-expected to see David Hasselhoff trot over in red trunks to meet us, pectoral muscles bouncing as he ran.

INTO THE UNKNOWN

I stopped only briefly to sample what this legendary city had to offer someone not willing to spend any money. I sat on the beach in Santa Monica, doing chin-ups to keep my climbing muscles alive, and slunk around the grimy, impoverished streets of Hollywood on Achilles counting dozens of people struggling to survive in the shadow of the fashion show at the Kodak Theatre near the Avenue of the Stars. Through the Oprah billboards, a few traffic lights and some ugly high-rise buildings, I could see the Hollywood sign on the scrubby hillside above the city.

The day's sightseeing ended only after I'd split the serenity of the monied and hushed neighbourhood of Beverly Hills, not on the bike but in the front seat of a Beverly Hills fire truck. Invited to sit in on a 'code three' blues and twos test, I sat grinning next to the driver as we sped through the streets, kicking up yellowing leaves.

I was getting damn close to Mexico. In an effort to learn more than my seven words of Spanish back up in northern California I'd spent a few weeks trundling along with post-it notes flapping on my handlebars or scraggy bits of paper wedged between my map and its plastic casing. On the paper would be the odd useful phrase in Spanish, maybe 'Is it safe to camp here?' or 'Where is the police station?' I mastered these phrases, then quickly forgot them, bored with learning before I'd even started. In my last and longest day's cycling in the States, I remembered only two phrases: 'One beer please' and 'Where is the bathroom?' These snippets of Spanish would allow me to survive, I reasoned, though it wouldn't be a particularly healthy existence.

I'd be lying if I said I wasn't a little nervous. For months I'd been listening to mildly disturbing roadside stories from a steady stream of Canadians and Americans, only a handful of whom had ventured into Mexico.

'You better be packin',' a farmer once said to me.

'What?' I responded, genuinely confused.

'Take a piece, ya know, a pistol . . . you can't be too careful,' he explained.

This small, friendly farmer in Oregon joined ranks of others recounting stories of misadventure in Mexico. If I were to believe everything I'd been told, crossing the border would take me into a land belonging only to a Tarantino film: vampires with chainsaws slicing up anything with a heartbeat, or a muscled vagrant in a waistcoat pointing a gun at my forehead and demanding my trainers.

Despite months of kindness from strangers having taught me to trust, these stories surfaced in the pools of my mind as I neared San Diego, covering 80, 90, 100 miles under the hot southern sun. I'd never cycled even nearly this far in a day on a machine as heavy as Achilles. It was exhausting work, and by the time I was 10 miles from the house where I'd been invited to stay, it was dark and I was lost on the outskirts of the city with insufficient energy to make sense of the map. My host, Keith, a man who on jogging past one day during holidays further north had invited me to stay, came to my rescue. With his family crammed into their car, they drove to where I was and Keith, pedalling powerfully behind me, made up for my failing legs, propelling Achilles up the stepped hillside to their house overlooking the city. One hundred and nineteen miles on a bike weighing eighty-seven kilos. I'd survived the day on energy bars I'd been given and my guts as a result felt sticky and sluggish. But I'd done it, I'd reached the end of the States, and in doing so, reached the end of anything I could predict, anything I was familiar with.

I stayed with Keith and his family for over a week, lounging and relaxing. It passed too quickly. 'One more day's rest, yes, that would be good,' I'd say to myself, testing how it sounded while sitting at the breakfast table, and imagining Keith's wife Cindy getting home and finding me still helping myself to their hospitality weeks later. No, I had to go, there was no good reason not to and on the morning of my fifth rest day, in an empty house, I had my mountain of gear in some semblance of order. What had they said about leaving the key somewhere? Oh yeah, open the garage, get the bike out, close the garage, lock front door and post key through letterbox. Last check inside . . . there, the key to warm relaxed San Diego life was now out of reach on the doormat. I had to go.

Despite the hotbed of cycling enthusiasts in and around the city and with Keith too busy to jump on I'd found no one to accompany me. It felt a little like I wasn't being taken seriously on account of how little Lycra I wore and the fact I didn't shave my legs. So, still vaguely thinking about turning around, I found myself begrudgingly cycling through the no-man's-land south of the city. I stopped only once, at one of the bad sandwich shops that sit wedged between sprawling truck dealerships in National City. Above the cement and glass-fronted buildings, I could see the Mexican flag waving lazily over Tijuana. After a cardboard sandwich and the alien sound of Spanish being spoken all around me, I pushed off from my last breather this side of the border. In a low-level silent but excited panic cycling through the dusty rubble-strewn scrub, I tried desperately to dredge up the remnants of Spanish words that might still be lurking in my head somewhere.

The US border police nearly all wore aviators and a tight-lipped, unsmiling, no-nonsense face. Through the wire fence I could see an endless line of cars trying to head north into the States. Unsure of border procedures for a tandem I coasted to the nearest officer, a man whose belly was only just being contained by straining buttons near his belt. 'Excuse me, where should I line up to go through the border?' I asked, smiling, uncertain as to whether I should join the pedestrians or the idling vehicles.

'It don't much matter,' the policeman said, staring past me as if I didn't exist. 'See that hole in the fence behind me?' he carried on, 'You can go on through that.' Behind was a section of fence that looked like it had been crudely cut away with bolt cutters.

'Really? I don't need to get an exit stamp or anything?'

'It don't much matter,' he said again, losing the already low-level interest he might have had in my enquiry. This interaction didn't fill me with confidence, but I went ahead as instructed and pushed Achilles awkwardly through the gap with no paper evidence that I had arrived in Latin America.

Despite cycling slowly trying to make sense of things, my heart was pounding and I was sweating. I hadn't been this on edge since finding myself in a run-down trailer park at 9 p.m. one evening in Oregon, dogs barking at me and a man wearing more than an average amount of garish jewellery promising to show me a safe place to sleep. I was all right then, so I'll be fine now, I kept telling myself as I got into increasingly busier streets, still no useful road signs in sight.

After about 25 minutes, near what I guessed to be the center of town, I pulled over onto the side of the busy fume-filled street, taxis and minivans belching smoke as they shoved through the traffic. I didn't know where to go but despite being nervous about attracting unwanted attention I shouted over to some sweaty, well-muscled car washers who'd paused in their work to look at Achilles. I smiled at them and said questioningly, 'Ensenada?' – I knew if I was cycling towards that city I'd be on the right track. They smiled back and pointed down a busy road on the far side of a large roundabout. 'Thaddawaay!' one of them added helpfully. I smiled, pleased to have had my first interaction in Mexico and survived unscathed, and cycled off into a cloud of leaded gas smoke and an onslaught of car horns. Five minutes later I spotted a large green sign for Ensenada which led me up another street, just as busy, between old, dirty buildings with layer upon layer of posters peeling off the rotten plaster walls. It would be a while before I'd be able to read this stuff, but the pictures suggested at least half of them were advertising boxing or wrestling events nearby. With every second I cycled the right way through this city, I felt, perhaps prematurely, that I was proving it was possible to travel in Tijuana without being robbed, raped or shot at. But looking at my cheap plastic watch I was worried to see it was 4:30 p.m., leaving little time to escape the city before sunset. I pedalled harder up a gradual hill that pulled at me until I was only crawling past pedestrians and fruit vendors pushing carts of pineapples or watermelons up the pavement.

'Gotta get out into the desert to camp,' I thought as sweat and fumes stung my eyes. Then I heard a shout on the pavement a few yards behind me.

'*Hola, de dónde eres?*' a man called out.

'Carry on,' I said to myself, no time for chat, glancing round quickly to check nothing had been lifted from the bike.

'*Bonjour, tu es Français?*' the same voice sang out again. Mmm, my French is better than my Spanish, but no, carry on, don't get sucked in, I told myself. 'Hello, where do you come from?' the man shouted louder now and with only a slight accent. This guy was persistent, spoke three languages and seemed very curious. I couldn't resist, already missing speaking my language, so I looked behind me, checking for traffic, before steering Achilles awkwardly in an arc, narrowly avoiding a scooter, and coasted to where the voice came from. Three men behind a taco stand waved at me, and I rolled to a stop in front of the clean stainless steel cart. I had forgotten about hunger until a mouth-watering meaty smell hit me from under the three steaming lids. I hadn't eaten since the grey sandwich on the other side of the border, and one of the men smiled as I shot a glance at the small menu hung on one of the metal stays under the word *Loncheria* in big red letters.

Marco, the eldest of the three, introduced himself. On seeing his broad smile, any remaining doubts about my security faded. Marco looked at my trailer and the whip antennae still flying my Union Jack and a left-over Canadian flag. 'You don't have a Mexican flag?' he questioned, still smiling but with a mildly concerned look on his face. I explained I hadn't found one yet, and that in an act of diplomacy I nearly always flew the flag of the country I was travelling through above that of my own. Marco nodded and said something quickly to his teenage helper. He wandered off round the corner of an empty building across the street.

Marco was explaining his language skills – he had a French wife and had travelled to France – when the teenager returned, a small Mexican flag hanging by his side. Marco took the flag, attaching it above the Union Jack, before carrying on talking. He was an experienced nurse, having worked in San Diego for a while, but he loved his taco stand and, unable to find another nursing job, he had decided to try and make a go of it.

The light was fading from the sky and casting an orangey-purple glow on the horizon above the pale flat city and coastline behind Marco's taco stand. I had stopped worrying about time now and had entrusted my wellbeing to Marco, not wanting to rush this encounter. Five minutes later, after following Marco's instructions and bumping along a heavily potholed street, I was sitting on a stool next to a filthy but functional mechanic's shop with a motherly cook, Esmeralda, smiling and questioningly pointing at different pots full of food, my reactions deciding the order of my forthcoming banquet. As she worked away, meat and onions hissing on a griddle through the serving hatch, I looked around me properly for the first time in Mexico.

So, this is it, I thought, trying to absorb as much of the surroundings as possible, still mildly dumbfounded as to how I had landed almost effortlessly in such good hands. With the evening, a kind of calm had descended. Not an actual calm, there were still car horns, shouts and an underlying activity on the street, but nothing was rushed, nothing pressed on me like earlier in the day. Little neon lights started to flicker on behind hatches and inside doorways, and elderly people took up their positions on the doorsteps, making the most of the cool while the pavement still radiated heat into the still air. The mechanics nearby worked slowly on into the evening, only pausing occasionally to saunter into the little liquor store for a six-pack of Tecate, the local beer advertised on almost every available square inch of whitewashed wall.

Esmeralda beckoned me towards the tiled bar top as she wrapped some frying meat up in a maize tortilla and placed it on a plastic plate in front of me. I wasn't sure exactly what it was, but it smelled good and tasted delicious. Within minutes, I'd devoured four tacos of various flavours, my favourite of which I guessed to be tripe. Esmeralda was lovingly wrapping up the eighth taco – brain, judging by the consistency – when Marco and his small crew arrived.

I stayed with Marco's family that night, but before arriving at his small apartment he parked up in an empty area of tarmac, the sea breaking heavily in the warm night on rocky shores 100 yards ahead of us. In the last deep-blue light on the horizon, I could make out a silhouette of All Saints Island 20 miles away. To our right was a red reinforced metal fence and beyond that the States, where a patrol car sat, lights dipped but looking strangely menacing.

Heading out of Tijuana the next day, towards El Rosario and beyond, old worries about the city had evaporated but thoughts of bandits on the isolated roads with big rusty knives held to my throat still played in my head, along with a tinge of anxiety about truckers. Before embarking on this journey, I'd read journals of other cyclists who had come this way, and a few enlarged upon 'the dangers and risks of the only north–south highway in the state'. Apparently the asphalt was 18 feet wide and the average width of a Mexican truck is 9 feet, excluding wing mirrors. The stories mentioned rocky cactus-filled drop-offs, evil truckers and drivers that positively relished the opportunity to mow down a sunburnt gringo on a bicycle. Other more recent journals documented exactly where bike tourists had been robbed. One cyclist, only a few weeks ahead of me, had apparently been the victim of a mugging about 50 miles south of where I sat.

But these stories slipped from my mind as Baja's desert revealed itself, a reddish-brown scrubland, the kind I'd only seen before in spaghetti westerns. Down the sweeping slope to my right lay two car wrecks a few hundred yards from the road. The roadkill I occasionally swerved around when traffic allowed had changed. I had left the raccoons and deer on the other side of the border and picked up a trail of dogs in various states of decomposition. The sun was hot, but this far north there was still a fresh breeze that kept me from melting. The price for this refreshment however was the putrid and nauseating smell of the next flattened dog, or the last, depending on the wind direction.

I passed through dust-blown brown villages, a haze of wind-borne sand hanging over them. *'Buena suerte!'* the people shouted as I passed smiling but still nervous about having to speak the language. I looked up 'suerte' in my almost untouched Spanish dictionary when I next sat down for a rest. They were wishing me good luck. Each time I heard it again I shed another skin of worry, letting it blow like tumbleweed back to the States where it had been sewn into me.

In the last tourist stronghold before uninterrupted desert, Marco and his family drove south to spur me on and introduce me to yet more food, the mouth-watering raw fish ceviche being a speciality here. That evening I sat on the coastal promenade of the city in the evening watching the lights of the cruise ships twinkling as their passengers sipped cocktails on the seafront. Before I left, André, a Mexican student, and Marco's five-year-old son sampled the delights of Achilles, Marco Junior bobbing up and down on the back seat, his little legs struggling to keep track of the pedals. Leaving the earnest child begging his father to let him come with me, I ventured from tourist territory into a land of smaller dusty communities and roads straighter than I'd thought possible. The asphalt often became masked by the rising shimmering air of a heat haze, undulations in the road ahead becoming mirrored and invisible. To the west, I caught the odd glimpse of the ocean, white breakers silently crashing down refreshingly in a gap between the giant sand dunes.

I was amazed not only by the quality of the food in these tiny little places as my buying of provisions got slowly more adventurous, but also by the proximity of the Internet wherever I was. I would pass through the tiniest, most insignificant little outpost only to find a crusty little sign creaking in the breeze directing me to a small shack that looked like a disused outhouse. Inside I would find a couple of bent and twisted wires leading down to two computers, old but in service, which would connect me, ever so slowly, to the 'interweb'. In one such hut on December 5, 2006, I received an email that bolstered me with a fresh dose of hope for company. The email was from Ari Goodman. 'Ari who??' I thought as I clicked on the name. Painstakingly slowly the email unfolded on the tiny screen to reveal a message from a girl I suddenly remembered.

'Hi, I'm Ari, the girl that cycled past you in Big Sur,' it read.

'THAT girl,' I exclaimed out loud, suddenly remembering a 30-second meeting with a small, outgoing cyclist wearing a Scooby Doo Lycra shirt. 'Huh, cool, maybe I'll hook up with you further south,' I remember her saying when we stopped on the side of the road. That was it, and I wasn't going to hold my breath, I'd heard that plenty of times before. But now it seemed like Ari was serious! I hardly dared believe that the forecast of over 600 lonely desert miles had suddenly changed. She said that she would likely arrive in Tijuana on Friday. It was Thursday. I panicked, scrabbling for my map, trying to predict bus stops along the long straight red line. Villages marked were few and far between, but there was one in particular in between a whole lot of nothing, called Cataviña. This was maybe two days of hard cycling away, and seemed like a good place to meet. I hurriedly typed an email saying this, then paid up and left, feeling a new-found urgency to get moving. I checked the water bottles on the bike's ample frame. I had nearly a gallon, enough, I thought, to take me through the day and cook with that night.

I had never camped in anything resembling desert before and I realised, looking up from the pale, sun-baked asphalt at the dry, cacti-dominated landscape, that I was looking forward to it. I had been nervous about camping in Mexico, but the soft landing thanks to my new-found friends in this country had allayed that fear. Besides, there was no one out here to disturb me, only snakes and insects with at worst a bite or sting, and only if I was careless. I made good progress that afternoon as the sun coloured the low-lying hills a beautiful orange. Then I pulled off the road near a gentle curve and barrelled carelessly through 20 or 30 yards of cacti to a small patch of bare dusty ground, big enough for a sleeping mat and hidden from the road by a thick tangle of spiny vegetation. The plentiful old dry cacti were weak, and it took three to prop Achilles up next to me. Only when I'd finished did I notice scratches along my arms and legs oozing blood gently where the thorns and spines had tried to prevent me from leaving the road. I sat down and jumped up again, two more thorns having sunk into my arse. The spines had gone in easily enough but clung tenaciously deep in my limbs with triple-barbed heads, tearing a small chunk of skin away when they finally gave up their grip.

The stars quickly shone bright after the sun went down and the heat from the ground disappeared into the sky as I primed the stove and lit the small pool of petrol. The fuel vapour hissed out of the small hole and the familiar welcome splutter of the blue jet of flame came to life, turning the small metal heat deflector red hot. Once my pasta was cooked and as the dull roar of the stove spluttered and died, the desert's silence was suddenly oppressive. Slowly though, my ears became attuned to the small crackles and shrill little screeches of insects living in the dried-out cactus husks. It was only 8 p.m., but with the hard desert cold and no one to talk to, sleep was the only option. I crawled into my sleeping bag and tried reading, my head torch lighting the pages in front of my nose, but my arms got cold and I gave up, slipping the book under my makeshift pillow and stowing my torch in the box.

Within a minute, after my eyes had become accustomed to the night, the darkness disappeared and the brilliant moon cast hard shadows of the cacti on the ground. When I woke a few hours later the moon had arced round and made the spokes of Achilles glint. I heard something, a rustling, a scuttling noise, and then I saw it near the back wheel about a foot from my bagged-up feet. I lay stock-still and watched unblinkingly. A scorpion? I wondered, knowing these things preferred to wander at night. Then it moved again, skipping and jumping a foot then stopping abruptly, sniffing the air. It was a mouse, and I watched it travel from the bush to my wheel, up onto the tire, up a silver spoke and round the chunky hub, disappearing behind the pannier then arriving on top of it before diving in like a child in a ball pen. Still groggy with sleep I wondered if it was making a nest in amongst my smelly leggings and sweat-stained T-shirts. Sleep returned after the mouse had come and gone a few times. Whatever it was doing, I sleepily reasoned, I welcomed the harmless company, and would at worst have to discard a shredded old shirt in the morning.

Early the next morning, in bone-cracking cold, I wolfed down the cold, glutinous remains of my pasta and checked my clothes, finding no sign of rodent damage. Then I wheeled Achilles slowly and more carefully this time back out of the scrub to the road, my scratches stinging as I moved.

I passed old ladies in tiny little settlements having already begun the morning chores, sweeping the dust from their steps or sprinkling water in the dirt of their yards as the sun rose. The 18-wheeler trucks that I regarded with a healthy respect sat sleeping bumper to bumper on the edges of these hamlets, where taco stands had kept them company the evening before. So far, the truckers that had passed me had saluted with a cheerful blast on their horns and had given me a courteously wide berth, swinging over to the other side of the narrow road. Soon after I had left the whitewashed buildings behind, the sun found me in the desert, causing me to sweat once more, dissolving the tide marks on my shirt and shorts from the day before.

A truck did, however, hit me later that day. I only had a few seconds' warning. The horn blast caused me to look round at the approaching truck. The driver was close enough for me to be able to see his expression – he looked totally void of emotion, chewing on a toothpick or a straw, gripping the wheel stubbornly, no intention of slowing down. Just yards ahead of the truck I felt the barrage of hot air hit me, then the sucking force as it whisked past me, inches from my shoulder. As the end of the trailer blurred across my squinting vision, Achilles sprang up, coming alive and jumping sideways in the air. I went with him, my foot catching a rock on landing, saving me from falling headlong down the embankment into the cacti. The truck's rear axle had connected with my pannier, I realised, breathing hard and swearing loudly as it rumbled away and the air grew still again. I was shaking with adrenaline as I assessed the damage, confused as to how such a sudden impact had only scuffed the pannier, not ripped it clean off. I laid the bike down and sat, still shaking, on the ground, breathing hard with shock.

I waited two days in the village of Cataviña surrounded by a city of house-sized boulders in the desert. I chased every bus down the dusty road like a dog. Doors opened, but Ari never appeared. The evening of the second day I resigned myself to continuing south the next day on my own, feeling foolish to have ever fostered the hope of this unlikely meeting.

Two days later, approaching the outskirts of Guerrero Negro, I moved slowly, bored by the now monotonous road far from the mountains and the coast. Up ahead was the junction and the road leading off at right angles to the town, and before the junction was a sign denoting the border of Baja California South. But there was something else, someone or something taking advantage of the tiny strip of shade it created. As I got closer I saw that it was human, lying half in a sleeping bag and reading. Closer still I saw, almost totally hidden by the sleeping bag, a bike helmet. A sleeping bag, skid lid and a book are not the standard chattels of a Mexican farmer, I thought as I rolled off the asphalt and bumped over the tussocky grass to the shade. Thoughts of company had all but disappeared, but the girl with huge sunglasses obscuring most of her face looked up casually as I stopped.

'Hello Dominic,' she said.

It took a few pregnant seconds to process what was going on. It was her! Ari smiled at me calmly, taking in my surprise and noting in a relaxed fashion, 'Lucky you saw me, I was so into my book you could have gone straight by and I wouldn't have known.'

After securing her modest backpack on the trailer, I wheeled Achilles enthusiastically back onto the asphalt, unable to wipe an ear-to-ear grin from my face. Company had made me happy again, just like that.

In the 20 minutes it took to reach Guerrero Negro, Ari recounted her journey south to find me. Having looked out of the bus window in the evening light of Cataviña she'd decided there was nothing there and continued in the night to Guerrero, a town with a few more basic amenities. With fluent Spanish she was able to ask around, and find out whether anyone had seen an unusually large, heavily laden bike with two saddles and only one person. With a 'no' from the town's nosiest old lady, she knew I had yet to arrive and set about waiting. I was impressed.

As we progressed south together, the keen Baja wind often blew in our faces, all but paralysing us and causing me to swear into the air, the sound clutched away instantly. Sometimes though it was a relaxing tailwind gently encouraging us in the right direction.

Early in our partnership we trawled the shelves of a small supermarket for a few days of supplies. The food labels might as well have been written in Chinese, the amount of sense they made to me. I had been in Mexico for a little over a week, and my Spanish vocabulary hadn't improved much. But with Ari's help I picked out obvious-looking necessities like tortillas, cookies, cheese, pasta and big juicy avocados. Then my eyes settled on some tins full of meaty treats – if the image was to be believed – in a dark tasty looking sauce. *Chipotles adobados* it read, in harmless-looking letters. I dropped two of them into the basket and walked to the almost sleeping checkout girl, looking forward to finishing the day's ride.

Fuel for fire was mostly easy to come by. In the enshrouding cold of the desert evening, Ari and I collected dead cacti, which burned easily on the dry earth. As the flame caught, scorpions that had taken up residence in the hollow wood crawled to safety and joined us a few feet from the flames, barbed tails arched high above their backs, ready for action if we threatened to tread on them. Days later, when we reached the coast of the Sea of Cortez, we'd burn driftwood on the beach instead of cacti, often cooking fish given us by a lone fisherman.

Fire, company, an emerging ceiling of stars and silence other than the crackling of flames, and sometimes a short-lived attempt to impress on my harmonica. Ari had changed everything, camping was once again pleasurable. Someone to share this perfect wilderness with was the vital ingredient needed to make me content, pushing any worry from the past or future deep into the shadows away from the fire.

The evening of our restock I rummaged in the food pannier, my fingers keenly curling around the two fat tins of meat, one after the other, then the pasta, and then a modest block of cheese.

I scooped out half an avocado and drank a little water as Ari told me who she was over the dull roar of the stove. She was 25 and on college vacation. She had come down because, well, why not – the temptation to take the plunge and do something different was too strong. The fear of the unknown that seemingly prevented many from joining me had not stopped her.

Once both tins of meaty sauce and pasta had been mixed in my largest titanium pot, I hurriedly spooned some into a separate bowl for Ari, then launched into the sauciest part of my mixture and scooped a heaped spoonful into my mouth. Juice and the odd pasta tube squirmed free as I chomped down. It tasted good. The smoky flavour made me smile, but only until my taste buds caught up with the action and alarm bells began to ring. The flavour quickly gave way to a burning sensation and beads of sweat appeared on my brow, swelling quickly like drops from a leaky tap. My tongue and the back of my throat screamed with pain as Ari looked on, grinning and curious, her first spoonful still only halfway to her mouth. Having gulped down too much of our meager water ration, I ran into the blackness of the desert, panting like a dog.

The next morning dawned the same as the last, hot and clear. Flies buzzed around the small pile of macaroni filth we'd been forced to jettison the night before. Still half asleep I let my tongue explore my mouth. It was raw, slack bubble-wrap blisters covered the roof of my mouth and my lips felt fat and swollen.

We stopped at a tiny store for water later that morning. While I browsed the shelves, Ari sheepishly asked the lady there what *chipotles adobados* was. The old lady blew out her cheeks and whistled airily, like a kettle letting off steam.

'It's hot,' she said, not telling us anything we didn't already know. The name meant smoked chillies marinated in chili sauce, she went on to explain, and used very sparingly, was a tasty flavouring.

'Sparingly?' Ari continued, 'like, say, one tin per meal?' The lady chuckled at our inexperience while she shuffled round the room cleaning. She made the whistling sound through pursed lips again as she dusted the rows of aging cookies in front of her and swiped lazily at the heat-addled flies.

'One tin lasts me a week,' she said before wandering off to fight the ever-present dust off some bottles too covered to identify.

9

One bad apple

DAY 266: 7,784 MILES

The sound of loud, tinny, Latin television invaded my dreams as I struggled to ignore the dawning of another day. Metal shutters clanked heavily open, and a harsh, unshaded light bulb caused me to squint puffily as it shone through my spokes.

As I became accustomed to the light, I took in my surroundings as if I were seeing them for the first time. I was sleeping huddled close to Achilles, outside a restaurant on the increasingly busy road leading into the town of Pinotepa, Oaxaca, southern Mexico. I had not had a companion since leaving the small fishing towns of the Pacific coast, a week earlier and 300 miles back. The last person to occupy my spare seat had been Lana, a girl who travelled with her little dog strapped into a bag on her chest. I missed her, and I missed the constant whispering company of the waves we'd cycled alongside.

After nearly nine months on Achilles, I understood my body and its day-to-day needs well. Needless to say, they revolved around food, and lots of it. Typically in the mornings, my eyes struggled to open until the need to pee became urgent. After pissing came food. Depending on how much I had had to eat the day before, my stomach acid crawled up my throat to remind me, making me feel sick and weak. So far in this part of the world, rice and eggs proved to be staple breakfast food, though sometimes I'd eaten tacos, and when necessary, animal parts that you'd need an anatomy book to identify.

TAKE A SEAT

The day I woke up in front of the restaurant was no different, until shortly after I'd relieved myself in the scrub behind the building. Priming my dry, crusty mouth, I fumbled around in my pocket for my wallet and a few cents that would buy me breakfast.

Mmmm. Nothing in there. I rummaged a little more desperately around in another likely 'valuables' bag. A few more seconds of confused filtering through old lighters, foreign coins and long-forgotten boiled sweets – now fused like cement to my passport or journal – was all it took to remember exactly why I was sitting there. I'd stopped prematurely the day before because I'd lost my wallet – I'd stopped to have a quick refreshment, only to find I barely had a penny to my name. I distinctly remember that numb, shocked feeling as I traced my wallet's movements back in my fizzing brain to the point where I had last seen it, nestling safely under a dubiously stained pillow on the bed of the cheap hostel I had slept at the night before.

My obscenities were no longer confined to my head as everything came flooding back. The taxi ride back up north 60-odd miles to check under the pillow. The taxi driver taking pity on the brain-dead gringo and returning my fare and adding a few pesos of his own. The army officer presenting me with a crisp ten-dollar note while he sipped a Fanta at the street-side restaurant. Despite the help of an eclectic collection of strangers, my wallet was nowhere to be seen, and the restaurant owner invited me to use his frontage as my home that night.

After a minute or two the confused, sweaty cloud dispersed from my sleepy eyes and I reviewed my current status. I retrieved the modest stash of money I had in the pocket of the jacket I was sleeping on, and found I had a total of ten dollars, four pesos and twenty centavos with which to make progress. Enough for breakfast and more in dirt-cheap southern Mexico.

'Is there anything else we can do for you today Mr. Gill?' the slightly nasal female English voice questioned after canceling my debit cards over the telephone.

'Well, ye-no, that's all, thank you,' I said, thinking better of sharing some banter with a bank clerk more than 3,000 miles away, and switching my attention back to the much warmer sounding Mexican noises filling the room around me. Breakfast had been cooked for me by the restaurant owner's children. After I'd devoured the fried *gorditos* – juicy, doughy pancakes topped with fried meat – they'd waved my money back into my pocket, then waved me off as I rolled into Pinotepa to buy some cheap biscuits and continue south.

That was it, I thought, once I'd dealt with that. The shit bit of the day was over with, and as I left a world of dust-spitting car horns and the sooty breath of almost roadworthy vehicles, the future seemed greener and fresher in every way. Soon I was out of town and rolling slowly but more quietly up into the hot, forested hillsides, sometimes saved from the searing jaws of the sun by a leafy canopy of trees. As I climbed in the still air the road lulled me into a humid trance. My eyes became glued to each drop of sweat that fell alternately from my chin and nose. The free-fall was either arrested by the crossbar of my bike, slowly rusting as a result of this steady bombardment of salty water, or by the gravelly tarmac. Once I groggily registered a drop exploding in the midst of a column of ants, sending those nearest into 'alarm' mode, doubling their pace and enveloping the moist dust where the drop had fallen.

By now I was used to being permanently soaked in a film of sweat, which had long since bleached any colour out of the back of the cheap Hawaiian shirt I'd bought back in Vancouver. In fact, a potent mixture of ammonia and salt saw to it that any shirt rotted off my back in a few short months in the saddle.

Up to now, the heat in North America never excessive, water had rarely been a problem. I drank two to three litres a day and even in isolated Baja had always come across a little shop full of sweets, melting chocolate, beer and usually water.

But as I laced my way slowly up into the hills, past reptilian roadkill, with the screech of exotic birds becoming ever louder, I gradually drained the three full bottles wedged into the cages between my revolving legs. I could carry up to about five gallons if necessary, but in my card-cancelling frenzy I'd failed to fill up in town, and by 2 p.m. I'd exhausted my modest water supply.

Before I was forced to suck the sappy juice from some exotic plant, my sketchy knowledge of the SAS survival handbook was saved from an airing as I cycled into the courtyard of a tumbledown adobe hut. On one side of the hut, set on the edge of a steep drop, a gap in the jungle canopy opened out onto a deeply rippled hazy green carpet of trees.

The hut was whitewashed, and under an adjoining palm-thatched awning hung a plump bunch of ripe red bananas. Painted in painstakingly highlighted and refreshing gold and blue letters on the squat wall facing me was the single word CORONA. A second prompt was not needed, and I quickly dumped Achilles and stumbled into the relative cool of the single bare room. In the corner, next to a lonely but miraculously operational fridge sat an elderly lady in a chair reinforced with washing line, a toddler playing with a plastic truck missing a wheel at her feet. Her face wrinkled into a welcoming smile as I entered, drops of sweat running off me and marking a straight trail from the doorway to the fridge in the hard pale dirt. But she beat me to it, and without asking, she reached over and retrieved an amber bottle. Even the slight sucking sound of the fridge-door seal made my skin prick with expectation, and as I saw the Corona emerge, images of mouth-watering beer adverts flooded into my parched skull, ice cool, condensation glinting, golden beads mirroring my sweat as they ran smoothly down the glass.

I gulped down two of them before remembering my limited funds, and quickly asked if there was water or a tap of some sort on the property. There wasn't. I thanked the lady and cycled off lubricated for the time being with beer, but wondering whether these two people during days at the 'store' lived entirely on a diet of bananas and Corona.

Travelling up the ridge line of jungle I didn't see so much as a streamlet, the lush, river-filled valleys that were once nearby having long since dropped far below me on either side. But after six more painful miles, I arrived, dehydrated, in a small community as the sun turned bloody and sank low over the trees.

Cycling into the village which the old dusty sign told me was Jamiltepec, it seemed as if I'd perhaps completed the slow, humid day's climb. By now my throat, parched and gritty, felt a little like my chain looked, coated in a dry layer of dust.

Tired, dripping with sweat and only too aware of my new status of 'nearly penniless', I slowed to a crawl, scanning the few people loitering on the tiny street, as I picked a victim to ask about somewhere to camp – I felt better somehow not hiding out and waiting for my inevitable discovery, first by the dogs, then children, and then everyone else.

'*Hay un lugar para acampar aci?*' I asked an old, gentle-looking man in a straw hat. He fiddled over the fishing line he had tied to one of the village's only lamp posts before looking up as if my enquiry as to where I could camp had lit a bulb in his head. He shuffled quickly into his yard, littered with rusting dismantled motorbikes, then disappeared into his small house, only to reappear almost instantly with an equally senior gentleman. They proudly announced, once back on the pavement, that I was welcome to camp in their yard.

A half-hour later, after refreshing my tired, burnt body with buckets of water in Antonio's outdoor bathroom, I was sitting on his porch with his grandchildren, Marian and Louis, handing out the only memories I still had of my country, a 20-pence piece and a little strip of Union Jack stickers which the two children held up to the bare light bulb to examine. I was rewarded in turn with the youngest of them singing the entire Mexican national anthem beautifully in the dry dirt in front of the house. Keen to squeeze as much as I could out of this cultural exchange, I stood up. 'God save our gracious Queen, God save our . . .' I sang, petering out rapidly after that, not even sure whether there was a time when I knew more than the first line and a half.

Sitting with the two tiny children and their lovely grandpa, I felt clean and relaxed. On the street, the village's taco stands were firing up ready for the evening feed. Like every evening in villages round here, people began to loiter, chatting after dark, having returned from a day's work. It seemed like the birds outside Antonio's house, until then sitting quietly in the trees, took it personally, raising the volume of their gabbling and squawking over the background sounds of spitting fat and tiny little radios hissing with static.

Then, just as I was thinking about sorting out the half-unpacked Achilles, propped awkwardly against a pile of worn tires, an old VW Beetle bumped into the yard, mariachi blaring out over the din of the clanking engine. Antonio looked at me with what I interpreted as slight anxiety. 'My little son!' he exclaimed in Spanish, trying to sound proud, and as he stood up, I did likewise.

His son was a small man, with – as with many Mixtecos here – probably about two thirds of a pot of gel combed into his shiny black hair. I greeted him with my usual enthusiasm, and shook his hand as he looked unsmilingly at me.

After a brief, hushed conversation with his father, he sauntered over and managed at a stretch to put his arm around my shoulder and walk me slowly this way and that in the yard explaining without a flicker of a smile that he'd be happy to treat me to a hotel room for the night. What? Why would he want to do that, I wondered? I didn't even think there was a hotel in this tiny place. 'Yes,' he carried on. ' You won't be bothered by little children, you can take a shower, sleep in a nice bed.'

I obviously didn't get it, whatever 'it' was. My Spanish improving but still lacking somewhat, I was unable to pick up subtleties or read between the lines. He stared – still unsmiling – at me as I explained clumsily that I thought his family was great and I'd love to sleep in their yard, it would be a pleasure.

As he retracted his arm and walked slowly to his car, I smelt the vapour trail of alcohol on his breath. Antonio shuffled up and urgently stated that he was very sorry but he thought I ought to go.

Then, all at once, I understood. But it was too late.

My world slowed down and my heart appeared to swell to twice its normal size and pounded in my ears. As I turned back round to gather myself together, the scene that greeted me was a million miles away from the serene family gathering with giggling children staring at the stranger in town.

The son stood in front of his off-white and tired-looking bug, holding a machete at his waist in one hand and a mobile phone in the other. My Spanish stretched just far enough to understand a one-sided conversation he was having with his friends. 'There's a fucking gringo in my house and he refuses to leave,' he said, still staring unblinkingly at a point between my eyes.

'I'm going, it's OK!! I'm going, I'll go now,' I garbled quickly, as the gravity of the situation took hold on my knees and my stomach simultaneously. At this point, from an onlooker's perspective, the scene would have turned into some kind of comedy sketch. To me though, it felt very far from being even a tiny little bit amusing.

Nervously and trying not to take my eyes off the dull blade being pointed my way, I stuffed things haphazardly back into my panniers and without shutting them or saying goodbyes, I pushed all 14 feet and 200 pounds of Achilles awkwardly past the VW and the drunk with a machete at least half his height. To my alarm, he slowly followed me across the yard. I pushed as fast as I could, though every pace just seemed to get harder, as if I were becoming slowly paralysed with fear.

'What the fuck is happening???' I thought as I barely made it to the dimly lit street, every tendon now straining to push Achilles forward. Antonio's son was still walking slowly towards me as I came to a complete halt.

A panic-stricken, temple-pounding investigation found the problem. In my rushed packing job one bungee had caught on a rear spoke and slowly but surely wrapped itself around my hub until I, well, stopped. If this had been a cartoon, I would, after a two- or three-second pause with brow furrowed, have been catapulted into the yard to land in a heap back where I'd come from. As it was, however, I got out my knife, now seemingly puny in comparison with what was advancing towards me, and cut through the bungee, each rubber strand seeming to snap away painstakingly slowly under my frantic, sawing blade. In what must have been a few of the longest seconds of my life, and all the while imagining an army of small Mexicans rounding the corner with bullwhips and bicycle chains, I cut through the bungee and scampered off down the street, Achilles free again to roll to safety.

In one five-minute period, the walls of my slowly building trust in humanity came crashing down around me. Everyone I saw in the street suddenly had eyes on me. They wanted to kill me, all of them. I was sure. So sure, in fact that I quickly found that there was a hotel in town and at 11 p.m., I felt the need to plead with the owner to give me a room for all the money I had, apart from fourteen pesos which I kept safe in another pocket. She begrudgingly agreed, took my money, and I wheeled Achilles into a dim, musty room and locked the door behind me, tempted to back the bed up against it in case the bullwhips and bicycle chains ever appeared.

That was where I stayed for the night, breaking out my emergency tin of tuna and sitting on my bed staring at the wall.

For the first time in about a year, I had felt threatened. For the first time since I rolled away from Prudhoe Bay, Alaska, that flight-or-fight adrenaline had pulsed powerfully and blindly in my veins. How can faith in those around you be smashed to smithereens by one little drunken man? I sat feeling ashamed and small, but unable to brush it off as a tiny blip on my otherwise smooth chart of progress. The walls had ears, the room felt flimsy and tinny and I felt utterly alone.

Despite, or perhaps because of, my mind exhausting itself with images of my violent demise, I drifted into a deep, dreamless sleep. I woke seven hours later to the sounds of birdsong and sweeping beating the light into the sky. The streets aren't always clean in this part of the world, but it's not because the people live in filth – in fact it is quite the opposite. They are compulsive cleaners. At least twice a day old ladies can be seen in front of their houses having finished sweeping inside and feeling the need to sweep and sprinkle water outside too. Their territory seems to vary depending on the severity of their habit. Some stop sweeping the dust around at the edge of the pavement, others carry on a little farther. I never tried it out, but I imagined if I had the misfortune to roll to a stop outside the house of a particularly conscientious cleaner while they were underway, Achilles and I would almost definitely get prodded with a broom until we shifted, with the dry mud and dust, a little further from the house. I rolled out of Jamiltepec, only pausing briefly for a four peso packet of cookies and a large bottle of water, careful to avoid the robotic efficiency of an operational broom.

Looking at my map, I could see that it would be two days of pedalling until I arrived anywhere likely to have a Western Union, my lifeline in financial emergencies. Still slightly numbed by fear though, I thought very little about it. I was pleased to be cycling again, away from an experience I was only too keen to leave behind.

It didn't take long for the road to envelop me again in its dusty embrace, and I changed quickly from victim to traveller on the move once more, a passing oddity for the Mixtecos clearing tenacious undergrowth in the fields or sitting sleepily in the shade of an adobe doorway. The landscape had become harsher, drier. The jungle had given way to fields of sharp, forbidding agave, each plant standing a few feet from the next for eight years, until a farmer could harvest the thick stem to chop and smoke and boil it. The liquid distilled from this process in homemade copper tanks dotted along the road was the potent alcohol of the region, mezcal.

As those sticky miles slowly ticked by, I thought again and again about the events of the last 18 hours. The edges of those memories had already dulled, leaving me more objective and philosophical. I sat occasionally under a palm roof with old men resting from the fields, or with a cowboy halfway to work on his horse which, like me, was running with sweat. Some pored over the finest details of Achilles, others were mildly confused as to why I wouldn't travel by bus. But despite perhaps a lack of comprehension as to why I should venture so far from my family, most wished me well and wanted to help.

More than ever before on this journey my belief in humanity was shaky. Should I trust, or should I keep myself to myself? After my run-in with the little machete man I wasn't sure. But it was those people I met on my little breaks who influenced my journey more than they will ever know. They have no email, maybe no telephone, I barely caught their names and I will most likely never see them again. But they twisted my fragile temperament easily, and thanks to them, the trust that had been so rapidly shattered sprouted fresh healthy shoots and covered the raw scars of the day before. A few pesos here, a free drink there and to smooth it off, a lengthy session of drinking mezcal in the midday sun out of a 5-gallon gas can, extracted with a siphon hose smelling strongly of gas. While maybe damaging my liver, those interactions renewed the confidence that had been snatched away. I arrived at the mid-sized town of Rio Grande with a few pesos more than I had left the restaurant with three days before.

It took me two more days to roll back to the coast, after stopping at a small post office for money wired from back home. The relief that came with the small bundle of cash spurred me to shell out for a celebratory ice cream, and the same evening I rolled into the coastal town of Puerto Escondido, a catchment for surfers from all over the world. At the cheap end of town I found a tiny concrete cell where the whistle from the small baked-banana cart blew steam until late into the night. Venturing by day to the expensive end of town I briefly tried surfing, with questionable results, and mingled with a small group of Swiss and Americans. After only a small amount of cajoling one of them, Lauren from Vermont, agreed to join me the following day.

Those few days were dream-like. Lauren is a lovely girl, intelligent and interesting, which helped. We made short hops in the suffocating heat and low-lying scrubby hills between hypnotically tranquil bays combed by powerfully refreshing Pacific waves. Soon, though, Lauren's company and the refreshing promise of a beachside camp became nothing more than mouth-watering memories as I turned inland once more, heading for Oaxaca. Scrub was quickly replaced by coconut palms, then small, broad-leaved trees, and after three days of constant hill-climbing I found myself in the stunted pine forests of the mountains. The air was fresh and cool, but stray dogs loitering outside each small village kept me clammy with nervous sweat. The first evening in the hills I was beckoned into the small basic wooden shelter of an elderly indigenous woman, and sat with her sucking honey from the leafy carcass of a bee's nest that she'd collected in a bucket from a nearby tree. The next evening I found myself watching a basketball match between what must be two of the shortest teams on earth, in the village of San José del Pacifico, perched high in the hills and bathed in the cool, blood-red evening light. For two more days I rode through the hilly pine forests, giving colourful basking snakes a wide berth on the tarmac and relocating an old, gnarled tortoise that sat quietly in the middle of the hot tarmac. Then the hills let me pass and dropped me into an arid patchwork of earthy red fields filled with maguey (agave) plants and in the distance, the white city of Oaxaca.

I reached the city the following day, its flagstone streets flanked by old colonial architecture bearing the scars of the very recent history of political unrest. Graffiti here, broken windows there, but tranquil and friendly by the time I rolled into town. From the stunning polished plaza next to the cathedral it's hard to believe that poverty exists at all in this region. But a short cycle up to the observatory on the hill allows you to look down on the edge of town, a drunken checkerboard of corrugated iron roofs and dusty, chicken-filled alleyways. Only then is it possible to consider that this is the capital city of Mexico's poorest state.

The far side of the city is also guarded by hills, more fields of maguey, more jerry cans containing petrol-tainted mezcal and more than a few lonely farmers in need of a drinking partner. After a week in the leafy colonial city I ran this gauntlet under the desiccating sun, the first afternoon disappearing in a haze of drunken dehydration. But then the hills changed. Huge orange and grey limestone escarpments protected the peaks and set my now wasted climbing muscles tingling. I dreamt of climbing those rocks that night while sleeping in a small village plaza huddled in a corner of the tired-looking bandstand.

By the time I reached the coast again it was as if it had undergone a remodel in my absence. It was not the sandy paradise that Lauren had abandoned me for. Sitting in the oppressively humid and apparently coastal town of Juchitán, the clammy air gave no hint of an ocean breeze, and tangled vegetal swamps hid the Pacific completely.

I sat for a while in the Parque Central watching the Monet-style flower stalls and the animated vendors. Huge leathery pods were filled with sweet-smelling flowers and buzzed with flies. Bunches of roses that would fetch a small fortune on the Portobello Road carpeted the pavement between stalls. A little further down the chaotic street others sold almost any consumable you could conceive of and their ranks were awash with the meaty smoke of *carnitas* and tacos from nearby food stalls. Everywhere there was the chattering and haggling of street trade, and above the flower stalls flocks of birds squawked and flapped over the din. The atmosphere was charged. It was just another day of trade for these people, but for me the seemingly chaotic activity was exciting and almost overpowering.

Juchitán is a little way off the tourist trail, and it wasn't until the following morning that I saw any pasty white skin other than my own.

TAKE A SEAT

It was 7:30 a.m. when Madja arrived, shaven head and bright blue eyes catching the attention of a small collection of children as soon as he stepped off the local bus. I'd met the Serbian back in Guadalajara, where he was teaching at the American School, and he journeyed with me away from the coast once more and up into the hills of my last Mexican state, Chiapas, famous for its large proportion of indigenous Mayans and a history of uprisings against the government.

From Tuxtla Gutierez, we cycled up steeply from the busy urban roads of the commercial state capital, where dry-fish vendors filled the streets, to San Cristóbal. Forty miles of gradual hill-climbing took us into fresh pine forests surrounding the lofty colonial city.

The tiny cobbled streets are home to numerous markets run by men and women in stunning indigenous clothes, revealing their glistening gold smiles as tourists struggle to speak their best Spanglish. The short but strong-looking local people weave their lives back and forth between a modest existence on the outskirts and tourism in the town's historic core. Like other colonial towns on the backpackers' trail, fancy bars in the center provide a comfortable environment for bohemian travellers. From a bar stool you get a good view of the live band usually pumping out reggae, but if you look behind you through the window you'll see small children confidently selling chewing gum to tourists wearing sun hats and money belts.

From this hotbed of culture, the road wound slowly downhill to the frontier, the invisible line denoting the end of my journey in Mexico. The end of mariachi, deliciously spicy tacos, the vibrant and only mildly irritating banda music and a culture I'd fallen in love with.

After a prolonged flick through my passport, the chubby immigration official looked up at me. Seeming uninterested she said, '*No tienes estampilla.*' I didn't have a stamp? I cast my mind back to Tijuana and dimly remembered being ushered through the gap in the fence. The back of my neck got prickly as I thought about the potential stick this might shove in the spokes of my journey.

'What can I do?' I asked the lady, who was listening in on her sweaty colleague mouthing off at some Guatemalan labourers. She turned her head back to me with a look of mild annoyance.

'You don't exist in Mexico,' she said.

'So you can't give me an exit stamp?'

'No, you never entered! You don't exist!' she kept saying, as if trying to deny the presence of a ghost.

'So, ummm, can I go to Guatemala?' I asked, trying to remain humble and polite.

'I don't care what you do, here you don't exist,' she said with a tone of finality. I wandered back to Madja who, having sailed through immigration, sat in the restaurant across the street. As we predicted after a short discussion, the Guatemalan checkpoint didn't mind at all that I was invisible in Mexico. They stamped my passport quickly and ushered me through to make room for the long line of men wearing wide-brimmed hats and holding machetes. Unlike us, these men would file north through this border to work in the slightly more prosperous Mexico every single day.

10

On and off the tourist trail

DAY 297: 8,364 MILES

The throng of money changers and local taxis and buses that congregates round the checkpoint meant we made slow progress until the other side of the border town, La Mesilla. The tiny streets were choked with the aptly named chicken buses, whose conductors danced around their charges singing vocally and scooping people on board. The old yellow school buses with customised and pimped-out interiors, now used to transport locals and their livestock, would pass us every ten or fifteen minutes in a flash of vibrant colour, fumigating Madja and me in a cloud of sooty smoke.

Huge canyon walls rose up on either side and fresh spring water gushed from the rock occasionally, while the precipitous hills grew up ahead of us. We had arrived in rural Guatemala, where children ran from their little wooden houses shouting excitedly, '*Ciclistas ciclistas!!*' and beautiful women in traditional clothes wove pricelessly beautiful textiles outside their huts with a simple loom hung from a tree. Initially Madja and I found it hard to spot the coffee that this region is famous for, but soon it dawned on us that the huge white 55-pound bags sold on the roadside were full of it. So much for any hopes of buying a handy travel-sized pack of beans.

Like almost every stoker before him, Madja appreciated reasonably frequent short rests to accommodate the sensibilities of his bottom. Not long after the border we stopped outside a small *comedor*, one of a handful of eateries we'd seen dotted along the road. A small man wearing a flat cap and a woollen jumper – a little like a Welsh hill farmer – quietly walked in from the road and sat down next to us. Like nearly everyone else he carried a machete in a handsome studded leather sheath. He sat quietly sucking hollow-cheeked on a Coca-Cola through a straw, watching us from under the peak of his flat cap. I offered him some peanuts from my bag, and he held out his powerful leathery hands to catch them. A few spilled as I poured them out, but after nodding a humble thank you, he carefully knelt down and picked them up from the dust, chewing on each one slowly and thoroughly.

Madja travelled with me through steep-sided hills dotted with patches of terraced agriculture and echoing with the thundering river and the honk of the chicken bus warning the locals of its imminent arrival. The bus never stopped for those waiting by the side of the road, it simply slowed down, the conductor leaning out and beckoning them on board urgently as if their life depended on it. The people would run or shuffle along and he'd drag the frailer or slower ones on board before the bus careened away again. Time is money for these bus conductors and stopping seems unnecessary.

Madja is an interesting man. When energy allowed, he regaled me with his story, including the escape from his turbulent homeland. In 1999 bombs began to fall on Belgrade when NATO's Secretary General, Javier Solana, ordered the bombing of Serbia. After some close shaves with officials in a small village on the River Drina, Madja and a friend successfully slipped across the border into Bosnia on a small fishing boat. Before escaping the country however, his training in the Serbian National Service had given Madja an attribute critical to the success of those days in the saddle. During particularly painful periods, he seemed to be able to switch off his brain, bow his head and power up the steepest of the hills with me. But ten days after he stepped off the bus to join me he left, even he had had enough, and with an aching bottom he returned to Guadalajara in time to teach his math class.

The next day, as I cycled along damp roads on hills roofed with huge anvil clouds, I missed the dry one-liners and intelligent humour that

Madja blurted out between military bursts of mindless pedalling. It was the beginning of the rainy season. Large spots of rain began to dot the asphalt, causing it to gently steam, as if hungrily anticipating the approaching downpours after months of scorching sun. That morning I'd left the small hostel early, trying to beat the massing clouds off the bike. My plan worked and the cool morning was dry, and I didn't stop until I was beckoned to a halt in the still air by an old man heading the other way on an equally aging bicycle. I stopped next to him. On the nearby, long since redundant lamp post, a cow was tethered. The man, in a well-kept Stetson, looked up into my eyes and said after a deep breath, 'How tall you are!' It's true that in Guatemala my, by Western standards, fairly average proportions were formidable. Then he tipped his hat, remounted his bike, and cycled away, leaving just me and the cow standing in damp morning silence.

In Xela (Quetzaltenango) I was received with open arms by the Cabrera family, despite only a moment's notice. The glamorous Cristy was a news anchor and wasted no time in interviewing me where I stood for the local news channel. Despite her high-heeled boots, she took a turn on Achilles, a cameraman filming from a noisy motorbike gunning its engine to clear the traffic ahead of us. Xavier Cabrera, Cristy's brother, lent me his powerful, karate-honed legs the next morning after litres of chocolate milk. We pedalled slowly out of the city's basin for nearly 30 miles uphill to Alaska, a small pueblito named on account of its relatively fresh climate high in the hills and shrouded in wisps of cloud.

For days as I travelled south of the village people would ask where I had travelled from and on answering Alaska, the small farmer or shopkeeper or child would look at me with a flash of recognition. 'Alaska? I have cousins there, that's a long way from here!' they might say. There was little point in clarifying which Alaska I was talking about, since bicycle travel to either one for these people seemed inconceivable.

Then, all at once, I slid back onto the well-rutted path of the backpackers' trail for the first time properly since southern Mexico. A land of beautiful lakes and volcanoes welcomed me as I crested a rise and looked over Lake Atitlán. Dropping down to spend the night by the edge of the glassy water, I wandered along the shore, the stars overwhelmed by the morse code of a million blinking fireflies. This volcanic basin has not gone unnoticed by the tourist trade. While locals sell textiles and bracelets to the travellers, bohemian entrepreneurs invite those seeking therapy into one of many 'reconnection centers' dotted around the lake. For the most part, high fences or high prices prevent the locals, garbage and stray dogs from encroaching on these miniature 'utopias'.

A day of cycling slowly out of the basin and into the next valley saw me entering into the rustic architecture, inflated prices and Spanish schools of Antigua, perhaps one of the most beautiful colonial cities in the world. This, it seemed to me, was a good place to set down roots for a while. I was tired again, and sitting down on a low wall next to a *mixta* stand and tucking into a grilled sausage, I planned my holiday.

I got a job, working at a mezcal bar run by an American, and through that I made friends quickly. Juan Manuel, a man who ran a jewellery shop in Antigua's stunning center, became not only my host but a good friend, and together with Viola, his Hungarian girlfriend, we explored the slopes of the nearby Pacaya volcano. We went at night, crunching over a honeycomb of recently cooled lava, cracks in this thin carapace glowing red with the river of magma still moving underneath us.

As in San Cristóbal on the other side of the border, the lives of tourists and beautifully clothed locals mixed right up until the edge of the historic center. Wandering around one of the most beautiful plazas I'd seen, the lilt of Spanish was drowned out by other more nasal conversations . . . 'What's this? Coffee? How much is it? How long will it take, because I have to go on a tour in a minute . . .'

'How much?? NINE DOLLARS??? Oh, nine Quetzales . . . you take dollars?'

And if the nonplussed Guatemalteco behind the counter didn't understand, the rasping English would be repeated, but louder.

Further out of town, life was more representative. Locals outnumbered the few tourists who strayed here, and bananas, *frijoles* and *pan tostada* outdo the American-style pancakes and French toast as breakfast food. Groups of indigenous women would wash clothes in a line of stone *pilas* near the stream, men would come back from the fields in the afternoon and life would go on relatively unaffected by foreigners.

I settled comfortably into both worlds, enjoying the familiar environment of a Western bar along with life at Juan's house, a short distance out of town. The mezcal bar was aptly named Café No Se: Café 'I don't know'. I stumbled out of it on more than one occasion feeling like I didn't know much after sampling the range of spirits and washing them down with *chapolines*, small dried crickets – a good alternative to peanuts. Working behind a bar made from the siding of an old chicken bus I met Vietnam vets, an authority on bumble bees and virile Latin guitar players, and I mixed with No Se's equally colourful employees. I gained interesting knowledge, I lost an incredible amount of sleep, and not surprisingly challenged my liver to step up a gear.

But after three weeks of building up a new and stable life around me, my time was up. If it had been up to me, I probably would have stayed longer, but it wasn't. Juan had galvanised his entire family from the city to make an outing of accompanying me to the El Salvadorian border, only a day away on Achilles. My last night at the bar was a drunken affair lasting until the following morning and ending at the house of two flamboyant and seemingly well-monied gay guys who were in possession of a Nintendo Wii. It was the first time I'd ever seen one and, too drunk to concentrate, I clumsily experimented with it. The world was advancing without my knowing anything about it in my own little cycling bubble.

I was grateful that I woke the next morning with a searing headache and tongue stuck to the roof of my mouth. It took my mind off what I was leaving behind as I forced some liquids down. Juan and Viola were coming with me, and once my headache subsided a little, the thought of their company for the day also lessened the blow of any sudden cutting of well-established roots.

Juan was first up, and once Achilles was out of the yard, with rust spots freshly painted during my rest in Antigua, he saddled up immediately, donning a plastic red nose, amusing his extended family in the two trucks following us. They all wanted a turn, Juan told me, even his 84-year-old grandfather, who had specifically requested a ride when he'd been told of my existence.

ON AND OFF THE TOURIST TRAIL

We rode uncomfortably through the cobbled streets with the trailer bouncing wildly now it was empty. Before we got onto the smoother main road bypassing Guatemala city we stopped at a small bakery, all alcohol having been sweated out of my system on the short ride, leaving room for hunger. Soon, two other acquaintances had joined us on their own aged but well-loved road bikes, and Juan leaned out of the back of the truck filming the at least partly Lycra-clad convoy. With the help of all these people, I rolled out from under the shadow of the volcanoes, and swept down onto the increasingly hot flatlands towards the coast, and one of the smallest countries in Central America. Miguel, Juan's grandfather, went as far as putting in two stints on the back seat, his left leg crooked and missing the pedal every so often. His face gave nothing away unless you looked carefully behind his well-trimmed beard. Underneath the cropped whiskers he wore a subtle smile.

Leaving these people at the border was not easy, and invisible claws from Antigua were tearing at my clothes. But as I rolled across yet another political line between cultures, I knew this would not be the last time I felt this way. I was being forced, through experience, to conclude that the vast majority on this continent are positive and loving people. Every day I would pass a TV showing crashes, robbing and abductions. Either, like a parting of the waves, I was riding through it protected, or the nastiness didn't exist in the volumes we are led to believe.

The pastures in El Salvador seemed greener, but the towns a little poorer. For the first night I stayed in a prison-like hostel on the recommendation of some locals, who said it was not safe to camp. There was something, a kind of fear, in the people here which I did not fully understand. I hoped it was the proximity to the border that gave the filthy town, aptly named Cara Sucia – Dirty Face – this uncomfortable feeling.

At least every few miles on the road I passed a small bicycle repair shack. Bikes seemed to be getting increasingly common, and cycling alone on Achilles I felt spoiled and selfish as locals passed by, sometimes three up and a child wedged in there somewhere, balanced cleverly on a tired-looking bicycle. Others pedalled along with pounds of fruit slung on the handlebars in plastic bags.

A day after leaving Juan and his family I reached the rolling coastline, cliffs and small river deltas competing for space on a shore choked with palm trees and black sand. The sooty exhaust sprayed out by passing vehicles no longer seemed warm to me, masked by the humid 109°F breeze. I sweated up hill after rolling hill, and flew down into countless valleys sweet with the smell of fermenting mangoes. Sometimes the troughs would be home to a small school, a handful of tiny stores or perhaps the house of a rich El Salvadorian with a swimming pool hidden in the trees.

Occasionally I saw small groups of people picking about in the dry undergrowth next to the clifftop road. When I stopped to see what they were doing I was proudly shown a plastic bag full of small crabs that lived high above the water in the dead leaves. They were, they told me, collecting ingredients for the local seafood soup.

At lunchtime I stopped at a bamboo shack on the clifftop, looking down on the black sand and surf of the sucking waves. I ate a small batch of crabs, the same as those I'd been shown, as part of a rich seafood cocktail similar to those I'd tasted in Mexico and loaded with a hot sauce I'd taken a shine to. I got going again after a therapeutic beer, feeling refreshed and with my salt-caked shirt now dry and crusty in the hot breeze. But after five minutes, just long enough to start sweating again, I was itching hard at a stinging sensation on my left wrist.

Once, I remembered, just once when I lived in London, I had had an allergic reaction to shellfish, causing me to run and madly scratch half-naked down Fulham High Street at 6:30 in the morning in search of a 24-hour pharmacy. It was happening again I was sure, but this time there was no hope of a pharmacy nearby and I knew that in minutes I would be scratching the flesh off my arm like an animal chewing a limb off to escape a trap. After 20 minutes of worrying, I dared to roll up my sleeve and monitor the damage. My skin had taken on a strange yellow complexion, redder where I'd scratched, with flecks of yellow coming off where my shirt had rubbed. It looked alarming. Were those yellow flecks skin? I couldn't tell until I looked closely and remembered that yellow colour from the *comedor* I'd stopped at for my seafood cocktail. A wave of relief hit me when I realised I must've spilled the Salsa Picante (hot sauce) over my wrist as well as dowsing my food with it. My throat wasn't going to swell and anaphylactic shock was not going to see the end of me . . . not here at any rate.

The small port town of La Libertad had a threatening feel to it when I arrived late in the day. Two-storey wooden hotels boasted surfboards, telling me I was still on the tourist trail but at a scale ten times smaller than the rut I'd left in Antigua. Shops and services closed up early to prevent robbery, an old man told me while putting the shutters down on a basic food store. The place looked like a depressed fishing village trying its best to get onto the world map of surfing with little to work with. As darkness fell and a handful of flickering streetlamps glowed yellow, my usual confidence faltered, and rather than venturing out, after a hurried fried chicken I lay in my room, a wooden box open on one side to the jungle. I was grateful at least for the erratic functioning of the fan blowing a warm wind over cheap Barbie-doll nylon sheets already soaked with my sweat.

On the less edgy banks of Lake Atitlán I had met an American Airlines pilot, Julie, who, with the benefit of work schedule flexibility, wanted to join me for a spot of cycling. La Libertad was to be our meeting point and two days after I arrived, so did she, at the more developed end of town I had not discovered.

I spotted her immediately. A blonde lady rummaging through a small mountain of kit on the pavement. A few minutes later we'd said hello and I stood looking at a pile of clothing made up mostly of sports bras and warm fleeces. I sweated just looking at them. Then Julie brought my attention to a couple of fancy collapsible wine glasses, a bottle of red to go with them, and a plastic container full of rapidly melting chocolate-covered coffee beans. Some of this, I decided, had to go, and Julie didn't take much persuading that the fleeces and half the collection of bras could be left with her friend driving back to San Salvador, the country's capital. The wine could be drunk, the coffee beans consumed and Julie needed her carefully folded flight suit and posh shoes to fly a plane out of whichever country she got off in. The novelty wine glasses stayed too and the following evening we toasted the journey and quickly shed the weight of a Californian Shiraz.

We stopped sometimes to harvest windfall mangoes that hadn't yet begun to rot under the trees. The sugary juice would cover our hands and arms, causing the dirt on the handlebars and dust kicked up from side roads to stick to us. Constantly in need of something refreshing to combat the temperature, we often stopped for small bags of coconut milk sold from under blue plastic awnings on the side of the highway. Once, as we rested in a pull-off home to a collection of food stalls, a lady came shyly over and invited us to eat. On principle I never refused invitations like this, and even though I had little appetite Julie and I wandered over and sat across from her and a plastic bowl full of a thick doughy mixture. She made us fresh hot *pupusas*, a Salvadorian bready pancake stuffed with pork or cheese. While I took the pork one I was given, Julie politely requested the cheese one.

Looking at the mixture in the bowl and the tepid cooking griddle as we thanked the lady and cycled away, I began to wonder about the wisdom of my distinct lack of pickiness. I had been sick once before, but that was only through sheer gluttony in northern Canada, where, passing a café that sold famously large cinnamon buns designed to be snacked on over a period of time, I had purchased one and wolfed it down, struggling to cram the uncooked dough at the center of this rolled treat into my distended stomach. On that occasion I managed another 7 miles before the world fell out of my bottom. For days the smell of cinnamon sent me into a cold sweat.

This time I managed a further 30 miles with Julie before the uncooked pork skin I'd consumed decided the roadside was where it wanted to stay. At 8 p.m. that night, camping in oppressive humidity next to a gas station, I doubled up in pain on the short spiky grass as my gut struggled to decide at which end to evacuate its contents.

That night I made countless delirious pilgrimages to the gas station toilets. Once, head bowed and cold sweat dripping off the end of my nose, I was dimly aware of a trucker snorting coke off the cistern in the next-door cubicle. Morning came painfully slowly, and I lay semi-conscious as the sky silhouetted the palms and forecourt roof. I eventually emerged from a dangerously dehydrated slumber when a fly dining on the dry salty sweat on my face tickled me awake. I was weak – I could walk, but I was slow and unsteady on my feet, having lost pints of fluid in the night. Julie had left me sleeping and spread the word of my predicament. Once I was tottering about our messy encampment, sleeping bags strewn on the grass, the security guard – the best reason for camping next to gas stations – arrived having shouldered his pump-action shotgun to deliver a large bunch of bananas. He told me he'd walked to his mother's house and she wanted me to have them. Even in my weakened, slightly delirious state this simple act of kindness coming from a man packing heat struck me as totally at odds with the region's reputation.

I didn't know whether it was possible to overstay one's welcome at a gas station but I felt like we were uncomfortably in between places and I wanted to move on. After only 2½ miles of trying to cycle, I felt dizzy and in danger of evacuating my bowels on my precious leather saddle. Too exhausted to care about abandoning Achilles, we parked him in a small church looked after by a family of evangelical Christians, and took a chicken bus to the small fishing village of El Cuco. There was a hotel there with something that resembled a comfortable room with cleanish sheets, so I limply pulled out the small wad of dollars I kept wedged inside my seat post for emergencies. No price was too high, I just wanted to sleep under the refreshing cool of an air-conditioning unit.

I spent two days in this strange community, where the ocean waves surged unchecked into the front yards of the fishermen's homes and small children played in the frothy shallows with flotsam, a lucky few with broken surfboards. Only rarely did I venture from the ice-cool haven of the room, paying my respects to the porcelain throne disturbingly frequently. I drank what I could, but despite taking some powerful antibacterial drugs I felt my muscle and body fat wasting away.

Forty-eight hours seemed like a lifetime, but the time came when I could begin to eat again, a teaspoon of rice at a time, but enough to feel strength flowing slowly back into me. The next day, with a few pounds left not so firmly behind me, we journeyed tentatively onwards through turbulent weather, mist hiding the hillside cloud forest. During the night, lightning freeze-framed the surrounding trees in black and white, and after two days we crossed into Honduras over a peaceful and stress-free border. We stopped often for me to rest. I was much improved but still weak and I felt old, breathing hard and leaning over my handlebars for long periods, steadying myself in preparation to move off again. Without Julie the bike would not have gone anywhere for those few days when my legs were watery, yet she didn't complain, she just took up the slack and got on with it, occasionally imposing flight-style progress reports on our trajectory through Central America.

'A very good morning to you, this is your second Captain speaking, Julie Kresko. I'm pleased to announce the forecast's looking good for the flight today, we're looking at high pressure with just a touch of turbulence in the late afternoon. The cabin crew will be bringing a snack around shortly of slightly overripe mangoes . . .'

On the recommendation of a local, we headed into the mountains, towards the fresher air and away from the main coastal road and the opportunistic crime associated with it.

The climbs were significant but as we rose the temperature dropped and the road was kind and smooth. One day, with rains threatening in the late afternoon, we set up the tent on a grassy shoulder backed by the damp jungle. A family emerged from one of the two houses on the opposite side of the road. They were having none of it and invited us unquestioningly into their small house on the hillside. As Julie and I packed the tent up again with drops of rain beginning to fall, Julie enthused about this stroke of good luck. I smiled in agreement but realised at the same time that I'd become complacent, accustomed to this level of hospitality from strangers after so many similar situations. I tried to follow her lead and jolt myself back in time, as if this kindness were new to me. I tried to remember what it felt like to be surprised by the generosity of the unblemished human spirit.

We were treated as members of the family and shared fresh cheese, milk and tortillas with Adriana and the children in their earth-floored kitchen, while outside the crickets and cicadas struggled to make themselves heard above the drumming rain.

What was I to give these people in return for their boundless kindness? I could give some token of my thanks, a flag, a bouncy ball, a few of my stories while we sat round the table sipping tea made with herbs picked nearby. Was this enough though? The prolonged taking without feeling like I was giving much back was starting to play on my mind. Achilles, however, helped to rid me of a portion of guilt when the rain let up. In the fading misty light on a deserted road, the handful of local families a little further round the gentle corner saluted us as the children of their neighbours sped past on a double bicycle holding onto their Stetsons or stopping their skirts blowing in their faces as they screeched and whooped. When I turned and saw the grins they wore, I knew I'd given, if nothing else, a few minutes of pleasant memories.

The cloud forest of Honduras and the organised armies of leaf-cutter ants marching around beneath their canopy soon gave way to an open scrubby landscape as we crossed a rope stretched across the road next to a currency vendor with the usual fat wads of cash and a well-loved calculator. This was Nicaragua, perhaps the poorest and most war-scarred country in Central America. Julie and I had crossed in and out of Honduras so quickly it felt like we were crossing between counties, not countries. And crossing those borders, quirky mannerisms and traditions change in the way you'd expect going maybe from Lancashire to Yorkshire.

The landscape here turned from a lush green to a scrubby brown as we descended towards the muddy shores of Lake Nicaragua, or Lago de Nicaragua, a body of water that half splices the neck of the Americas. For the last three countries, beautiful green eyes and paler skin that I'd first noticed only occasionally in the heavily indigenous Guatemala had gradually become more prevalent. We were far from the Atlantic coast, and though small pockets of Miskito native culture are still present here, the architecture as well as people's complexions are powerful reminders of the Spanish colonial influence.

Granada, the historic capital of Nicaragua, had streets flanked by archways that reminded me of Antigua. The difference was the tourists – there weren't any here, and the lack of money in their absence meant the once-grand architecture was in places crumbling, with paint peeling off the shutters on the windows.

When Julie wandered out to the lake front I took advantage of the tranquil plaza to write. I found writing was my constant, something that kept me grounded whilst everything around me changed from day to day. As I sat at a chipped green wooden table and thought about the stories I had gained in the last weeks, two children joined me on rickety chairs. I asked them their names and held out my hand. Paolo and Junior shook it, and then, done with pleasantries, asked me for money. 'Para comer,' they said. Money for food.

I didn't give them any, instead I slid my half-full glass of chocolate milk across the table, which they sucked dry before politely placing the empty glass on the kiosk counter to be washed. They were eight and ten years old, they said, before asking about my strange handwriting full of words that were unintelligible to them. As they pored over the pages of my rapidly filling journal, I watched them. One or two sores blemished their dark brown skin, and Paolo's face was scarred, perhaps from falling into a stove or fire. Then they looked back at me, curious about me now, about my pen, the St. Christopher around my neck. I stopped writing, more interested in talking to these two. They spent a few minutes in hysterics as they pointed my video camera at each other and examined the results, before they bade me farewell and walked slowly away, arms over each other's shoulders.

From Granada, Julie and I cycled round the huge Lake Nicaragua and took a small ferry to the dreamlike Ometepe Island, where, on the slopes of Concepción Volcano only the downpours of the rainy season silence the sounds of the cloud forest and jungle we'd become accustomed to. The animals' silence never lasted long though. Even as the plants shed the last heavy drops of water, the forest creatures came out of hiding as we went hiking up into the mist. Lizards and geckos skittered away from under our feet and a dung beetle took advantage of a break in the clouds to roll its perfectly spherical ball of shit across the trail. Looking up as we threaded our way beneath the forest canopy we could see troops of howler monkeys staring curiously down at us, pursing their lips and letting their slow, rasping barks sound across the valley.

11

The Pan-American ends

DAY 354: 9,365 MILES

Julie, free to fly away whenever she wanted, had been with me for six weeks. It had given me a chance to get to know someone, to wake up and not have to second-guess how my companion worked, how long it would take them to get ready or in what order we'd pack Achilles to ensure our respective necessities were close to hand. But the six weeks we spent together also made me aware of a change that had crept into me without my knowing. I was so accustomed to having a constant change that I never had to surmount the obstacle of familiarity. For couples, the exciting start is called a honeymoon period, but for any friendship it's the same. There was never long enough to have to overcome it, most stokers only stayed with me for a week, two at the outside. At the end of six weeks I took Julie for granted and I became ratty, almost resentful, that just by being there she was preventing a string of possible companions. It was unreasonable, nasty even, and I knew it, but I found this subtle but ever-present unappreciative mood hard to control.

Before sunrise in the seaside town of San Juan del Sur, Julie left me. She said she needed to get back home for some work but might fly out again soon. I wondered whether that was the truth or whether I'd been sufficiently grumpy to put her off the idea of returning. Spending 24 hours a day within inches of a grumpy man can be very persuasive.

Crossing into the northern and most Americanised end of Costa Rica, my stomach was far from settled. While my bout of Salvadorian Montezuma's revenge had cleared up completely, another disorder with some similar symptoms had taken hold. Gluttony.

Addictively greasy deep-fried chicken became a regional staple as I journeyed into a land with an increasingly Caribbean influence. It was the sudden and traumatic effect of eating piles of this that upset any Central American equilibrium my stomach had established. Travelling over the spine of green mountains from the Pacific to the Atlantic, I felt I was well on the way to being able to compile a *Michelin Guide to Gas Station Toilets* and nearby establishments in which to source tissues.

But it wasn't just my eating habits that changed as I ventured deeper into Costa Rica. As if to display tropical superiority over its poorer neighbour, the moment I crossed the border the fields seemed greener and the trees taller as I sweated away from the gringo-filled beaches into the heart of the mountains. Toucans cocked their heads and stared with great effort over their huge yellow beaks as I passed. Once in a while humming birds would mistake my now faded Hawaiian shirt for nectar-filled flowers. After a brief hover, they'd flit away realising that the stench coming off my dripping garments was not what they were looking for.

Exotic animals only increased in frequency once I'd decided to take a road less travelled. After weeks of rolling on tarmac I wanted some kind of physical adventure, a small challenge to occupy my mind and give it something new to chew on. So, despite yet more warnings from the locals about uncrossable rivers and poisonous snakes, I shunned the touristy highway and skirted along the south side of a huge lake on an initially good if slightly muddy track. For two days I toiled, in the shadow of the volatile Arenal volcano, through increasingly difficult conditions. The track turned into a shallow river, then deep mud, then a small rocky path cutting a tiny hole through the dense vegetation. I pulled Achilles achingly slowly through the jungle, sometimes stopping in knee-high mud to summon new reserves of energy and extract my rapidly disappearing bicycle from a swamp, and other times trying desperately to keep momentum through the lake-like puddles, my pannier bags half submerged and dragging me down. When I stopped for a moment, giving up my struggle with the jungle, I listened. The bouncing, rattling and scraping of my bicycle was replaced by birds, insects and monkeys, all seemingly mocking me with their screeches and cries. Then the chiding hisses and howls were suddenly joined by the 'pfffffsssssss!' of something right behind me. The cumulative effect of hundreds of jolts and bounces had blown out the valve on the inner tube of my back tire, and I settled down to fix it in the mud, an interesting mixture of ants and weird flying insects biting me as I did so. I got another puncture shortly after I'd fixed the first, but the second was caused by a tack from a discarded horseshoe.

That night the volcano added a bass line to the constant cacophony, sending ominous rumbles across the lake to my perfect camp on the shore. From where I sat eating a tin of sardines I'd picked up in the last village, red balls of rock could be seen falling, as if in slow motion, hundreds of yards down the ash-strewn mountain, breaking up and sending the few surviving trees up in a distant haze of flame.

For two consecutive nights I watched the light show from my tent vestibule as bats dodged and rolled, feeding on mosquitoes fat with my blood. The next day, after I'd woken to the noise of a pig chewing the empty sardine tin I'd left in the dirt, I found tarmac again. It was a relief, the adventure I'd craved so much three days previously had more than tested me. Just when I thought the deep impassable river was a myth, I'd found it after 50 miles of mud, thorns and punctures. It took me three trips to ferry bike and equipment across the river – it came up to my waist, and the powerful current was enough to see me on the brink of toppling over on the uneven and slippery boulders. I left the heavy and awkward bike until last, keeping my shoes on and whittling a branch to steady myself with. On the closing stages of the good dirt track skirting the base of the volcano, though far from where the hot ash continued to fall, I joined another man on a bike, a middle-aged Costa Riceño. What he was doing seemed unusual. He was riding to his friend's house 30 miles away. But not because he had to – there was a regular and cost-effective bus. He just wanted to have some fun. So far on my journey through Central America, I'd found fun to be a luxury most people couldn't afford.

Back on the well-developed roads the surrounding forests were dominated by huge adventure holiday resorts that catered for tourists willing to pay for rafting in the morning, cookies and milk for the kids, a quick toucan tour and then some rappelling and a snake-handling session before tea. I often pulled into these all but empty holiday camps to try to get water or some provisions. Almost without exception they proved impersonal and most of the time unhelpful.

Slowly though, as I edged southeast down onto the hot, straight roads of the lowlands, the Caribbean influence grew. The dark skin became a little darker, faces more of African origin than Latin. The pumping 'cumbia' music being vomited from passing car windows or front porches became displaced by the dulcet tones of a reggae star, while the red, white and blue of the Costa Rican flag was increasingly challenged by the black, yellow and green that have come to represent Rasta culture.

Jamaica seemed to almost fuse with this country in Puerto Limon, one of the busiest east-coast ports in Costa Rica. The world-renowned symbol of the ganja leaf adorned clothes and cars. As I stopped to get my bearings, an old dreadlocked Rasta sauntered past with cracked glasses, mumbling lyrics in thick patois. 'Emancipate yourselves from mental slavery, none but ourselves can free our minds . . .'

The rhythm had changed completely, and as I rolled along the quiet palm-fringed coast towards the popular Puerto Viejo, the ever-present tourist population only encouraged the laid-back beach culture full of Jamaican rum, Bob Marley and coconuts. But I didn't arrive there alone. Ten miles from the small beach town the road turned back to dry stony dirt next to a tiny thatched bus shelter. I cycled past, and only when I glanced back on hearing voices did I notice two men with large, conspicuous suitcases. I circled and stopped next to them. They had been among the countless numbers of backpackers that volunteer every year on turtle conservation projects along this coast, but they were done, ready to start the alcoholic segment of their holiday. Jim, an Italian New Yorker, was keen enough to head the short distance into town on Achilles that he proceeded to drag his suitcase over. Within minutes it was balanced precariously on a now very top-heavy trailer and when we bumped unsteadily off, the trailer pivot arm flexed worryingly under the weight. We made it though, while Jim sat readjusting his baggy jeans occasionally and describing for the camera how we met in a thick New York Italian accent.

Jim was sweating heavily behind me by the time we rolled into Puerto Viejo, a small, sleepy town forced into slow mode by weed and humidity. Bikes prevail here too, just like in the rest of Central America, but here it's different, they're cruisers. It's as if all the tired but still trendy Californian beach bikes are shipped down here to be given a new lease of life, one where the paint job no longer matters, and the tires are let down a bit to mirror the low-pressure lifestyle.

Jim introduced me to his friends, and soon I was relaxing with them, lounging on beaches and sucking on the energy of the town when it came alive at night. The lights from beach-side open-fronted bars cast shadows on the trampled beach, but the glow was swallowed up quickly by the lazy ocean, black and warm. This holiday atmosphere wasn't a cultural novelty, in fact I'd already found it in dozens of tourist destinations along my trajectory. But it did allow me to take a little break from transience once again and recharge my mental batteries.

It didn't take long though for the ugly side of vacationing to come out. After a relaxed night, I walked back to the hostel and witnessed an American on what seemed like a cocaine-fuelled rampage in the village's dimly lit dirt streets, fighting with stray dogs and punctuating garbled sentences with crazed shouts. The spectacle made me sad, but suddenly pleased I could escape tourist craziness on Achilles whenever I wanted.

But the rot of that one bad apple didn't seem to spread amongst the friends I made, and Adrienne, a lovely girl from the Appalachians, jumped on for a day to accompany me across the quiet, bridged border into Panama. She was a placid girl and long-suffering as I made stereotypical inquiries about her knowledge of the backwoods and funny-looking folk playing the banjo.

We rolled into a small grassy park backed by a mangrove-edged river. There, on the swings next to a gaggle of curious kids, sat our friends from the hostel, the statuesque and beautiful Miquel, Jake and Jimmy,

having arrived not long before us. We knew that to get to Bocas del
Toro – the Bull's Mouth – you have to cross a stretch of water, but I
expected something a little bigger, more official, than what we found.
The dock was no bigger than a boathouse you might find on the
lakeside of a large country residence in the UK. Between the walkways
sat a fibreglass boat with an outboard which we commissioned to take
us to the hooked tongue of the bull's mouth. The kids helped pack the
boat in return for a pedal round the swings, and unlike the bumpy
cycle to the dock, the boat glided and hummed through the water, our
V-shaped wake breaking over floating vegetation on the edge of the
straight jungle channel. Occasionally I saw a small, isolated hut on stilts
and a canoe hidden in the bushes, but otherwise it was just us, speeding
along the waterway and out into a delta solid with lilies big enough for
birds to sit on. And then, after we had motored across the open gulf
under sun filtered into rays by rainy season clouds, the boat nudged into
a small gap between perhaps a dozen other launches and deposited us
on the small, darkening main street of Bocas.

It was an even more relaxing sanctuary than the last. I spent two more
days on all but deserted beaches, the hot wind kicking up the waves
and swaying the palms behind us. Drawn by the thuds of windfalls, I'd
occasionally saunter to the trees to retrieve a fallen coconut. It would
take maybe 20 minutes to get to the white flesh and milk with my tiny
knife, but in the heat the reward was well worthwhile.

I wanted to leave this place early in the day, before the tepid but
hammering afternoon rain got going or the heat cranked up. A sunrise
departure, however, proved impossible, when I wandered out of the
hostel bleary-eyed to find my bike where I'd left it locked to a flimsy
drainpipe, but the tires flat. Strange, I thought, but rolling the bike a
few feet into the courtyard I found out why. The rubber of both tough
tires had been slashed, not punctured. A clean 4-inch cut had been
made in each, making the tires and tubes unusable. I usually only
carried one spare at a time, but since a delivery in Panama City I'd had
two spares, so despite making my blood boil, the problem was fixable.
I worked quickly, detaching the wheels and standing Achilles on his
handlebars while I replaced the tubes and tires. It looked like the work

of a drunken tourist rather than a local and I could only think of one person who might bear a grudge, since I'd made friends with Miquel, his ex-girlfriend . . .

As I worked the sun came up and I began to sweat, reattaching the wheels, leaning over the bike to lock things back in position and reattach bags and bungees. As I did so, stripped to the waist, I began to itch. It got quickly worse and my eyes stung as I rubbed my face and scratched my reddening chest. I thought it might be heat rash, but it was pretty acute, and increasingly painful. Then I realised something was missing from the bike. I'd attached a canister of bear spray in a small holster to my handlebars. It had been pressed on me by the mother of Sarah from way back up in Whitehorse, Canada. She wouldn't let me leave without it but only recently had I felt it might be useful, not for bears but for the countless stray dogs that snapped at my ankles as I rolled through villages. Everything suddenly became clear. The canister was missing, and when I found it back near the drainpipe in the dirt, it was nearly empty. Running my finger across the frame of Achilles I found it was covered in a brown residue of bear spray.

This set me back, and very real irritation made leaving at least one of the otherwise pleasant bunch of tourists a little easier, as I headed for the hills and comparative solitude. It would have been nice to share the afternoon rains and painful hill climbs with a friend though, Miquel maybe. But no one's travel plans fitted in and loneliness crept up again quickly to gift me with hours of post-company depression. On numerous occasions during the lonely days I wondered, not for the first time, what the hell I was doing. Hour upon hour of hot, badly paved highway, or hairpin after hairpin of power-sapping climbing . . . what was the point, when sometimes I struggled to remember the last time I'd enjoyed riding like this? But constant movement doesn't allow this question to linger for long, and during one such pity party I stopped at a tiny store to force the negativity out with sweet bread. I stood outside next to three men chatting and laughing. One of them introduced himself as Lorenzo, who laughed harder, with a twinkle in his eyes, when he heard about my project. Five minutes later after pumping up his bald tires for him, I followed him down a little muddy track towards the river hidden by the trees. We arrived at a small wooden house on stilts, where his wife was cooking and his daughter Ruth looked to be doing homework at the only table and chair on the dirt floor. Before my sweaty Lycra had so much as touched the old tarp tied at each end to make a hammock, a coffee was thrust into my hand by Lorenzo's wife Elizabeth, and the family politely shooed away the five dogs and numerous chickens that shared the ground floor with them.

That evening we ate fried plantains and pork and played dominoes, with my bike-light piercing a hole through the gloomy dusk. Later, a bed was prepared for me in the only upstairs room. Despite the fact that there were only three mattresses on the wooden floor, the idea of refusing their offer of a bed seemed a little rude. So, not long after the fifth game of dominoes I lay there listening to the sound of the night here in yet another family home. The dogs stirred and sniffed the air occasionally, and a chicken adjusted herself on the eggs which she had recently laid in the corner of a small box downstairs. Sometimes, Ruth told me, the hen laid eggs in the box where she kept her school books. Lorenzo, or perhaps Christian, his son, lay close by, snoring slightly, and the timbers under us creaked slightly as someone rolled over in their sleep.

The next morning Christian and I walked up the river barefoot in torrential rain to fish. With chewed-up banana as bait he quickly reeled in five fleshy *sábalos* which formed the core of our lunch, my farewell meal with all three generations of the family, including Eulogio Cabrera, the most senior, at 84 years old. He told me stories of hunting for rabbits in his youth and stumbling across pumas, his eyes sunk deeply in his small skull but dancing brightly and projecting those memories at my face. He laughed when recalling his childish mistakes, and smiled proudly when he described the ingenious ways in which he had provided for his parents decades ago.

While he talked from the comfort of the only chair, I looked from face to face of his children and grandchildren, propped in the corner or sitting two abreast in the hammock. The whole family was watching and listening equally proudly, despite having heard these stories many times.

THE PAN-AMERICAN ENDS

After a lunch of fish and rice, during which the family insisted I sit at the small table while they perched around the open-sided room, Elizabeth pointed to a small carton she'd prepared for me. It was a *mono*, she told me, telling me to take it for the road. My Spanish was pretty good now, and I knew what a mono was. A monkey. What was I going to do with a monkey's head? (The box was too small to house an entire animal.) The family laughed when I questioned it, and politely, after wiping the tears away, explained that in Panama, mono also means packed meal. I thanked them before retrieving my camera, propped filming in the crook of a tree, and rolling the bike up the muddy path towards the road.

It rained almost constantly for three days as I made the return trip to the Pacific coast. I squelched as I pedalled, my shoes only water-resistant when it came to retaining moisture. In the brief periods of no rain it was hot and humid enough for sweat to slowly displace the rainwater and form a greasy film on my skin. Then, hours later on the vegetated ridges, the wind whipped the heat away from my core, causing me to don all four layers of sodden clothes while the mist swirled through the palms and over the precipitous jungle. Waterfalls sprang up overnight, huge plumes of water spouted from the greenery above the road. Down in the steep valleys I could hear the rumble of a raging torrent, but the thick canopy of trees kept me guessing as to exactly where it was.

After the rain and roads had taken payment for my Caribbean detour, I arrived, on June 25, my birthday, in the medium-sized town of Gualaca. I was 25 when I first set off on my journey. I caught a fish for my 26th birthday, alone and content, next to a small Alaskan river. My 27th birthday was shared with a litre of chocolate milk and a small group of volunteer firemen and women at the Gualaca fire station.

Fire engines, I was learning, since they adorned a fair few of my Panamanian sleeping quarters, have a certain beauty about them. The polishing the volunteers give them allows the red paint and chrome to flash in the sunlight during the day and reflect every lux of the dim light bulbs at night. They get North America's best cast-offs down here, Freightliners, La Frances, Internationals, but every single one is caressed

139

and cleaned as if it were the cutting edge in fire-fighting technology, providing a stark contrast to the dusty streets outside.

It wasn't always the giant garages I'd sleep in though, sometimes in the cities I was invited into the plusher dorms, fire station libraries or small band-practice rooms where the *bomberos* might be found watching a staticky image on a television in the corner. In the poorer units, I'd arrive and maybe interrupt a game of chess played on a board scratched out of cardboard using bottletop pawns. The closer I got to Panama City the more facilities improved, and I all but forgot that the early days of my fire-service sponsored camping was in stations that didn't even have a water supply.

Once, only a day out of Bocas del Toro, as I was told to be sparing with the water tapped straight from one of two dormant engines, I pictured the scene at a future call out . . .

'Errr, Captain, number two tank has run dry!!!'

'Que??? It's a 2,000-gallon tank and we've only been here three minutes!!!'

'Yes sir, it's just that Alejandro took a bath yesterday and José volunteered to do the dishes, must've been a bit overzealous rinsing the soap off sir . . .'

Meanwhile, a small village is burned to the ground. But Alejandro is clean and the dishes are ready for a new meal. I didn't, however, bring the topic up with my friendly hosts.

On the night of my birthday I lay near the two engines and an ambulance, sweating next to the big rubber tires until first light when the dogs, hens and people in the surrounding houses began the new day like the last. Unusually for me, I felt homesick for my friends and family. Each day on Achilles found me out a little more, physically and emotionally. I rested after my birthday, recharging for a day, searching in vain for a yellow fever vaccine, as I would need proof of immunity at future border crossings, and enjoying the large range of food available in this small city. Once, on the second of numerous visits to a range of tiny bakeries, I wandered over to inspect a nice-looking piece of sponge with chocolate and coconut all over it. I put the change needed to purchase the cake on the counter, smiled briefly at the shop lady who had a slightly bemused look on her face, and walked out, ripping the paper off my treat. A few seconds later, the lady made a 'ppssst' noise, having rushed to the door. I had become accustomed to this attention-grabbing sound, and turned casually to see what it was she wanted. Only then did I find out that I had apparently not deposited 35 cents on the counter top at all, but one washer, a spare part for my bike, and a Nicaraguan penny. I apologised, grinning and embarrassed before dropping the correct shrapnel in her palm. Looking up she shot me a great big Mestizo eye-wrinkling smile. I was pleased I'd tried to pay in washers, the smile was worth a dollar alone.

More than a year had passed since I left the wide open spaces of northern Alaska, my memory banks reserved for the journey back then a blank slate and waiting to be graffitied. Slowly, spaces had been filled up by signatures, memories, experiences, both deliriously happy and painfully sad. Cycling closer again to the west side of the skinny country of Panama, I felt like space was running out. On bad days I'd feel sufficiently road-weary to be full, bloated even, with new experiences and unwilling to take on more. I was only a day or two away from Panama City, not even close to being done. And, to add to this rain-soaked introspection, I was approaching the only roadless section of the Americas, with no plan as to how to tackle it.

The Panama Canal stretches for nearly 50 miles from Panama City to Colón, allowing the waters of the east and west to touch navigable fingertips just once in the entire length of the Americas. Two bridges span this canal at the southerly end, the larger being Puente de las Americas, from where one can see the skyscrapers of the financial district beyond and, a little closer, the downmarket barrios forming the seedier but more characterful part of the city. I was relieved to arrive here with only the bridge separating me from another rest, and prepared to cross this milestone, readying my camera for action and priming my legs to ride the incline which ended halfway to the far shore.

Suddenly though, a whistle came from behind me, and a young policeman appeared out of nowhere, running down the hard shoulder of the Pan-American Highway. I would have to turn back, he told me with a tone of finality. Bicycles weren't allowed on the bridge. I smiled at him, and said quietly that I'd cycled rather a long way to get here and wasn't too keen to turn back. After rubbing the downy hairs on his teenage chin, he hailed a passing government truck, and instructed the driver to take me over the bridge and into the city.

So that was it. As the wind whistled through my hair and I travelled at a speed I was no longer used to, I thought about the Central America I was letting slip quickly away. After the truck dumped me on the far side of the bridge and I pedalled into the metropolis, a young racing cyclist rolled up alongside and introduced himself. Glenn, a lithe, friendly character, was to become my unofficial guide for the next few days, facilitating TV interviews, tours on the tandem down the causeway to the exclusive yacht clubs and ice-cream parlours. That first evening Glenn agreed to come out for a drink with me, and on scratching his head and procrastinating about where to go, he became set upon the idea of heading to El Bocas Toreno, a bar he had not ventured to for a while.

'Venga,' he said enthusiastically as we took advantage of one of the many old buses, customised with risqué paint jobs and panel-vibrating music to cater for the driver's taste. It propelled us jerkily into what I found out was the slightly less up-market area of the city.

Avenida B in the day is a chaotic patchwork of stands, fish markets and porn shops, not really allowing room for vehicular passage. At night, it was dead, garbage the only sign of the day's activities and the odd drunk sleeping where he had been sleeping for the last week.

On the dank waterfront, a dimly lit entrance with a few people loitering outside was Glenn's target, and after pausing as if to ensure that this really was the place he remembered, he gestured me in with a grin on his face.

It was incredible. An awesome visual feast of drunks, scantily clad women of all races, ages and statures, and a continual stream of men fresh from a 14-hour shift on a fishing boat or in the city. It was of course a low-key whore house, the interaction between the men and women nonchalant and matter-of-fact.

At any one time, at least seven men, usually older men, sat dozing at tables, beer in hand. They appeared to take sleeping in shifts, for as soon as one woke up, another would lapse into unconsciousness elsewhere in the noisy bar. Once conscious, the old man would do one of two things: order another beer, or summon a girl over and after a few words, with the cheeky grin of an 11-year-old boy, was willingly led away, not to be seen again for about five minutes.

Once reseated, the old man again allowed his chin to slump slowly to his chest, and with the fingers of one hand curled around a beer bottle, he'd go back to sleep.

I was informed that anything I could ever want in this little wonderland would cost ten bucks. Despite unbeatable value, I decided to save my money for food over the next few days.

When I gave myself a chance to lay out my maps on a café table after two days of journey-free thinking, I looked up my route options further south.

Not far south of the city, the road ended at an area shaded dark green. I ignored this problem and looked further south into Colombia and Ecuador. But when I extracted my Peruvian map I lost the will to look further. The southern tip of this continent was still an impossibly long distance from where I was slumped sucking on a papaya milkshake. The reality of my situation was that I had little idea how far I had to go. Looking at a world atlas it seemed as if I was about halfway to my goal, but I knew only too well that a few hairpin bends and detours could change all that. I put the maps away, defaulting to denial, pretending I wasn't about to leave again.

As I wandered the city sometimes with Glenn, I made friends. The owner of the nearest bakery soon became a very valuable acquaintance, as did the nearest café selling the cheap but filling standard fare. I watched huge freighters rub shoulders with decrepit old fishing boats at the mouth of the canal and occasionally was overwhelmed by a huge supermarket, such as I hadn't been into since northern Costa Rica.

I ventured a little way from the city too, but not on Achilles. Celia, one of the friends I'd made here, worked in the city but lived a little way out, as do most of the city's employees. Her family invited me to their house a half-hour bus ride away, where I was looked after like a member of their clan in return for English tuition and fixing little Jason's bicycle. This I did enthusiastically and that evening like moths to a light bulb, friends of Jason – Celia's son – came with their bikes too, asking me to change things, or make things work that had stood dormant since their big brother had left home years before. Fixing bikes was a job I enjoyed. My small collection of tools empowered me with the ability to give a tiny fraction back as I went, and that evening I settled down to sleep on the couch, while a small handful of children were still out in the dark skidding, squealing and chasing each other on rickety but functional bicycles.

12

Sailing to the proudest country

DAY 381: 9,818 MILES

The Darién Gap is an area of almost virgin jungle 125 miles to the east of Panama City, bordering Colombia and spanning the width of the country. Due to the swampy and waterlogged geology, as well as the fairly constant paramilitary activity in the area, the Pan-American Highway has never been finished here. No roads exist, only a mysterious network of rivers, paths tangled with vegetation and tiny indigenous villages provide those who live there passage to the outside. It also provides a leafy and all but impenetrable stronghold for the heart of the region's drug trade and associates, or *narcotraficantes*. It's this that keeps people out of this region. The harder the Colombian and US military try and combat the cocaine trade, the deeper into this jungle these terrorists go. I looked at the map and the series of little names that was dotted along the north coast. I'd heard stories of people catching boats from village to village, making their way along the edge of the gap. I'd heard other stories of people who had walked straight through with little other than a machete, but needless to say the majority of stories that have littered newsstands and bookshops for 50 years describe kidnaps, murders and many years in a humid and vegetal purgatory.

This kind of adventure appealed to me – dragging my bike through the vegetation, hacking as I went with the machete I'd picked up in Guatemala, maybe talking paramilitaries round to helping me or giving

145

me a lift down a river hidden under the jungle canopy. I knew it might be a little naive, but I liked it and actually dared to foster the thought, more than a year of good fortune having bolstered my confidence in people. Anyhow, there was a silver lining to a hostage situation, it would allow me time to recuperate on a fruit diet and become fully fluent in some of the less regular rules of Spanish grammar. Another appealing aspect of this option was the likelihood of an insect laying eggs under my skin and the resulting larvae erupting from one of my limbs a few weeks later. As far as I was concerned that's one of the boxes an 'adventurer' has to tick before he truly comes of age.

Then I thought about my bike. It hadn't got any lighter and I had trouble pushing it across a parking lot, let alone dragging it through a dense tangle of mangrove swamp. A hundred and twenty-five miles? I remembered, all of a sudden feeling foolish, the time it had taken me to travel the 30 miles of muddy tracks in Costa Rica. I'd lose the will to live before I'd even managed a few days in another, altogether denser, jungle I realised. The idea slowly drifted away as I gave it up to search for an exciting alternative. In various email sessions in the city collecting news from home and contacts further south, I learned of a friend of a friend of a friend sailing round the world with his family. As luck would have it, and as far as anyone could tell, it was possible the family was on their boat in my neck of the woods. On one email there was a mobile phone number. Two days before I left town, I punched the numbers into a pay phone on the street. After a few drawn-out rings there was a click.

'Hello?' An English voice in one ear sounded incongruous with a thousand Latin sounds flowing in the other. The speaker introduced herself as Alice, wife of Pete and mother to Ruben and Olive. They'd been expecting my call. I felt as if I were being watched by the secret service, monitoring my every move and ensuring I made progress without upset. They were indeed on the north coast of Panama, and agreed to help get me to Colombia. Clutching the phone with my shoulder, I scribbled the name of an island I'd never heard of and agreed to meet them there in four days.

I had no idea where it was, or how to get there.

* * *

SAILING TO THE PROUDEST COUNTRY

I spent the next day recovering from a small stomach bug, packing and checking over the map. The name Alice had given me wasn't even an island on mine, but there was a track marked that headed north along the edge of the Darién region. The next morning I said goodbye to Celia and met Glenn, fresh from a night's work as a croupier at a tourist casino. Clad in his flashy Lycra and reflective shades, he co-piloted me quickly along the busy highway east out of the sprawling city. It was a short journey of extremes, one moment dry and impossibly hot, and the next with an almost solid wall of rain causing us to pedal quickly to a concrete bus shelter before we drowned in the spray bouncing off the tarmac on the Inter-American Highway. The city traffic disappeared and only a handful of buses overtook us as we dodged downpours and hopped quickly between isolated bus shelters. Glenn lived up to his pro-rider look, piston-like silky-smooth legs ensuring we made good time down the straight, humid road. Once or twice I'd be surprised by a spontaneous 'It's fantastico,' sung out from behind me in camp-sounding Spanglish. Glenn had obviously warmed to Achilles.

Only a few miles short of the Darién we arrived in a tiny community. About 50 yards before the little cluster of wooden buildings a track led steeply up into the jungle on our left. Looking for other possibilities and finding none, I guessed this was it, the track that would lead me to the coast. A man in the city had told me that motor canoes sometimes took people from the beach to the San Blas islands, the biggest of which was the island Alice had mentioned. I desperately hoped that man had known what he was talking about, as I hugged Glenn goodbye. He was smiling through a layer of rain and sweat. He'd loved the ride, he told me, and wished desperately that he could come further. He sat down heavily on the bus stop bench, exhaling and struggling to describe his yearning to do more cycling. For him though, the casino called, and if he didn't return that night, someone else would have filled his place and he'd lose his job. I waited with him until a city-bound bus carried him off. The guy hadn't slept for more than 24 hours, nor would he for a further 12. His appetite for cycling was evidently a lot bigger than mine, and I quietly saluted his enthusiasm while trying to muster a little more of my own.

TAKE A SEAT

The next day, after being allowed to sleep in the kitchen of a basic restaurant swarming with mosquitoes, I began to think, casino or no casino, Glenn was wise to retreat from a task that left me fried and half dead after less than 10 miles. Still suffering slightly from the aftermath of another unidentified fever, I struggled to push my bike inch by inch up 17 percent rocky tracks and then to maneuver it carefully down a similarly steep descent and across a muddy quagmire, and repeat the process many, many times. The jungle closed in. The rains came, the rains went, and still I pushed, like a high-altitude mountaineer, pausing every ten steps to suck air. I began to question why I hadn't paid $100 to take a ferry from Panama or Colón.

But when I stopped long enough to look around, I gawked at the pockets of mist and cloud caught in the tight green valleys below, partly obscuring one or two simple thatched indigenous dwellings. The Kuna people inhabited this strip of land as well as the archipelago I was heading towards. I'd seen a few in a supermarket back in the city, hard to miss with their brightly coloured dresses and intricate beading halfway up their calves and arms. That day however, as I mostly pushed Achilles slowly forward, it was only howler monkeys that sounded their disapproval at my presence in their territory until I stopped at the only building I'd seen close to the muddy track.

It was the water barrels I stopped for. I'd seen them under the eves of the building with a cloth stretched over the top to filter the plentiful supply of rainwater from the roof. The building was a tiny school. Señora Laura, the only teacher in the Cartí Llano area, told me this building was the daytime home for 18 local children, whom I could see behind her poking their heads round the door frame, giggling at the outsider. I noticed two of the girls wore traditional Kuna dress, making the other bouncy children look drab in their surprisingly clean shirts and trousers.

For the remainder of the day and night I rested with Laura and her family, and partook in preparations for what must have been one of the most isolated Children's Day celebrations in the country. Shortly after I arrived, parched yet soaked from the rains, I sat in the only classroom while the children excitedly put the final touches to a huge paper chain made of newspaper. Once there was a squeal of delight from a young boy in wellington boots who had found a naughty picture in the small strip of paper he was gluing. Laura quickly quelled the excitement and removed the offending boobs, allowing the paper-chain production line to gather pace again.

Sadly, the thought of missing the boat ride to Colombia forced me to leave these children after sleeping in a classroom with a 'Barney the dinosaur' revolving slowly from the ceiling above my head. By first light the moths of every shape and colour fluttering around the light bulb outside had disappeared.

After taking part in the opening celebrations, a sack race, some singing and the crowning of the Cartí Llano queen – a small, timid girl who wore the simple paper crown as if it were forged from the purest gold – I rolled away for more muddy torture.

The mornings were worst. Whatever it was that had invaded my gut left me feeling weak and nauseous for a few hours after waking, and I used up my last polite smile waving the adorable children goodbye. Only 4 miles on, on a road that made me flounder in deepening mud, I lost the will to continue and sat in the mud retching pathetically. For a quiet minute I was grateful I hadn't ventured into the Darién. If I wasn't strong enough for this 'track', the jungle would have killed me.

It was a pick-up truck – rare in this region – that came to my rescue. In return for 20 bucks that I extracted from my seat post and waved limply at the driver, I got a small pineapple and a ride in hammering rain through clay-like mud to a swollen river. It took an hour for the truck to mostly sideslip 9 miles, and I sat in the back occasionally connecting violently with the roof each time a tree root or rock stood proud of the mud. I slumped, only semi-conscious, grateful the truck had come and far too weak to care about wimping out.

Sliding out of the truck once we stopped, I immediately sank up to my calves in mud, but looking groggily around I saw I was far from alone. Twenty yards away idling in the fast-flowing muddy water was a wooden canoe, a rusty outboard lazily pumping out blue smoke. Six Chinese men were loading coolboxes on board and shouting in Mandarin at one other. Floundering in the mud I found a spot for

Achilles and my bags near the bows, and walking out from the bank, I climbed in after them.

The leaky craft propelled me slowly along with the Chinese fishermen – apparently restocking their restaurants in the city – between knots of fallen trees, past local Kuna men paddling smaller dugout canoes to the sea. With waves threatening to breach the bitumen breakwaters we crossed the open water to arrive at the principal island, El Porvenir, home apparently to one of the only telephones in the San Blas archipelago.

Leaving my pile of cycling equipment on the small dock under the watchful eyes of three giggling children and an old man, I entered a maze of tiny dirt alleyways, picking up some tomatoes and finding the telephone guarded by an old lady with a small box. After paying her a 25-cent surcharge, I walked into the phone box and put another quarter in the slot. Pete, the skipper of the boat I was meeting, picked up after one ring and in a thick Kiwi accent instructed me to meet him in an hour at another island, smaller, but apparently with an 'immigration hut'. Hurrying out and thanking the guardian of the phone box I enlisted the services of another motor canoe, complete with pilot, to take me to the island, 45 minutes away. My equipment had been left untouched by the kids as I knew it would be. I'd long since stopped worrying about people taking my stuff. It rarely happened, and anyway, to hold on to a small-minded distrust on a journey like this would have been way too tiring.

During the crossing I huddled in the bows next to Achilles watching tens of islands near and far glide slowly past. They were all your typical picture-postcard tropical paradise, the thatches of huts showing themselves behind a perimeter of palm trees and then the pale strip of sand. There are 365 of these islands in all, the driver told me when I asked, shouting over the sound of the motor, and together they made up the majority of the Kuna Yala, the land that by law belongs to the Kuna people. Perhaps specifically due to this isolation, these people have managed to maintain one of the most intact indigenous cultures remaining on Earth.

As the sun broke out from behind a cloud we nudged up against the rickety dock of my island, and soon I was sitting alone on the sand, with

Achilles never having looked so useless. There were two huts, perhaps twice as many palm trees and not a whole lot else. But, right on time as I was wrapping my chain to protect against salt, the handsome 44-foot *Yamana* cruised round the beach into view. All was going according to plan.

Twenty minutes later, after getting a dozy policeman in one of the huts to give my passport an exit stamp, and crossing the 50 yards of water in Pete's dinghy with Achilles balanced precariously across it, I was in the boat's cockpit with the Grant family, a bubbly mixture of English and Kiwi blood that would take me east for two to three days along the coast, depending on conditions, Pete said.

That first night at anchor in the sheltered water between three islands there was a storm. Jagged rods of lightning shot down into the black water around us but we were untouched, and the anchor held firm. The next day, with little wind and the steady throb of the motor underneath us, a school of dolphins jumped playfully around our bows as we travelled away from the last of the islands. In order to sleep that night Pete and his family entrusted me with the responsibility of piloting their craft for three of the thirty-one hours it took to get to Cartagena, the walled city that Sir Francis Drake plundered four hundred and twenty-three years before our arrival. For those three night-time hours, I sat at the helm of *Yamana*, transfixed by her movement through the water. Phosphorescence sparkled in the wash of our wake and the genoa billowed in a keen and steady wind in front of us. It was peaceful, and the slap of waves against the hull and the inviting red glow of the compass in its own oily sphere accompanied me in the darkness while the others slept. I discovered the magic of sailing, having at last left my mild sea-sickness behind. Stars winked down reassuringly as electric storms lit up the horizon to starboard. If I stood on the metal bar underneath the skipper's chair, I could see Achilles through the plastic cockpit window lying safely on the foredeck. We were hours away from landing in Colombia, where the Andes rise up and crease the continent lengthways until it runs out, well over 5,000 miles south.

A day later, surrounded by gently swaying masts, I sat in the marina bar catching snippets of adventures on the high seas. Conversations were about sail dimensions and bilge pumps, good ice-cream cafés and how the Bahamas are at this time of year. I heard very little about the country we were in. The real Colombia began outside the gated compound a few streets away, but even there, like most of Cartagena, it's impossible to get an idea of the culture and colour of the place – it's too wealthy, too manicured by the influx of tourists and high-living Colombians.

I suppose it was inevitable, with New Zealand and Australia spreading their countryfolk liberally across the globe, that I should snag at least one on my voyage. And so it was, after approximately 10,500 miles, when Pete stepped up to the plate and left *Yamana* to accompany me to Medellin, where he'd reunite with Alice, Ruben and Olive. Pete towered above any locals we met and his lithe figure and bright blue eyes attracted curious glances wherever we went. He seemed to try and hide under the peak of his Cuban baseball cap, about as effective a camouflage as a willow sapling might be for a fat man with an afro.

The road gave us a few days' grace while my new second mate was broken in and I lost my sea legs. I found Pete on the morning of the third day having washed in the bucket shower in the corner of our concrete room. He was mixing moisturising cream and arnica in the palm of his hand with a hopeful look on his face. He stood up, and reached down his Lycras as if to check for his prostate while looking up at the ceiling with his face twisted into a curious wince. I asked no questions, just laughed, made sure the camera was pointed at him, and hoped like he did that the tincture would do the trick.

It wasn't long before the prelude to the Andes punished us and the topography stripped a few more precious ounces of fat from my lessening frame. Despite these very physical obstacles, pain was more easily forgotten with a combination of lively conversation and beautiful landscapes. Outside the towns and cities we cycled through undulating lush green fields, dotted with trees and cowboys, or *vaqueros*, wearing stripy Colombian sombreros.

Once we'd cranked slowly up into the highlands closer to Medellin, Colombia showed another side of her varied land. Cool alpine meadows stretched through the hills, with pine trees lining the road running near the bottom of wide valleys, but always seemingly deviating to take in a viciously steep rise of 6 or more miles. We rested a day in the hillside town of Yarumal, swept with a fresh breeze and a cold night air I'd been dreaming of for months whilst sweating in fire stations or gas station forecourts. I sat for hours the next morning, watching very elderly men take on the gargantuan task of ascending the steeply sloping plaza. Two old friends sometimes crossed paths, one on his way up, the other descending to a nearby café. They would take off their sombreros, steady themselves on an iron railing, and launch into conversation so animated it was hard to believe their senior status until their wind-hardened faces creased into wrinkly grins. *Hermano, mi hijo, primo . . . *. Brother, my son, cousin – everyone was referred to as a member of the family in this way, and so it was that, for 48 hours of drinking aniseed-flavoured liqueur (aguardiente) in the cafés with the old men, and dancing enthusiastically in the entertaining local bars, Pete and I were absorbed, albeit briefly, into the Yarumal family.

As we cycled through the outskirts of the hilltop city the following morning, it dawned on me that, in a country famous for coffee, I'd seen very little – it wasn't even in the giant white sacks I'd seen in Guatemala. It was as if any shops selling the shiny brown beans had been replaced with small workshops that made and sold coffins, of which there were many in each town. Could it have been a small spelling error somewhere high up in national bureaucracy? Either way, 'Fancy a coffin?' became a commonly asked question between smirking Pete and me each time we passed an old man knocking together a wooden box. It was especially during the painful or hungry periods that infantile humour would keep us entertained for hours.

Medellin, my first sizeable Colombian city, held delights of its own. It was here, in between the brown hills and neighbourhoods built at impossible angles on their slopes, that I found myself at a Colombian house party. Pete, who had reunited with his family after a good five-day stint of arse-numbing riding, had said to me that, in his opinion, some of the best experiences when travelling are to be had in the houses of locals. That has always been my feeling, and even as a large bull mastiff savaged my hand while I tried drunkenly to rescue a piece of paper from its mouth, I found myself thinking how true those words were. Once we were sure the dog hadn't caught anything from me, the small but perfectly formed party (which fortunately included a nurse and a large supply of iodine) resumed pace and barbecued meat was brandished to soak up the cartons of rum and aguardiente.

This country was quickly becoming my favourite, and only once, the previous evening, had I seen any hint of Colombia's shady reputation. Invited for dinner, I went to the expensive quarter with some Colombians Pete and I had met at a café on the road days before. Propelled through their city in a plush four by four, I wound down the window, amazed by the thickness of the glass.

'It's bullet proof,' the driver said when he saw me fingering it.

'Why?' I asked. 'Are you an important man?' He laughed along with his friends in the back briefly before falling quiet, then changing the subject.

When it rains it pours they say, and having had a drought of Antipodean company for so many months, Achilles suddenly became awash with them. I found my first Australian companion, Max, in a hostel in a leafy residential sector of the city. A quiet man by his country's standards, but quietly persistent in his enquiries about a free seat on Achilles. After I'd ensured that he didn't have one of those hats with corks on it, we journeyed together further into the hills where the coffee that had been so elusive began to outdo coffin shops. We cycled into 'El Cafetero', Colombia's coffee district, every single person in this cycling-mad country beaming and waving at us as we passed like a goods train, labouring heavily up gruelling hills. Within a day and a half Max turned from an intelligent geology student with a very pleasant manner to a deranged and exhausted shadow that, when breath allowed, offered up brilliantly dry one-liners. We occasionally came across military checkpoints. Each time I mentally checked where my hidden money and the spare copy of my passport were. But each time we were waved through by smiling squaddies until the afternoon of the third day, when we were halted next to a large crowd of people at an intersection surrounded by the rich greens of farmland. The lazy-looking soldiers ushered us over with the crowds next to stands of confectioneries and there, after half an hour of chatting to curious locals, we witnessed a bicycle event that dwarfed my journey in notoriety. The Tour de Colombia is said to be the most gruelling bike race on earth, and after thousands of miles on Achilles, the speed at which the blurred and colourful peloton flashed past left me speechless. By the time we arrived in Armenia and sprawled our belongings about the house of our hosts Victor and Anna Maria, Max's body was already in its shut-down procedure.

The following morning after a deep, dreamless sleep in a plush bed, sitting with a glazed look on the sofa, Max began to speak.

'You know every so often we pass a donkey on the side of the road?'

'Yup,' I said. I'd seen countless donkeys since Mexico, farmers often owning them to haul loads, but I wasn't sure what he was getting at.

'Well, you know they always look kinda sad and long suffering, like they have nothing left, like they may expire at any moment?'

'Errr, yes . . . ?' It's true, that was a fairly good description and it fitted every one.

'Well,' Max began with a tone of finality, 'that's what I feel like.'

It wasn't the first time Achilles had had this effect on someone, but the rolling Colombian landscape had made this section of the road particularly debilitating.

The following day, while Victor the architect took time out to guide us around Salento and other beautiful, almost Swiss-style, villages that exist around the coffee industry, Max followed us obediently, as if he'd had a lobotomy. Once a hammock presented itself at the beautiful family finca, a short drive from the city of Armenia, and, without even sampling the delights of a table full of food, he collapsed.

13

From pocket-size to parent

DAY 418: 10,882 MILES

It was approaching the end of August 2007. It's the month that brings a soft but persistent breeze to Colombia. As the leaves of banana palms began to slowly flap, or the cheap nylon pillowcases displayed at a dusty roadside stand rose and fell, every small child's senses became alert to the new aerobatic adventures that awaited them. High above the trees, we could see a tiny twitching movement, something darting from side to side like the head of a serpent moving through invisible grass yet making no headway. If I could have seen over the trees I would have been able to make out the oranges and greens or blues of a small plastic kite, and I could trace its line down, over the banana palms and avocado trees, over the rich green coffee plants nestled in between, down to the hand of a small boy, his face upturned, staring with a furrowed brow up at his flying machine.

In the small towns Max and I had seen kids who lived on the street gather together and run along the curb, a handful of battle-scarred paper kites chasing after them. Out in the fincas and fields the children had grander kites that soared high over the plantations, a fragment of hexagonal colour in a sky of billowing clouds.

This was the Colombia I had silently worried about for months. Drugs. Paramilitaries. Crime. Kidnappings. Corruption. These were the words I had associated with this place weeks ago, when I first arrived. But with the tranquillity that surrounded me I couldn't help but start to replace these words with others. Happy. Curious. Well-educated. Proud. Smiling. Latin America is a happy land generally, but Colombia is up there on the podium. Even construction workers leaning on their shovels and watching us go by made the happiest clowns look like mere amateurs. Yet despite my observations, the headlines were full of things like 'Britain is now the second biggest donor of military aid to Colombia', or perhaps 'US steps up backing for drugs war'. As true as all this may have been, I discovered a country that, at least in the world surrounding Achilles, was saturated in nothing but kindness.

Within two days Max was able to walk again, still pale but smiling and well enough to help me cook a last supper for my hosts. Victor, on hearing that my back seat was soon to be empty, took it upon himself to find me another companion. After shepherding the two of us around for press calls, he answered a continual string of calls from those responding to an article advertising a ride on Achilles. By the time we were in the midst of cooking lasagne and garlic bread on our last night, he'd narrowed down the applicants to two. One was, as far as he could discern, a gay hairdresser, the other a business student, female, and a couple of years older than me. As any proud and virile Latin man would have done in this situation, Victor made my choice for me, and the following morning, after visiting a school where chanting students made me feel like some kind of rock star, Sonia Beatriz Lotero, my first Colombian stoker, introduced herself. She was tiny, and for a moment I wondered whether my seat post would drop low enough to accommodate her. After a few minutes twisting and pushing with an Allen key however, seat and handlebars were lowered sufficiently for my pocket-sized companion to mount, and we cycled away from the city, waving once at the students and Max, Anna Maria and Victor standing behind the slowly closing school gates.

We quickly left the coffee district behind, and the road dropped down the east side of the hills back to the flat roads heading towards Cali. Sonia had no fixed time to head home again and wore a broad grin, bobbing up and down merrily on the back seat. She was no sportswoman, but she was trying, and being so light I only felt the slight extra weight by late afternoon, when she had become exhausted.

I asked her every so often if she was OK, if she was enjoying herself. The melodrama of each of her responses made me think she might have been taking the piss, but each time I turned round she was wearing an earnest, almost profound expression. After two days experiencing life on Achilles she told me, when I asked, that this experience was definitely one of the best in her life, right up there with giving birth to her baby daughter. It was news to me that she had one, and her answer confused me. Was the experience as painful as giving birth to her baby daughter, or as life-changing? Sonia was a nice girl, but a little too nice, and unusually intense. She was pretty in a small kind of way, but people in this country were rarely unattractive. Back in Medellin an innocent trip to the supermarket had turned into a lengthy gawking session on the steps outside, where I stood stunned by the beauty of these people. Another time when Pete the Kiwi and I had stopped at a small wooden restaurant in an isolated village, our pre-breakfast hunger was completely destroyed by the sheer beauty of the woman who wandered out and began to sweep the floor. It was almost offensive. I wanted to eat fish and rice, not sit drooling open-mouthed and incapacitated by a woman sweeping in a bikini. Thankfully, Sonia was not that irresistible, otherwise I might have been tempted to have her sit up front. I'd tried that with Cassie back near Prince George simply because she'd asked me. Two hundred yards later, after two capsizes, she'd retreated to the stoker seat once more.

As we cycled on the broad highway towards Cali people pressed the local marshmallow-like gelatine into our hands or quenched our thirst with sugar-cane juice on the roadside. By then Sonia had attached a yellow plastic clip-on radio to the front of her shirt that was already struggling to contain her ample bosom. The radio emitted a tinny noise that Sonia seemed to enjoy. It reminded me of the kids back home who wander around with their mobile phones playing a similar tuneless sound, like white noise but infinitely more irritating. Still, I stomached the noise until the traffic of Cali drowned it out and it took all my concentration to navigate around hand-drawn carts and the erratic dart of taxis.

Right from the moment the fire station turned us away I disliked that city. I didn't give it time. We were only there a night, having to fall back on a faceless tenement block hotel next to a bingo hall. Sonia wanted to go dancing – Cali is apparently famous for salsa – but somehow the traffic, filth and relative unfriendliness of the city had made me irritable and unwilling to pay the small entrance fee to the bars, let alone make a pathetic attempt to dance. Every time I'd strutted my stuff anywhere near salsa territory in the past, I'd become annoyed about the fact that I wasn't born with that hip-swinging sexiness in my blood.

Achilles was beginning, after three days, to make Sonia's un-conditioned frame suffer. Past Cali the hills began to rise again, and pulling Sonia and our gear became hard work. In the late afternoon after leaving the city Sonia resorted to whimpering on the back.

'I'm dizzy,' she said. 'So dizzy.' Perhaps unfairly I had little sympathy, figuring she was just being dramatic, but 5 miles before we reached a little town I stopped abruptly, unable to tow her along any further. She took a taxi and met me in the small square a little later as the ice-cream vendors were wheeling their carts out to cater for the late afternoon Sunday family crowd.

That was the end of Sonia's ride, but she wasn't satisfied – she wasn't going home. The lure of a transient gringo seemed too great. Instead, she took a few bags the following day on a bus as I pedalled more easily and less irritated up the steep hills towards the colonial hillside city of Popayán. Somehow I suddenly enjoyed this time on my own. Time to think, with no tinny radio or cries of exhaustion. It sounds horrible now I write it, but such was my life on a tandem. With more than half my journey spent cycling solo I had become used to my own company. I tried to be as tolerant of stoker habits as possible, but the smallest irritant only a few inches behind me would spread through me like a virus until isolation was the only cure.

After a day of steady climbing, saluting the few passersby, one with half a pig draped over his scooter handlebars, I arrived in Popayán mentally refreshed and ready to be nice again. In the large plaza surrounded by ornate Spanish churches I found a blind man, a tandem bicycle and Sonia leaning out of a little red hatchback waving at me. She had found family friends and with them an invitation for the two of us to stay at their house. It's always nice not to have to worry about searching for a place to sleep in a city, and after Sonia had remounted Achilles, we followed the red car to the outskirts.

A few days before I'd left Panama I had received some welcome news. Just as my brain, usually impenetrable to homesickness, had begun to wonder about my family again, my father had agreed to fly out to Quito in Ecuador and provide the first nepotistic help on the back seat. I was excited and anxious. I felt the same as during the days leading up to a visit from my parents in boarding school when I was 8, nearly 20 years earlier. But he was flying in to Quito, and that was still days away. I wouldn't cycle there in time for his arrival, and besides I was in no hurry to leave the comfort of Popayán and the Chaves family. Their son Marco soon became my partner in crime, waving at his friends as we cycled about town doing errands on Achilles.

A month before, Ecuador had seemed like a good place to reunite with my father, since it was past the worries that Colombia represented. But now I had witnessed the more positive attributes of this country, I began to feel like I wanted to expose him to them. So, I formulated a plan. The bike would stay in Popayán while I bussed to Quito and then back, having picked up Gill Senior. This bought me more relaxation time, and in those days before waiting for the bus, I reflected on what I'd seen of Colombia. Whatever happened on the apparently dangerous section of road between here and the Ecuadorian border, I was grateful that I hadn't followed the example of countless others, and bypassed the country. I could have had no better introduction to South America. The hypnotic lilt of the Colombian accent made everything sound as sweet as the juice from the roadside stands, and without exception every stranger treated me like a friend. True, I'd been nervous at the first few checkpoints, but soon the soldiers became a source of food, chat and contacts. The landscapes were fresh and inviting, but, and this was the only but, I chose not to think about the hills ahead, where the small introductory creases of the Andes would turn into the true, jagged folds of the second largest mountain range on Earth.

I tried to film the arrival of my father from a vantage point on a balcony above the arrivals door at the airport, but as I saw him, young-looking and holding a reassuringly light-seeming duffel bag,

After three days, I reached my first real uphill challenge – the Brooks Range – still with an empty back seat.

Robert and Christine Hager, who sheltered me from the fierce rains at their fish camp.

In Ocotlán (Jalisco, Mexico), my companion, an Ocotlán resident, had organised a parade in my honour!

The Mexican hills took their toll.
I barely smiled for the camera!

Some days I carried on giving
rides until late into the night.

Julie Kresko and Achilles
nearing Nicaragua.

Adrienne, my smiling Appalachian girl,
helping me cross over into Panama.

Cycling alone in the hills above Medellin, Colombia.
(photo by Pete Grant)

The children of Leticia Morocho all doing their bit on a punishing Ecuadorian hill.

Luis Senior takes time out from sorting maize kernels to pose in front of his house in Los Piños, Ecuador.

Adam couldn't help himself; he just had to pick it up.

Two of thousands of children to take a shine to Achilles – Peru.

Grinding slowly up Duck Canyon (Canyon del Pato), Peru.

One of many only slightly uncomfortable campsites with Barney and Adam.

A dry campsite in the Sechura, Peru.

A shepherd's son in southern Peru. They start them young . . .

Porters on the Inca trail near Cusco, in traditional dress.

Carrying Achilles across the corrosive salt water at the edge of El Salar de Uyuni, Bolivia.

White with salt, Adam and I emerge burned but unscathed after our Uyuni salt flats experience.

Arriving in Concepción, Chile.

Fighting off the cold with a fire in the forests of the Carretera Austral, Patagonia.

After days of black ice and snow, Joselyn and I cross into Chile for the last time.

Alonso poses as me two days from our goal on Tierra del Fuego.

Tired, relieved and emotionally empty, I arrive at the sign that marks the end, with not one but two companions.

I let the camera fall on the strap around my neck and ran down the steps. I still remember that hug. It's a rare feeling hugging one's own family with simple pleasure, uncluttered by a meeting later in the day, getting to the shops before they close, or family politics.

We journeyed back to deep within Colombia together, catching up on the last year and two months of each other's lives while a string of buses dived down and coughed slowly up the arid canyon lands near the border and then the lush green hills that we knew we'd face again on the bicycle. After more than ten minutes travelling up one hill I registered my father looking out of the window with a perplexed grin.

'I'm not sure what I've signed up for here,' he said, only partly in jest. I was worried too, since these would be the longest climbs I'd tackled so far.

Approximately 24 hours on various buses gave me a different and perhaps more normal insight into the world of the traveller. You're constantly entertained by a steady stream of food vendors hopping on and off, or sometimes a smartly dressed sales person presenting a well-rehearsed speech about the product they pass around for inspection, a small box of tablets that is – as unbelievable as it sounds – able to cure anything from mild asthma to anal fissures.

These colourful characters, changing at each stop, operate on a reliable backdrop of Steven Seagal, or perhaps Arnie, fighting highly skilled Chinese gentlemen on the wobbling television at the front of the bus. Outside, people with no voice look up at you and rivers go tumbling silently under bridges below your feet. In fact, there is a whole hilly landscape of life, people, villages, sounds and sights that the bus traveller only experiences in fast forward, with the monotonous drone of the bus clanking through its gears as the soundtrack.

The attractiveness of bicycle travel struck me then more than ever before. No windows blocking out life's real accompaniment. No travel-induced sleep causing you to miss the small stand selling bright, shiny mandarins or mouth-watering fruit juice. From the seat of a bicycle, everybody and everything has a voice, a smell, an influence on your immediate future.

Once we arrived back 'home' in Popayán, it was a hard place to leave. Sonia was there to greet us and hand over the stoker's baton to my father while he bedded into Colombian culture. With the help of the Chaves family and countless locals, some sitting tipsy outside the local liquor store, he had a crash course in Colombian, sampling the local moonshine, soup and hot chocolate, and sitting with Marco and his friends helping to assemble the small model airplanes he'd brought over from the UK as gifts. Then we left, Sonia, Marco and family standing in front of their house and waving. Marco had given me a small Indian head on a string which he insisted I hang round my neck for luck.

'Take care of the Indian!' he shouted after us as we disappeared past the school, off the dusty street and onto the main road heading uphill out of town.

Within minutes sweat began to darken the smart khaki shirt my father had bought specially for the ride, and only his pasty white legs were left suggesting he was new to this game. Unlike my journey out of Armenia with Sonia, the hills gave us no grace, ramping up steadily the moment we left town. First there were 3-mile hills, then 6-, then 15-, as the surroundings became drier and we looked down on small oasis-like farms in ever-deepening arid valleys. Gradually though, my father's worries about the dangers of Colombia evaporated as mine had done, as countrymen both old and young embraced our journey and helped propel us onward with smiles and fruit, stuffing it without asking into the lids of our pannier bags. The opening stages of our journey were only marred by one blatant show of aggression, directed at my father.

Dogs are not uncommon here, and would bark warily at my strange three-wheeled contraption as they had done since the barren northern plains of Alaska, sometimes chasing the trailer's flags a short way past their property. On our second morning together I was preparing the bike for departure outside a quiet little hostel in El Bordo, with the morning sun warming the cool air and sending thick misty rays across the courtyard and down into the valleys to the east. My father was packing his meager collection of belongings in the store room when suddenly I heard a commotion. From a darkened corner of the room he was in, a dog I'd heard there protecting week-old pups had launched herself at my father's delicate legs. It sounded big and I remembered suddenly how easily canine teeth had sunk into my hand back in Medellin. I'd already begun to run across the yard to help fight the animal off when I heard a chuckle, my father's voice – he was apparently finding the mauling funny. Arriving at the doorway I peered into the shadows and saw my father staring down at something that had attached itself to the bottom of his trouser leg. It was a Doberman – well, half a Doberman. The owner sidled up casually moments later, explaining that while the dog had inherited the aggressiveness of a Doberman, it had the body of a Chihuahua, rendering the attack spirited but ultimately futile. While under slightly different circumstances my father's cycling could have been hampered by deep tissue damage, the dog's savaging had left only saliva stains on his technical hiking attire.

As we got closer to the border, the towering hills lifted us up onto a rolling plateau of vivid and irrigated greens, sewn together by old fences and agave hedges that could from a distance be confused with the south of England. By the time we got there, however, the hills had taken their toll on my father. We'd had our downhill treats, overtaking everything on the road and reaching 50 miles an hour with Achilles' weight for once proving stabilising and beneficial, but on the unending inclines my father's stubborn perseverance had stripped his body of energy as he doggedly pedalled upwards, head down, not daring to look up. The evening of our toughest day he sat in our tiny hostel eating fried fish and rice, looking ten years older than when I'd met him at the airport.

The following morning we sat in the same place, eating the left-overs he hadn't been able to finish for supper. While we ate, a nearly toothless elderly man shuffled with a dignified gait up the road in an oversized, crumpled beige suit and a small black trilby perched on the top of his head. He said hello to everyone in the cold morning air of the hillside village and he shot out a warm grin as he checked up on the health of the village's inhabitants, all at least 20 years his junior.

My father felt mildly sick, he said. I could see looking up the road that the hills by no means abated, and the 12 or so miles to the border would, I decided, be too much for him. His mind could do it, but his body had suffered enough punishment for what was supposed to be a holiday. I hailed a taxi that idled nearby and as my father climbed in the back, I gave the driver instructions to deposit him at the border.

Weeks later, in the comfort of a plush Ecuadorian town, I received an email. My father had taken the trouble to describe his experience with me, and for the first time I read a detailed account of the more technical aspects of a stoker's world on my journey:

> There are bound to be ergonomic reasons why one should keep one's head down; after all, raising up one's noddle just to have a look around must use a lot of calories and, anyway, one risks a stream of invective from him up front for having upset the delicate balance that keeps us on the road, so best to keep eyes down and one's mind in the tiny little world that soon closes in around one.

I realised as I read that he had a point. Memories of snapping at dozens of benign and well-meaning stokers flooded back. My father perhaps more than most broke down the technicalities of being a stoker, measuring his upright posture by monitoring where the drops of sweat falling from his nose fell. He took in everything while his head was bowed. The fading logos on the water bottles, the stroboscopic effect of the whirring chain. Everything.

> I've discovered that stoker sanity can be kept on an even keel by looking up not more than every 270 yards, that way the interminable bend/hill combinations crawl past in a reasonably progressive way . . . oops time to shift the bum. Now this is one operation demanding supreme skill and timing if him up front is not to be upset. There we are, the cheeks gently eased back on the saddle . . . now who could have noticed that? But oh no, here's the inevitable wry comment 'What's going on back there?' Oh well, soon be time to shift the hand grip again . . .

The more I read, the more guilty I felt, and I made a mental note to try to be more forgiving in future.

* * *

FROM POCKET-SIZE TO PARENT

After I'd cycled to over 13,000 feet and descended and ascended the sides of countless gruelling valleys, my father and I crossed the Ecuadorian border together. The taxi had propelled him over the worst of the hills to the border's immigration building. When I saw him sitting on a bench waiting for me, despite the aging effects the cycling had had on him, I was increasingly grateful that we had shared those days in the saddle. The father–son relationship had changed after nearly 28 years. I was able to look after him here. I was his translator and guide, principal propulsion unit and occasionally slave-driver.

'I want to stop NOW!' he shouted at me once when I refused to stop for a much-needed bottom break a stone's throw from that day's goal. It reminded me of those walks when I was little, when I was the one having a tantrum. But the intimacy of those few days is something I'll always be grateful for. To have had such an uncomplicated friendship with your father is, I realise, something that the majority may well never experience.

After passing smoothly through immigration we settled ourselves at a small café a few yards into Ecuador for lunch before the final six miles to Ecuador's border town, Tulcán. My father had decided to cycle those first miles in Ecuador rather than take another taxi.

At the café, where dogs loitered for scraps and one sleepy drunk rested on the pavement, we met Victor Hugo, not in fact the man famous for glorifying the French Revolution, but a small, dark man with a neat and greased side parting and a shoulder-buttoned woollen sweater to keep him warm in the thin air, cold despite the equatorial sun. The meeting would have been inconsequential if, after 330 yards of struggling again up Ecuador's first little challenge, we hadn't stopped to see him running after us, his old leather shoes 'pat-patting' on the road. Had we forgotten something? Nope. The man simply wanted some exercise. He caught up easily and jogged alongside us, only pausing to mop his perspiring brow, comb his hair carefully or run into an isolated little church and then quickly out again as if he'd caught Jesus in the middle of changing his loincloth.

I had no idea what this Colombian man was doing – he said he was a footballer, but, with respect, I doubted it. Either way, I admired his tenacity and was pleased to have his grinning face alongside us as we crawled up and away from the border. Soon we reached the plateau and Achilles began to inch away from Victor until the glint of his shiny hair dulled and then disappeared as we cycled past lines of gas vendors selling gas out of glass Coke bottles and waving siphon hoses as if Achilles might indeed benefit from a refill.

Tulcán was the end of the road for my father, after pedalling me through some of the most demanding landscapes I'd encountered. The sadness of waving him goodbye was dwarfed by the renewed sense of family I had embraced and the warmth that came with it. He'd also left a couple of new pairs of cycling shorts, which was almost as gratifying.

I cycled the remaining distance to Quito alone. As I made progress, religious festivals coloured the night in small villages, fireworks bouncing off the walls of the San Gabriel Church as the entire village celebrated some virgin or other and the crowd applauded as sparks rained down on them. One year, two and a half months after departure, I reached the equator, where a huge stone sundial marked the progress of the sun's arc through the sky, and the distant mountains that guarded this invisible border into the southern hemisphere only occasionally poked through the clouds. A favourable tailwind propelled me easily back onto the warm tire tracks of the tourist trail, and back in Quito I landed in a life of comfortable coffee lounges and rum-and-Coke nights that entertained a backpack-toting population of travellers. The tourist trail, irrespective of the country, has a generic feel, and as they had done in Mexico and Guatemala, little children wandered the streets, weaving in and out of congested city traffic selling chewing gum. My eyes followed one boy skilfully preying on a couple of blonde girls. He rejoiced when a sale was made, his little hand shooting into the air with a small silvery coin held between two soft and grubby fingers.

14

The whisper of Sansa

DAY 450: 11,674 MILES

Not long after leaving the comfortable pizzeria-filled confines of
the tourist quarter, I left the metropolis of Quito behind and skirted
Cotopaxi, a vast volcano to the east that remained shrouded in
cloud while I passed underneath. Heading towards Baños, Ecuador's
equivalent to Bath, a city nestled in a lush valley surrounded by
hot springs, I stopped for the night in Latacunga. A compact and
pretty city, it had all the things I had come to expect – markets,
bus terminals, bustling commercial streets (never short of bootleg
DVDs) and at least one tranquil leafy square that in the evening or
all day on Sunday would likely be full of families sitting on the low
walls chatting, or walking slowly around with children brandishing
balloons or ice cream bought from the street vendors. But Latacunga
also had something I had not yet come across. Having resigned myself
to shelling out about four dollars for a cheap hostel, I searched the
streets and asked a few people for advice as I usually did in towns
and cities. A man with a bicycle scoffed mildly when I mentioned my
budget before leading me to a building with a large, official-looking
wooden arch leading into a courtyard. CASA CAMPESINA it read, in
large, well-maintained letters over the door. The man cycled off and
I bumped Achilles awkwardly up the curb, then the step and into
the courtyard. A friendly meeting with the short man who ran the
establishment told me that this was a hostel for farmers in town on

167

business and would cost the princely sum of 75 cents, or $1.50 if I couldn't rustle up any photo ID. I'd hit the jackpot! When I returned at 8:45 p.m., having eaten, I found a group of perhaps 30 men and women crowded round Achilles where I'd left him propped on a large clay urn in the center of the courtyard.

I hung back for a second to watch the spectacle. There were tiny old men wearing baggy suits that might have fitted them 20 years ago, their frames now bowed with age and the muscles worked away, leaving indestructible leathery sinews to keep them moving like the strings of a marionette. There were taller young men, some scruffier and with cheeky grins, pushing and nudging like schoolkids trying to encourage mischief. The women wore trilby-type hats, their beautiful black hair usually braided in one or two plaits down to the waist and sometimes tied together at the bottom. I was the only stranger there, and this hadn't escaped the group's attention. One particularly small old man turned round and nudged his neighbour, saying, '*Mira, el gringo!*'

I introduced myself and muscled into the happy throng to stand next to Achilles. I felt a little like one of those people demonstrating interesting but useless items of kitchen apparatus outside a cheap supermarket. You know, like the egg choppers that cut five slices at once, or kitchen knives with massive handles and tiny blades so people can't cut themselves, or anything else.

Where was I from? What was the flag? Why two seats? I got all the normal questions in a quick-fire round and then some more unusual ones, technical questions about the gearing or what spares I was carrying, oh, and why my wife wasn't travelling on the back.

'Because I haven't found one yet,' I blurted out to keep them happy before our boisterous meeting was cut short by Franklin, the boss, standing on the steps to elevate himself from the crowd. At the sound of his voice the men and women, like brainwashed convent girls, shuffled into two quiet lines. Just then a stocky, rosy-cheeked drunk tripped over the step at the entrance and rolled into view, getting to his feet and grinning apologetically before joining the end of the queue. Franklin gave him a stern look; it was five minutes after the curfew and he was tipsy, but he let him in anyway.

Most of the men and women knew the drill, and those in front and behind me in the line looked at me reassuringly when Franklin began to read out the numbers we had been given. Responding to these numbers, the women made their way one by one upstairs and after a few minutes all was quiet again. Then the men started moving forward. I heard my number and followed suit. I followed the shufflers – some of the older ones with gammy legs having to be helped upstairs – to the large washroom, where I was told I had to wash my feet in what looked like one of a long line of urinals. A faded and peeling paper notice on the wall clearly stated that they weren't. Only pausing to dry my feet on an old pair of jeans near the bathroom entrance, I shuffled onward, half expecting to be shaved, de-loused and given a pair of stripy pajamas. Instead however, I ended up in a large dormitory full of bunks. Immediately a small chorus rang out.

'Come and sleep here!' random men smilingly chimed.

'Why must I sleep next to you?' I teased one of them.

'To talk,' he said, looking hopeful, and that straightforward answer won him the dubious pleasure of a bed next to the stranger in town who, after a day's cycling, hadn't showered – the procedure for that seemed festooned in complications.

For the next two hours a gradually dwindling set of voices in the dark quizzed me about how to say obscure phrases in English. Whenever I translated and calmly said for example, 'I've got a lovely bunch of coconuts,' I would hear giggles and bed slats creaking as old men convulsed in silent amusement. But, one by one, the questioning voices and chuckles disappeared and a less than peaceful night chorus of throaty snoring began. From the sodium glow of street lamps outside there was enough light to look across the top bunks from where I lay and see the silhouette of a hat on each chest as it rose and fell in the rhythm of sleep. The bronchial cacophony only faltered occasionally over the next six hours, when an offender's next-door neighbour took action. I would hear loud but unaggressive swearing or a slap to the face, followed by a satisfied chuckle as the snorer stopped snoring for a second and sleepily swore in retort before his head returned to the pillow and the cycle started all over again. There was a definite odour in the room too. It wasn't stale sweat but more a well-used woollen smell, or one of old felt or soil ingrained in clothes that were washed only as often as time allowed. Localised around my bed, however, was the more unpleasant acid stench of old perspiration that has invaded synthetic sports gear.

By the time morning came, at exactly 5:45 a.m. when the fluorescent tubes blinked on, I felt that, while I had barely slept an hour, I had been close to being accepted among this bunch of men, who were rising, indifferent to the fact that dawn was barely creeping in through the window, putting their hats on, stretching and shuffling out. Most would head out onto the street selling fruit, nuts or trinkets for the day, making enough money to stay another night and hopefully take some back to their family in the country. I was, in comparison, impossibly rich, having no need to work and instead bumping Achilles sleepily back down the step onto the street to head south into the jungle. I shall never forget the night in that dormitory, the simple, unquestioning and straightforward way in which they treated me despite our differences. Any brave promises of joining me on the bike that I'd heard in the darkness the night before had, by the time we had all wiped sleep from our eyes, vanished. These people had to work, there was no time to have a play on a strange bicycle, other than perhaps a brief and wobbly circuit of the small courtyard before hefting a huge bundle of alfalfa or other produce and setting off for the day, the concept of international bicycle travel inconceivable. Playtime, I was increasingly beginning to realise, was not an option for these people. Hence, I rarely picked up a companion when I rolled through communities in the countryside. Fields needed plowing, corn dehusking, cows milking, children and the elderly caring for, none of which can be done easily from the uncomfortable back seat of a stranger's bicycle built for two.

Alone, I swept down roads flanked by mineral-rich volcanic soil growing leafy crops, the rumble of the boiling river growing ever closer. My wheels rolled from tarmac onto soft black dirt, where only days before a volcanic eruption had triggered a mudslide that had carried the road down the hillside while people slept.

* * *

Baños was a local tourist hot spot, the hot springs and volcano attracting domestic tourists from the city as well as travellers like me. The only colonial main street was lined with sandwich boards advertising climbing trips, rafting adventures or competitively priced pizza, all in English, or something resembling it. Unlike in Latacunga, I was unlikely to be able to afford a hostel here, and so fell back to my well-practised 'plan B', hanging out in the small square, where Achilles would receive curious glances, and tourists and locals alike would come and talk to me, perhaps bringing with them an offer of accommodation of some kind. It worked, and on this occasion the good Samaritan came in the form of Rodrigo, a local hotelier and textile shop owner who applauded my efforts before cycling with me up the hill out of the small town center. We arrived, not at his hotel, but at a house that lay empty and bare at the foot of the volcano, which was billowing fumes that mingled with the clouds brushing the tops of the deep, tangled forests above us.

Rodrigo, a thickset bald man with a friendly round face, trustingly gave me the keys and after I'd swept a thin layer of volcanic dust off the bare floorboards and shifted some broken old furniture, I laid out my mat and sleeping bag, occupying a house that had lain vacant for more than a year, since the threat of volcanic eruption left this part of the small city, being directly in the line of a mud or lava flow, largely empty.

I spent three days walking in the valley, from the thundering waterfalls deep in chasms where a permanent mist of water vapour encouraged vines and mosses to grow, to the muddy slopes of Tungurahua, whose crater puffed above me in the cloud. The dense knotwork of foliage on the volcano's steep slopes caused me to claw through the muddy ash, squeezing through gaps in giant root systems that had grown up since the last catastrophic eruption.

Rodrigo, obviously inspired by my unique journey, decided to abandon his family and join me as I journeyed through the jungles that nudged up against the foothills of the Andes. Christophe, a French cyclist who had until then been travelling in the opposite direction, chose to accompany us too, deciding companionship outweighed any vague plans to head north. He had meandered his way here from his homeland, and talked of adventures in the Sahara, camping with the nomads and searing heat that seemed almost inviting early the next morning, when blue skies allowed the warmth to escape upwards, leaving the air sharp and still. For the first time I saw, as the three of us cycled downhill through the streets, Tungurahua's summit, a solid-seeming plume of steam rising lazily in the cold air from behind the crater's rim.

With Rodrigo sitting behind me, his head bowed in an air of focused exertion, we skirted cliffs dripping curtains of water, vapour bending the light into rainbows around us as we followed the river easily down to the warmer jungle basin. We stopped in the humid, dirty air of Puyo, an ugly little town on the edge of the jungle 50 miles from Baños, where we sat on the large tilted kerbstones with local children, gulping down large mouthfuls of sugar-cane juice out of plastic mugs from a nearby mangle, whose operator sat next to a stack of scorched sugar cane ready to be crushed between the rollers. Rodrigo was tired – it was the first time he'd done any exercise for some time and we slowly pedalled into town with no aspirations to travel further that day. We shared cheese sandwiches with kids and a couple of flirtatious teenage girls in the park, before retiring to a small bar, where we sat for too long, steadily drinking late into the evening, watching the street transform, small food stalls being wheeled out, lit by dim bulbs wired to a car battery and ready to cater for the evening crowd. Drunk now and with the blind hunger that comes with it, we stumbled, pushing the bikes to the long line of stalls, and sat heavily on a rickety bench next to a few others slurping at their soup or chewing on chicken bones. As we greedily wolfed down food, a rat scuttled across the two by four behind the vendor, glancing down at the pots of food, then moving on before it was swiped at with a cleaver glinting under the weak light.

At 2 a.m., weaving dangerously to the town's outskirts, we found a basketball court on which to sleep and removed our sleeping bags, too tired to bother closing up panniers or organising our new quarters. Rodrigo was just sober enough to decide that one of the crude benches in the spectator stand was preferable to the dusty court where Christophe and I already lay comatose, half in our sleeping bags and half sprawled on the more refreshing concrete.

We were woken by laughing children taking the short cut across the court to school. I opened my eyes just wide enough to let the stabbing light flood in and register the boys dawdling past, wondering what these gringos were doing on their turf. I closed my eyes again, too late though to prevent pain from flowing into my cranium – the pain of a full-blown dehydrated hangover, my mouth dry and leathery, all moisture having dribbled out into the dust, causing it to stick to the side of my face. The hangover and arse-ache that accompanied any initiation day on Achilles spelled the end for Rodrigo, who was craving the comfort of his own bed sooner than he'd expected. Christophe and I carried on alone, still desiccated despite gallons of cane juice, but worsening roads over the next few hours painfully jarred our respective hangovers into submission.

I enjoyed cycling with Christophe through the thickening jungle, listening to his stories and telling him mine. He was relaxed and more carefree than me, not worrying too much about where he travelled, just taking in the surroundings as they washed over him. He had no definite goal, and would go home when he felt like it.

Passersby became less frequent, but we'd occasionally bump comparatively noisily through a community of small wooden huts and see a family maybe walking home from a small plantation, each with a machete in hand, the smaller children having to clasp theirs with two hands so as not to drag them in the dirt. The jungle had an overwhelming noise, but soon the constant tinnitus-like screech of cicadas and crickets, like that of the mosquitoes in Alaska, disappeared, our brains scrubbing it out and only aware of it occasionally, when we stirred briefly in the middle of the night under a starry, leafy sky. Then it was deafening again. The screech of an owl, rodents exploring nearby, a frog chorus or my French companion briefly rolling over noisily in his sleep.

After two days of jungle travel, Christophe and I stopped outside a tiny bamboo hut that a sign informed us was a bar. We wandered in, our bodies still vibrating slightly from our slow progress down the rocky track. Inside the bar it was dark, but small, elongated dusty shafts of sun that filtered in through cracks in the bamboo walls allowed us to make out a large, intimidating insect nailed to a wooden joist and the standard scantily clad Pilsner girl that decorates every establishment selling Ecuador's most popular beer. There was nothing else, and the small, hollow building had an ominous feel as our feet tapped back out across the loose planks, the whirring of myriad unseen insects suddenly oppressive.

As our eyes struggled to adjust to the equatorial sun, we saw a woman squatting on the track. She had walked 2½ miles from the nearby village to visit the lady that ran – or apparently didn't run – this little drinking den. As we remounted our beasts of burden, she called after us in the thick slur of indigenous Spanish, 'Be careful around here.'

My wheels scrunched the small stones underneath them as I stopped to enquire lazily why care needed to be taken in this relatively remote region.

She looked at us, with an air of mild concern for the foolish outsiders. 'Sansa' was the word she let slip from her mouth, the 'S' being enunciated and dragged out in the jungle by the cicadas. She told us that people sometimes go missing in the jungle here, sometimes tourists – two Swedish girls had disappeared a couple of years back. This woman believed, as did a handful of other locals we questioned about it, that these disappearances were due to the supposedly long since discontinued practice of Sansa amongst some remote, purely indigenous communities.

'Sansa?' we questioned, not familiar with the word. Rather than explain this to us, she let go of the plastic bag sitting on her knee and raised her hands to her face. She traced a line across her neck with the forefinger of one hand while tugging at her hair with the other, then made as if to crush her head between her palms.

'Head shrinking??' Christophe said, looking at me and grinning with amusement.

The woman nodded, figuring we'd got the idea, and let her hands return to the bag on her lap.

'Be careful,' she said again, as we thanked her and cycled slowly away, any trace of a grin fading fast from our faces.

What had been a placid, stony road flanked by vegetation now looked and felt threatening. I let Christophe cycle off ahead. His head, I thought, was marginally bigger than mine, and he had blond hair, surely prized in these parts by head hunters, given its rarity. The jungle had somehow now grown eyes and ears, and while I sweated constantly every day, the sweat now pricked at my skin while I juddered along, scanning the thick wall of trees on either side.

Hours later Christophe made a discovery, only revealing this to me while we were cooking our pasta that night by the Rio Pastaza, fireflies scoring the darkness and for once the sound of a large river drowning out the insects. He extracted from his bag the cleanly severed head of a child's doll, with blonde hair and no eyes that he'd found on the track. Suzy, as she came to be known, became my first bodyless companion, riding on my second seat, and arming us with some bargaining power should we come across any head-hungry natives. Perhaps it was Suzy 'the head' – our one link with those that practised Sansa – that kept us safe from the invisible tribes for the next three days, for we saw not one single shrunken head necklace or string of ears or anything else out of the equatorial norm, arriving at the steep hills that marked the end of the jungle unscathed.

We stopped at this division between landscapes when invited to sleep in the covered yard of a family home. On stopping, we had apparently also signed up to play a game of volleyball with the rest of the male population of El Partidero, the tiny village that looked out over the jungle. Low, dark clouds were heavy in the air, but only higher up the dusky mountain did rain fall, coming down in silent misty sheets a few miles away.

Our hosts paraded us proudly around the village's floodlit court, Christophe and I towering easily over the people there. We were obviously, that evening, the secret weapons, the champion attackers to destroy the diminutive opposition on this lofty battleground.

Any hopes, however, of us guiding our five-man team easily to victory against a team of twelve-year-olds were dashed by our clumsy style, as we lamely tried to smash the ball over the net, more often sending it bouncing down the hillside. Each time we did this a small boy scuttled off in hot pursuit to retrieve it, until, fortuitously for us, it fell irretrievably into a chasm.

For three more days we journeyed purely uphill, the road snaking up the sides of huge green valleys, and the rain mixing with our sweat, causing rivulets of salty water to saturate everything by mid afternoon. Achilles continued to buck irritably under me as I did my best to guide a now stripped-down and comparatively featherweight 185 pounds of bicycle up some of the toughest roads I'd encountered. Christophe within a mile could pull slowly out of sight on the uphills, with a lighter bike and only two wheels, not three, to judder on each slippery pebble.

We arrived in a small village near Las Palmas, Achilles having picked up two small girls hanging on with broad excited grins and unable to reach the pedals. Their brother skipped enthusiastically alongside as we got closer to the house of their unwell grandmother, whom they were going to visit.

The children's mother, also walking alongside with two empty jerry cans as I struggled to balance and move impossibly slowly up the last short steep hill, suggested that Christophe and I stop for a break at the house – she was a teacher in the local village and was curious to know more about us and where we came from. So two hours later, still unwilling to pass up opportunities to meet new people, we sat, incongruous in our brightly coloured jackets, on a double bed that filled the tiny room upstairs in the grandparents' house. The grandparents were in the bed, tucked up together under the thick woollen blanket, and the rest of the extended family sat, squatted or stood wherever there was room, a few limited to poking their heads through the door of the mud-walled bedroom. The entire family without exception had beautiful, warm dark faces, and for at least an hour we had a 'Q&A' session, the granddad taking every opportunity to make fun of our stature or Chris's thinning blond hair.

The following morning, having stayed in the half-built house of Uncle Luis, we found ourselves trudging up a steep, muddy track through scrubby alpine pastures into the low cloud and mist back towards his family home, a structure of mud and cane, dark inside with a rickety ladder up to the attic, where we arrived to find the grandfather, Luis Senior, sitting on a pile of maize, ripping the kernels off a cob. Once out of bed this man had transformed, frailty gone and with all the strength of a hill farmer half his age. The kitchen was dark, and when the fire was lit, tendrils of smoke wound up through occasional rays of sunlight, into the eaves and out of a hole in the wall, mixing with the moisture of the air as they went, to leave shiny black creosote deposits on cobwebs and clotheslines, mementoes of 1,000 cooking fires over a handful of generations. Under the raised clay stove *cuys* – guinea pigs – squeaked away, busy copulating and rooting around in the potato peelings and alfalfa provided for them by Alicia, Luis's sister. At last, I thought, at the mention of guinea pigs, the opportunity to eat some properly weird food. As happened without fail on 'rest' days, my body defaulted to 'caterpillar' mode, feeling sluggish and only able to carry out one activity with any degree of proficiency. Eating.

Due to my enthusiasm, I was in charge, under Luis's expert guidance, of dispatching two guinea pigs, killed only for special occasions. That day, Christophe and I *were* the occasion, being the first tourists they had properly rubbed shoulders with since two Brazilian air force pilots had crashed twenty miles away in the hills and been rescued on horseback by Luis and his father. That explained why their house had the furniture of a military aircraft – plundered from the twin-engined wreck and brought to the house, seat belts an' all.

I killed the rodents as instructed, though not deftly, with a relaxed blow to the back of the neck which should have killed them instantly. I winced as I had to do it a second time before dipping them in boiling water to loosen the fur and plucking it out from its skin. An hour later we consumed every last bit, intestines painstakingly cleaned with a knitting needle by the younger Luis's wife in the small stream outside. It was rich, like rabbit, and along with the corn and potatoes the grandfather had prepared earlier it provided a meal fit for statesmen, let alone two grubby cyclists incapable of plowing the small sloping field with a wooden plow and a cow under the despairing eyes of the locals.

That afternoon we rode bareback, our feet dragging on the ground as Luis's diminutive horses struggled to carry us uphill to go fishing. Alicia and her son were our guides and tutors for this exercise and I was quick to point out to them after tentatively poking at my sore inner thighs, that they'd forgotten the fishing rod, and nor could I see any nice trout-filled streams. The 11-year-old chuckled like an old hand and guided us over to a small runnel of water hidden in the wet tussocky grass. He produced a plastic sack from under his holey jacket and proceeded to thread a stick round the mouth of it to keep it open. Holding it in the water, spanning the tiny stream, he instructed us to splash around upstream, slowly walking towards the bag. This brilliantly simple maneuver secured us three small, silvery trout, in a watercourse so small I'd have been surprised if it had stocked tadpoles, let alone fish.

After dark, back down in the valley, I noticed Luis eyeing the lock knife that lived on my belt – the one indispensable tool I owned, used constantly during cooking and bike maintenance. But nothing is really indispensable here, I was beginning to realise. If these people could do so much with so little, I could probably do without it. After a moment's thought I handed it over to Luis, whose eyes lit up in gratitude, weighing it in his palm for a moment before clipping it proudly on his belt.

I saw Luis completely by coincidence two weeks later while I took a prolonged break in Cuenca, a beautiful Ecuadorian city sitting midway between the jungle plains and the high mountains of the Andes. He had had to make a rare journey to town to fulfil some slightly spurious bureaucratic requirement of the kind that South American governments seem so good at inventing. I asked Luis how he was finding his new knife.

'What?' he questioned, apparently surprised that I should ask such a question. 'I don't use it,' he continued. I was confused until he explained that it was safely tucked into his box of prized possessions. There were two items in this box, he said proudly: his new knife, and a military torch given to him by the stricken Brazilian pilots.

At first, Cuenca feels like a town that is in many ways encapsulated in a bubble, protected somewhat from the rest of Ecuador by a film of affluent culture. The walls are old and white, and every alcove and small doorway is filled with a mixture of expensive little cafés, the odd shop selling Panama hats, and telephone kiosks. The grand cathedral, never finished, stands as broad as it is high in sandy-coloured brick, its domes hiding behind the stocky towers looming over the central park. Vendors of religious trinkets and a faithful collection of shoe cleaners collect beneath its arches every day, while indigenous families mix with the upper crust or gaggles of flirtatious teenagers wandering at leisure along the wide shady paths cutting diagonals across the square.

You don't have to stray far, however, to find another side of this city. Sitting on the steps leading down to the river was Johanna, a weathered 84-year-old lady, munching on a piece of bread or maybe a chocolate given to her by a passing stranger. And, when I walked across the river, past the military hospital and down the Avenida de las Americas, I came across a small family sitting on the grass that separates the pavement from the wide concrete street, surrounded by rubbish. Slowly they sorted piles of waste paper and boxes, poring over the ripped and dirty pages of an electronics catalogue, perusing the vacuum cleaner selection or admiring the shiny image of a stereo with 'megabass'. They lived vicariously through the garbage, probably not ever having half the money needed to purchase the plastic stereo or even the batteries to power it.

After six weeks relaxing in Cuenca I was ready to leave. Besides, any excuse I had to stay just a little longer had disappeared. Another camera had arrived to replace the one that had been stolen while I was guarding it a little too casually in an Internet café, and I had repaired Achilles, replacing the front fork, which had developed a crack. Achilles had been well made and I was surprised to find a weakness, until I figured out what must have caused it.

Back in Mexico one day, riding in a heat-induced stupor through monotonous banana plantations, the bike had abruptly disappeared from under me, and the folk music I'd been listening to grew faint as my headphones were ripped from my ears. I was flying for an instant, hitting the corner of a high-backed banana truck on take-off and then, fairly gracefully for a wingless animal, travelling a few yards before belly-flopping in a ditch full of dry grass.

A second passed before the pain hit my brain and I writhed like a trapped rodent. The truck's door opened and I registered the blurry outline of a fat, drowsy-looking Mexican wiping sleep from his eyes and walking over to me.

'Why did you do that?' he asked, rightly confused.

'Aaaummpghhh didn't seeeeaarrgh,' I responded, clutching my shoulder, still writhing in the maddeningly itchy vegetation. As I pieced the last minute together I realised I'd completely zoned out – that truck could have been parked there for weeks and I wouldn't have known. I'd been looking down. The driver roughly tried to help me to my feet but I resisted, needing a minute to ascertain if I had broken anything.

I looked up to see the man get back into his truck before burying my head in the prickly grass again. He drove off, covering me in fumes and leaving the miraculously barely damaged Achilles alone in the road. I never saw any signs of the crack at the time, but that impact I guessed must have caused the beginnings of a hairline fracture in the fork. After getting up and experimenting with movement, I found I'd broken nothing other than a chunk of dignity.

Christophe had returned home, knee problems having developed, but I had the promise of more company, though not on the back seat. On the morning of departure I wandered from a new friend's house down the cobbled streets to my next companions' cheap hotel. I had met them for the first time two days previously in the same hotel room, after initial email contact. I'd have had to be blind and perhaps lacking a sense of smell not to realise that Barney and Adam were a very 'special' breed of British gentleman. The room was strewn with seemingly random items: a snorkel, a Ray Mears book entitled *Bushcraft*, a pair of well-worn football boots and a 5-litre water bottle, two thirds full of urine. In the corner were two bikes ready for action. One of them, Barney's, was normal and fit for purpose. Almost every inch of the other bike, however, was covered in stickers that warranted closer inspection. On doing so I found images of a furry cat, Saturn, Jesus and a small shoal of sperm stuck along the top tube. The bike itself had seen better days, but the stickers must to some degree have made up for the structural shortfall.

Adam, the bike's owner, sported an Afro and a full black beard that reminded me of an old comical portrait, the kind that could be flipped upside down to see another gurning face. He told me while fuelling up on empanadas at our favourite café that he'd made a bike trailer out of an ironing board and some bicycle stabilisers he'd 'borrowed' from his Pakistani father's hardware store in the small village of Keyworth. He decided, though, to leave that behind on our journey together and make do with the two school backpacks strapped to a flimsy pannier rack and a pencil case to store valuables tied onto the handlebars. Barney had at least one fairly functional pannier, but even so, the two of them made me feel vastly over-equipped.

We left in convoy, rattling slowly down the cobbled Avenida Presidente Cordova onto tarmac and down to the river. It felt good to be moving again, but Achilles' 200 pounds felt heavy as my legs reacquainted themselves with cycling. The other two were in no hurry though and like a comedy duo, bags flapping and rubbing, they charitably pedalled alongside.

After our first day together, Barney's pathetic tires had been punctured twice but we'd covered 30 miles despite a late start, and cycled some distance up a steep track to camp in a meadow near an isolated house blasting out Bob Marley from tinny speakers. The air was damp and by dusk the eucalyptus trees were enshrouded in fog, droplets of water collecting on Adam and Barney's brilliantly inadequate tent. They'd reinforced the single-skinned shelter with a large white sheet of plastic that became ripped within minutes of erection; it looked more like a poorly rain-proofed pile of building materials than a tent.

There was an earthquake that night. The spindly trees shuddered and the night song of birds fell silent while the ground seemed to move in slow motion. The following day, after swimming in the frigid plunge pool of a waterfall on the mountainside we found out that the epicenter had been over 600 miles south, where a month or so before a larger quake had reduced Peruvian coastal towns to rubble.

We coasted slowly out of the mountains, camping the following night amongst tomato greenhouses in the dry earth, Adam lighting a fire with paint thinners and recoiling with a scream as the solvent vapour ignited, forming a brief carpet of flame around his feet.

We passed through the 'Bananero' near the coast, one of the world's largest banana-growing regions. It was hotter now, and humid with the wall of huge leafy banana palms blocking the view for miles on either side.

It was as if Adam had been sent to give my journey a new lease of life, contractually obliged to provide at least five daily doses of infantile hilarity. That day, on a deserted stretch of road, he'd decided to strip off and cycle stark bollock naked, waving his small camera around as he went. About 200 yards from his clothes, scattered in the gutter, a local bus rumbled quickly into view, leaving Adam no option but to pedal along sedately, smiling and waving as dozens of Ecuadorian faces pressed up against the bus window, wearing a look of confusion as they sped by. Barney hung his head theatrically as he was prone to do, groaning slightly at the absurdity of it all. He was thousands of miles from home, on an ill-equipped machine, accompanied by a man wearing only football boots on a bike adorned in sperm stickers. Adam was no ordinary bicycle tourist.

Together the three of us passed through the dusty, once prosperous, gold-mining town of Portovelo, exploring the mines, some dangerously unstable shafts still operational. Since the Americans had left in the 1950s, the area, once with the best economy and services in the country, was reduced to a ghostly carcass with a small population, the men of which risked their lives for 12 hours a day in 104° heat, scraping what was left out of the bottom of the cramped shafts. This usually amounted to sufficient gold to trade for food, but little else.

Camping next to a shallow river one evening a couple of local boys cycled up to our camp, interested in our equipment. After a chat, one of them became keen to join us the next day on his own bike, and sure enough the next morning there he was, and once we'd pushed our bikes, fully loaded, through the shallows and back onto the road, we pedalled off, the four of us, but still with one empty saddle behind me. André was 16 and wanted to travel when he had saved enough money. Few Ecuadorians travel – very few are financially able to and those who can rarely have the traveller's spirit, the Latin culture centering on family and the desire never to be far from them. Our new companion didn't last long; due to his pedal snapping off he was forced to coast back home after only an hour. He did, however, briefly try a stint on Achilles while I wobbled alongside on his machine, which felt like a toy after the weight of the fully laden tandem.

His face gave nothing away, but his pedalling got gradually slower. I asked him how it was. '*Facil, si, genial,*' he said, smiling and calm. For something that was apparently easy he was pedalling slowly I thought, and at that moment, André ground to a complete halt, failing to put a foot down and keeling over into the large storm drain. He wasn't the first to find that it took a little practice to master my juggernaut of a bike. But even then his Latin bravado remained intact.

'That's good, nice bike,' he said as he picked himself up while I held the handlebars and seat and leaned away from Achilles to get all three wheels back on the road.

With Barney and Adam, my journey became a healthy mix of crude schoolboy antics, companionship and cultural enlightenment, albeit mostly in some back-street pool hall or with local teenagers during a rest-stop game of soccer in the local park. Once, in a hunger-fuelled bad mood, I stopped with them at a tiny shack offering snacks and manned by three kids. Five minutes later, Adam had volunteered to provide a human target for a child playing with a catapult. My bad mood vaporised as I watched Adam hop around in hysterical pain, a large welt forming on his calf.

It was exactly what I needed to keep me on the road. Companionship like theirs made the good times incredible and the bad times bearable. I could at least rest assured that if I was wet, they were probably wetter, and if I had a puncture, they were probably about to get three, so I became less self-pitying and instead shared my superior equipment and supplies with the bicycle-toting clowns.

Close to the Peruvian border we parted company but with promises to meet three days further south. Adam and Barney had spied an obscure petrified forest on my map close to the border but further inland. And so, not wanting to endure more mountains than necessary

TAKE A SEAT

on Achilles, I sped down to the busy potholed disarray of the Tumbes border crossing. South, over the barrier and past the battered armoured police vehicle, the road stretched away in a straight line, disappearing into the beginnings of the vast, sand-filled, treeless landscape of the Sechura Desert.

15

The bicycle clowns

DAY 523: 12,136 MILES

The heat was unbearable, and the blackness of the new, sticky tarmac only added to it, gently cooking my underside as the sun grilled me from above, gusts of warm air scouring me with sand as I rode. The wind became stronger but more refreshing when the road butted up against drab straight beaches, where a palm-thatched shack selling basic refreshments could usually be found. The vendors moonlighted as fishermen, closing up shop and venturing out through the surf to trawl their lines out of small rowing boats, hanging their catch to dry off on the shack's timbers in the heat of the afternoon.

The popular surfing town of Mancora proved rich in potential stokers. The town forms an isolated tourist trap, an ugly settlement that fills a few miles of sand squeezed between the Pan-American Highway and the ocean. Despite the distinct lack of palm trees and turquoise shallows – the Atlantic waves churn up the coarse sand, making the water a greyish brown – the beach provided a relaxed Peruvian staging post where I could reconnect with the boys, finding them sitting at a plastic table in a small hut. Adam's face was buried in half a watermelon, sucking at the juicy flesh and only briefly raising his head to acknowledge me, black seeds stuck in his moist, scraggly beard. Barney was tucking more delicately into the local delicacy, ceviche, raw fish garnished with fried corn kernels and onions. On the table lay Adam's trusty snorkel.

TAKE A SEAT

That afternoon Barney and I sat on the beach while Adam trawled the shallow waters for interesting marine life, returning triumphant as a pearl diver with an unpleasantly fragrant puffer fish and a catfish – both had been dead for days, maybe weeks. The ensuing gathering of stray, hungry dogs on our patch came close to scaring away our neighbours and new friends, a small international bunch of beautiful tourists. As it was, Philippa the English rose and Erin the Californian boho-chic photographer were brave enough not only to suffer the gag reflex brought on by the catfish but to sign on that night, after one or two cheap tequilas, for a desert stint on Achilles.

At last the following morning and for the first time in over two months, I pedalled slowly south with a full complement of bums on Achilles, Philippa sitting tall and leggy behind me as Barney and Adam trailed after. Adam wore a $1 pair of 'Gucci' sunglasses, picked up from one of the many vendors who walked the length of Mancora beach with huge portfolios of spectacularly ineffective eye-wear.

The road was hot and monotonous, often disappearing completely in a heat haze, oncoming traffic appearing to float on a mirror until we got close enough to see the hot fumes belching from their exhausts. Some vehicles were of a greener variety, heavy carts rolling on the salvaged axle of a truck and pulled by an unfortunate donkey propelling a driver and huge stacks of firewood slowly but surely towards some distant shack. Firewood, like water in this place, was something of a commodity.

When we did come across a town, the four of us would stop and restock at small supermarkets, buying a 5½-gallon water bottle – the kind designed to fit office water coolers – and decanting the contents into smaller bottles that would then be loaded onto the bikes. Achilles provided most of the carrying capacity, gaining at least 30 pounds in weight at each water stop.

The eye-catching company of both Philippa and Erin – they swapped over in a small town two days down the coast, Erin having travelled by bus to join us – made the dead, parched landscape of the Sechura a little friendlier, not only for us but for each local vehicle that passed by, the drivers' eyes glued to the pale skin and pretty face glowing with a light sheen of sweat behind me. Dragging the girls out of throngs of adoring young men when we stopped in small communities was not an easy task, and neither Erin nor Philippa escaped without at least a handful of marriage proposals. But like so many of my companions, Philippa certainly didn't escape the painful price of a ride on Achilles. After only a day in the saddle, Philippa's groin became something of a sore point. Swapping my streamlined seat with Adam's 'shopping bike' saddle didn't seem to help, nor did the loan of a pair of my padded bike shorts. But Philippa soldiered on in the dry 'paint stripper' heat with, as she so eloquently put it, a 'very sore vagina.'

Two days after she ducked out and headed back north on a bus, Erin did likewise, waiting with us in the sparse shade of a thorny tree next to a local lady sitting on four sacks of maize until an old white taxi pulled up. The driver crammed the lady, Erin and the four sacks on top of the four existing passengers, and drove heavily north, the suspension struggling to keep the tires from scraping the rusty wheel arches.

There were no fences in the desert, so camping was possible along almost every inch of the road. Very few people lived outside the infrequent communities, but the further south we went, the more we could see huge, ugly warehouses, long and squat out in the desert, three or four in a row. With this sight came a stale, dry smell of death – they were battery farms supplying Peru's insatiable appetite for chicken and chips, a cost-effective meal we often took advantage of in the towns. But it was the wind that proved more unpleasant than these occasional sightings, ripping at my flags on the trailer and necessitating riding in an ungainly peloton, taking it in turns every couple of miles to break trail and suffer the full force of the headwinds. The desert experience turned into a war of attrition, attacking us slowly, dehydration and mild stomach disorders frequent occurrences due to a constantly opportunistic diet, taking whatever the villages en route provided in the way of sustenance. Comparing notes on recent and often worrying fecal deposits made up much of our evening conversation as we sat around my roaring stove. But it didn't usually stop at just idle chat, each conversation was often backed up with evidence from Adam's rapidly growing photographic library of turds – the presence of the girls had curbed this obsession but only for the four short days in their company, and even then Adam was unable to contain his excitement when returning from a particularly colourful toilet stop. Though I pretended not to, I quite enjoyed this scatological chat. It punctuated the long dark evenings with bursts of uncontrollable laughter while we cooked or removed the latest batch of thorns from our tires.

In desperation, doing our best to escape the maddening heat and headwinds of the highway, we opted to take a tiny road marked on the map that appeared to follow the coast. For one and a half days we rode on a beach threatened by rising tides, or pushed our bikes through deep sand between ghost towns guarded by dogs, nervously backing away and barking at us as we cycled past, often getting bogged down in drifts of sand collecting in the wind shadow between tumble-down buildings. On our way out of one eerie village, one resident silently staring at us from a doorway, Barney and I found ourselves billowing through a deep trough of white feathers that had, like the sand, drifted into a small hollow from one of the chicken warehouses in the sand dunes round here.

We camped on the isolated and windswept beach, pitching my tent between two small dunes that afforded only the slightest protection against the wind. Brewing a much-needed tea while huddled around the spluttering stove, Barney and I were greeted out of the darkness by two figures, one in a wet suit, walking up the beach. Juan and Redin, crab fishermen from a town nearly 20 miles north sat with us and gratefully accepted drinks and cookies before leading us back to their moto-taxi – the three-wheeled taxis that are so prevalent in these parts. Next to the vehicle was a basket about a third full of small crabs, which they explained they got about 50 cents for. Not a bad living, I thought, until I realised I'd misunderstood them, they meant 50 cents a kilo (or couple of pounds). They'd spent three hours so far, Juan standing chest-deep in the frigid black surf casting a circular net, and they'd maybe collected four pounds, six at a push. A couple of bucks for a soaking, hypothermic night on a beach didn't seem right, but I wasn't about to give them a hand.

The two men smiled and thanked us for the tea as we left them to spend a few more hours on the dark beach and wandered back to our flapping tent with Achilles propped solidly beside it. Adam was missing, and it was perhaps fortunate for him that he'd suffered mechanical failure early on in the beach journey, causing him to go back to town for spares. In the afternoon the following day, after bouncing Achilles over a beach of pebbles, up into the dune-encrusted tracks inland and then back out only to find huge crumbly cliffs and a high tide blocking our already crawling progress south, Barney and I collapsed on the rocky headland, devouring a small bag of mangoes we'd been saving for emergencies. Not wanting to believe the painful progress we'd been making was in vain, I found an old man wandering the sandy streets.

'How far is it along the beach to Puerto Chicama?' I asked him, knowing that in that town there was an asphalt road heading inland once more.

'Mmmm, about two hours,' he answered as we stared at the coast ahead, every fifth or sixth wave crashing up against the base of the steep rocks.

'Do we have time to get there before the tide blocks the way?' I asked, though I thought I knew the answer.

'If you leave now!' the old man said. But I'd heard that kind of blind optimism before from these people, who all too often say what they think you want to hear.

'Are you sure?' I asked, fixing the man with a more serious look.

'No,' he said with the air of someone who's had the truth beaten out of them.

It was settled then. We'd covered a pathetically short distance on the beach in an effort to escape the deadly monotony of the highway, but we'd failed.

I looked inland at the scrubby hills separating us by about 12 miles from the road, before taking a last look at the ocean, emptying the sand out of my shoes and trudging off, pushing the bike back the way we'd come.

It was as if, once we'd battled our way back to the black top, the Pan-American Highway was punishing us for our unfaithfulness. The headwind had doubled its efforts and, still without Adam, there were only two of us to divide the misery between. It was only by keeping our eyes locked on the asphalt and forcing our minds into a different place as we pedalled that we made progress, doing our best to ignore the desert as it inched by.

We made it, eventually, to the colonial town of Trujillo and the haven of 'Lucho's Casa de Ciclistas', a house open to bicycle travellers, fast or slow, local or otherwise, and from the cozy base of his workshop, draped in rims and frames and pedals, all fifth- or sixth-hand and ready to be used again, we explored the vibrant markets and incredible archaeology in and around the city. The Moche people, pre-dating the Incas, had made this place their home, building huge cities and temples out of the same type of mud bricks still used today. When the Incas came, these civilisations slowly fell into ruin, their successors taking the most skilled and able of craftsmen to work in new cities. And so, little by little, the desert breached the solid protecting walls, reclaiming the city in a sea of drifting sand. It's hard to fathom, looking out from the still ornate, excavated remains, how much more is out there, buried under the mind-numbingly monotonous miles of desert sand through which we had travelled.

Lucho, a powerful cyclist himself – perhaps the most famous and able Peru has ever conceived – helped propel me for a day, a day when the building dunes continued their west to east progress, inching their way across the highway in ever-moving sandy ripples. With his waxed and powerful quads stretching the drive chain behind me, we cruised along the gradual inclines, easily leaving Barney and Adam, who'd fixed his bike, miles behind within only an hour. Lucho happily commented on how good it was to have had the fortune to ride on Achilles – he'd heard about me from a tiny stream of cyclists making their way south ahead of us. News travels faster than one expects down this dead-straight highway.

Like an expensive firework, Lucho's assistance was explosive but brief, and after lunch at a small roadside stand he shook my hand powerfully, wishing me well for the road south, before boarding a small bus to head north back home, still clad in his garish Lycra. He had to get back to run his small audio equipment business, and keep his family living in the modest but comparatively privileged manner to which they had become accustomed.

THE BICYCLE CLOWNS

But he'd done what was necessary to propel Achilles to what was nearly the end of this stretch of desert. The three of us had decided to head inland up what was known as Duck Canyon to the small city of Huaraz, a mountaineering Mecca that nestled beneath the blindingly white corniced ridges of the Cordillera Blanca.

Weeks before, the idea of ascending over 10,000 vertical feet from the sea to the spine of the Andes had scared the shit out of me. I remembered the climbs of Colombia, most of which were only half that height and still endless, testing me nearly to breaking point. But now, after constant headwinds and not a single bend in the road to allow a fraction of respite, the climb and a change of scenery were a prospect that excited me. Besides, I thought, the companionship of Adam and Barney was bound to take the edge off the hills.

We spent our last night in the desert at a truckers' hostel, backing onto a mechanics' yard, home to scrapped trucks being scavenged for working parts. In a corner of the yard grew a small gnarled tree, and to the tree a moth-eaten monkey was chained.

I'd seen a lot of things along the way that we Westerners would regard as cruel, but somehow this hit me harder than usual. This monkey was doubtless from the Amazon basin on the other side of Peru, where trees are as ubiquitous as sand is here. In the dusty parking lot the monkey brainlessly moved from the ground to the first branch, then the second of his tiny tree, and returned to the floor, having wrapped his long chain once round the trunk. He'd pause to nibble an old mango, dust sticking to it where the skin had been peeled away, then he'd repeat the same path as before. Sitting on a concrete step in the cool evening watching the skinny animal breaking its routine only to shoot me a nervous glance, my thirst to leave the lifeless vacuum of the Sechura grew stronger.

Slowly at first, then dramatically as we swung left away from the regular rumble of goods vehicles and onto a dirt track, the scenery changed from harsh desert to low scrubby hills where plants grew in the shade of rocks. Then our small convoy crossed an old iron bridge over a canyon where murky and powerfully eddying water flowed around house-sized boulders. A river. I hadn't seen water as inviting as this since the waterfalls of Ecuador, the cold, salty grey of the Pacific seeming almost as forbidding as the desert since we'd pedalled south of Mancora.

After swimming and letting the dangerous currents twist us from one whirlpool to the next we pedalled, refreshed and clean, past lush rice paddies and tiny irrigated pastures, a vibrant leafy green beneath the towering dust-coloured peaks. It was nice to look up and be greeted by views of jagged ridges and a manageable chunk of sky rather than the endless sky of the desert and a limitless supply of air for the wind to use against us.

As we climbed above the deepening gorge and twisted between the foothills of the Andes, holes began to appear in the hillsides, some only yards from the road. We discovered when we emerged from one covered in soot that these were primitive abandoned coal mines, and as we bumped further up into the valley we saw tiny conveyors clanking dirt out of other tunnels above us. In a tiny village in the midst of it all everything was coated in a layer of sooty dirt, including a small family of ducks waddling uncertainly amongst the legs of three fruit stands crookedly standing side by side.

As we hungrily devoured the town's meager supply of biscuits, I watched a man staring at us, black from head to toe except for his blue miner's hard hat. I walked the few steps towards him and pointed a packet of biscuits in his direction. His blackened hands reached for one and he nodded weakly in thanks before his teeth flashed impossibly clean against his soot-stained skin. Despite an exhausted, stupefied stare, the man began to talk. He had worked all night, he said, as he did every night. During the day, he lived a semi-conscious life, not bothering to wash the coal off his leathery skin. His gravelly voice prompted me to ask about his health. All the miners had lung problems, he said, but they had no choice. In this beautiful but isolated valley, it was what they did, the only source of some meager income, and what their fathers and fathers' fathers had always done. All the while he stared up with glazed, unblinking eyes at the nearby hillside, at a tiny black hole where a conveyor spilled coal into one of a handful of waiting carts.

THE BICYCLE CLOWNS

We left the miner with a small packet of mint chocolate biscuits that I doubted would do much to rid the gritty taste of coal from his mouth and cycled away, a sheet of thick fumes from a passing truck screening our departure from the filthy village.

Above us, the road steepened and Achilles skittered, losing traction often on the rocky road, but any feeling of effort or pain was spirited away by the view and the sheer exposure of this road, hewn roughly into the side of the canyon. Gone were the days of my legs being too weak to control my pedalling over loose ground as they had been back in Alaska. After about 14,000 miles of practice the subtlety needed to maneuver Achilles sympathetically over gravelly patches was now second nature and I found myself able to keep pace with Barney and Adam, who stopped occasionally to commandeer my video camera, sprinting ahead for a short distance to shoot my all-important wides, putting Achilles in context, a speck of movement on a backdrop of rock.

What was quickly becoming my favourite road since the beginning of my journey was characterised by the crude tunnels blasted into the rock through which we travelled, disappearing into black holes at least every mile up the 24 miles of the deepest part of the canyon. The tunnels necessitated the donning of head torches, which between each hole made us resemble boy scouts, massively over-prepared for the onset of night-time hours before sunset.

There was little motorised traffic on the road, the few vehicles that passed were either trucks servicing the hydroelectric dam above us or the twice-daily clapped-out bus driven by a local with balls big enough to make this dicey journey in a vehicle too big for the track. On this stretch of precipitous road the three of us were forced to camp on a small pull-out a foot away from a sheer drop to the river below, nearly dry now, water only existing in stagnant pools. Adam and Barney, closest to oncoming traffic, rolled a large boulder in front of their pathetic tent in a vague attempt to protect against a gung-ho bus driver swinging wide around the corner above us.

The next morning, as quickly as the first gaping tunnel swallowed up my tattered British flag, flying war-torn from my trailer, the holes ceased. The welcome asphalt returned and the horizons expanded to reveal fields, greenery and farming people of the Peruvian sierra, where schoolchildren blocked my progress until they had been rewarded with a ride – sometimes jumping on two at a time before I'd even come to a standstill. Once an old man grinned with delight as he was given a circuit on the back around his little farmhouse shop where I bought more life-preserving biscuits, having left the others behind fixing punctures.

Like those I remembered in Ecuador, the mountain people in Peru proved to be very different from those on the coastal plains. It was as if the topography provided a lofty barrier to development, life continuing up here as it had for many years, families often walking slowly down the roads from their fields on small terraces above, with knotted shawls full of grass or firewood slung around their backs. The responsibility of carrying the baby seemed usually to fall to the hunched 'tough as old boots' granny, plodding with bent back but still impossibly strong.

Expressions varied on seeing Achilles. Some were indifferent as they trudged along or hacked at the earth near the road with mattocks, but some faces broke into a wide-creased grin as they waved at me enthusiastically, attracting my attention by whistling shrilly. I'd wave happily back, this interaction picking me up during small, perhaps rain-soaked, psychological troughs. It had been the same in the deep north of Canada or Alaska, where instead of whistling, a trucker would tug enthusiastically on his horn, saluting as he sped by.

From Huaraz, after a brief attempt at satiating my climbing appetite with the boys – efforts largely hampered by route-finding errors and the rain clouds that claim the Cordillera every afternoon in the wet season – we kissed goodbye to these most regal of ice-fluted mountains and followed the road up, over damp and freezing moorland with a river below us to the east meandering along the wide valley floor slowly enough to freeze in places.

The three of us knew this misery would end at a small village called Conococha, where the road angled to the right and the contour lines on my map bunched up as the thin red line hairpinned its way back to the west coast. The discomfort it took to reach this frigid little village was, however, unprecedented, the altitude and cold sapping my energy and causing me to halt, almost too weak to dismount, and consume, one after the other, a can of evaporated milk and a small bottle of olive oil I kept for such emergencies. The boys were miles ahead of me with more palatable morsels stashed on their lighter machines, but my hunger was such that these curdling liquids did the trick, slipping down easily, almost pleasantly, allowing me to pedal the remaining 5 miles to the village, the wet cold of which wasn't equalled by even the wettest winter's day recorded in England. There was no rain, only a hanging, clingy moisture that stuck to me, seemingly well below zero. To make things just a little less pleasant, there was very little glass in the windows of the place where we lodged: not enough to stop the cold from invading our bodies, despite having to penetrate three layers of the thick llama-wool blankets we'd bunched around us.

We survived the night though, and after a few cups of the local coca tea (also called maté) we were quickly rewarded with what the map had promised us if we got this far. After a mile or so more of the damp, cold ridge line, and with my joints aching from the trials of the previous day, the road rolled downhill and out of sight through a notch in the hillside. A moment later, the hanging mist had cleared and before us was nearly 10,000 vertical feet of descent, the hill dropping away from us in one folded valley, the colours changing as the alpine plants gave way to grass, then rocks and sand in the base of the valley far below. Achilles handles a little like a motorbike at high speeds, stable and smooth, and his weight carried me quickly away from the other two, whistling through the hairpins then down the straights, my eyes watering and the tires singing as I reached silly, uncontrollable speeds. To brake too much was to risk overheating the rims and melting the inner tubes, something that didn't bear thinking about at 60 miles an hour with nearly 220 pounds of bike to plow me into the rough tarmac. So, like on so many hills before now, all I could do was let Achilles run and then brake hard and fast before each hairpin, grateful I didn't have the extra weight of a stoker to contend with.

But despite the small safety issues, it was fun, and to travel so fast was exhilarating after days of climbing at a snail's pace. The overwhelming feeling was one of progress as the temperature slowly rose with the fast drop in altitude. Within an hour, the roadside was dotted with cacti, and in small hollows and dried riverbeds, clumps of rushes or banana palms grew, a tiny bit of subsistence agriculture near a small shack indicating we were getting closer to civilisation again.

That day we reached the coast, where we feasted on chicken and chips in a small, dirty town amongst sugar-cane plantations, to celebrate our safe passage through the mountains. Barney was leaving the following day, having exhausted his available holiday time. So we made that last evening together a long one, traipsing around the town, from small eatery to bar and back again for seconds, amazing the locals not only by the fact that we were so, well, foreign, but by our capacity to eat chips.

Later, we sat in the small square watching a bunch of children playing football. Girls and boys ran around in the square at midnight, parents either wandering around town or at home, unworried as to the whereabouts of their babies – everyone takes a shared responsibility here for the children in town.

One kid, the fattest on the court, took control of the game: a player, self-appointed referee and water boy, in charge of refreshments and eating almost constantly when the ball bounced to the far end of the square. Then his continuous barking orders and encouragement stopped suddenly as Adam worked his magic with some local girls who found us something of a novelty. The boy, perhaps eight years old but huge, put his chubby hands on his knees and bent over, retching then puking plentifully over his shoes and the polished concrete. Looking up with an expression of mild inconvenience, he cast around until he found a piece of dirty cardboard with which he covered his pile of vomit before indicating to the small girls looking on that it was safe to continue play. Before Adam, Barney and I wandered drunkenly back to a hostel of sorts, we saw the boy taking another quick snack during a short break in play. It made me feel nauseous, regretting the last quarter chicken I'd wolfed down with a generous slathering of mayonnaise.

Adam and I reached Lima in time for Christmas, my second Christmas on the road. It was December 23 when we rolled literally off the edge of the desert which had all but throttled the life out of me with its sandy grip on and off for the last 1,200 miles. Topping out on a painfully large wind-blown hill, the sand streaking the road seemingly liquid in its movement, my eyes were greeted with something other than a drab brown and hazy pale blue sky. The dunes dropped away in steep, crescent-shaped ripples to the sea 2,000 feet below. Beyond the sand there was a darker, flat land dotted with industry and little spots of painstakingly cultivated greenery – lack of sand dunes didn't mean there was any more water; the mains supply, where it existed, was regularly cut off for days at time.

We met Pedro, our Christmas host, in the fume-choked madness next to the airport entrance. He emerged, parting a throng of street vendors selling fruit, gunning his dirt bike loudly, his ample frame making the machine seem toy-like in comparison. He greeted us with the enthusiasm of a lifelong friend, his Californian accent only coloured slightly by his native Spanish. Both Adam and I, sweaty and dusty from the street, received a big, clean-smelling bear hug.

We had first met Pedro and Alicia over 620 miles further north in the heart of the desert, where we'd stopped at the only tumble-down adobe homestead for miles. I remember having to fight towards the promising blob in the distance for hours and being grateful when I got there, the wind clawing with breathy fingers against every inch of Achilles' dented frame. I remember camping in an empty, roofless outbuilding, its walls providing a sanctuary from the wind. It was here that Adam spied a beautiful black, yellow and red striped snake curled up in a corner of the room. Black on yellow, the snake is mellow? Or was it black on red, you'll end up dead? None of us could remember the life-saving mantra, so Adam went ahead and picked it up anyway, a crazed and terrified curiosity taking hold, before evicting it from the premises.

Pedro, Alicia and their dog had stopped at the dusty pull-out the next morning in the hope of finding a *paradero*, a small truck-stop selling water, at least. They found us instead and invited us to their home in Lima, 'For Christmas if you arrive in time,' Pedro said in English learned growing up in Los Angeles, California.

TAKE A SEAT

We thanked them for their kind offer, not really expecting to be in Peru's capital around Christmas time. Besides, Pedro cut a strange and maybe threatening figure. His arms were covered in what looked like gang tattoos, and his meaty frame only just folded into the seat of their tired-looking hatchback.

In the days after a lovely Christmas spent in a family home with Lima on one side and the dusty, shanty-filled hills on the other, Pedro told me about his teenage years in the States. While we sat at a street stand sipping on Peru's life blood, juice made with *lucuma*, guava, *guabana* and a million other delicious fruits I'd never heard of, he explained the tattoos. He'd got mixed up in the underbelly of LA gang culture and spent time in juvenile detention, and his father, despairing, had sent him back to Peru. Since then, Pedro had found religion, and it seems to have worked for him. If every God-fearing person I'd met along my journey had acted with such unquestioning hospitality, many a man or woman would have been saved from having to endure the unpleasant experiences that I'd heard about in second-hand backpackers' horror stories. Sadly, a large proportion of the evangelicals and missionaries that I'd met on my journey seemed to preach fear and, perhaps in a misguided attempt to unite, discourage people from trusting in each other, trusting instead exclusively in some misrepresented God.

Pedro tried to accompany me out of his city, where only a few blocks from the Presidential Palace poverty and disrepair come out of hiding and spread themselves outwards in a patchwork blanket of plastic sheeting. Alas, his ample backside and heavy frame, more used to the comparatively plush suspension of his Chinese import motorbike, let him down only 2½ miles from his house. He felt physically violated, he said, by the expensive, ergonomically shaped saddle.

After spending a firework-filled New Year with more new-found friends in the small seaside town of San Bartolo – a city dwellers' retreat on public holidays – I progressed south along the coastal road, alone again, Adam having chosen to head into the hilly forests to the east of Lima for a while. With no one cycling alongside, my mind focused again solely on my surroundings, sucking them in, the sights, the smells, sometimes twisting the stimuli into abstract and stupid thoughts until

I was left thinking about something completely different. Weekenders' bars and beaches were all too quickly replaced by a new wave of harsh and unforgiving desert, where tiny and infrequent shacks made of palm matting sold only gas, the tiny families living there often waiting days for water.

I crept south past piles of adobe rubble lying where it had fallen months earlier during the powerful earthquakes that razed most of the region of Pisco to the ground. Rows of aid organisation tents lined the roads in towns and villages, the unstable remains of houses still in use behind them. Six months after the worst of the quakes, some areas still remained cordoned off, containing acres of uncleared, unsearched rubble that was said to carry the sickly stench of tens if not hundreds of missing corpses, left buried with insufficient aid to extract them. An old man scavenging litter in the rubble told me people like him still come across body parts in the ruins.

By now it should have come as no surprise, having experienced the same phenomenon further north, but in these areas of destruction and poverty, unfettered smiles and generosity were plentiful. People busy literally rebuilding their lives frequently enthusiastically beckoned me over to chat, bought me lunch or presented me with a Coke from an antique delivery truck that still did the rounds through the now unbounded streets.

The catastrophic earthquake hadn't destroyed the people's resolve, nor had it changed the weather, the wind continuing to erode my enthusiasm along the dead-straight coastal highway, only letting up occasionally, when I would sprint forward for an hour or two, or as long as the lull would allow.

The going was sufficiently mind-numbing to cause me to make a mistake, one I had made time and time again, somehow forgetting each time any lesson learned.

On reaching some deserted gas station or excuse for a café, flies buzzing lazily round the counter and vultures congregating 30 yards away near the outhouse, I'd ask the sleepy salesman about distances to the next landmark marked on the vague map fastened to the box on my handlebars. Latin Americans rarely work in distances, they work in time – I knew that. I also knew they were, understandably, unable to guess at what speed I was capable of travelling on Achilles. This and the fact that Peruvians, like their neighbours, often tell you what they think you'll want to hear, make asking distance questions a dangerous activity that can result in a complete and tearful meltdown in the middle of nowhere. Months earlier I had learned that, unless each landmark had been moved without anyone's knowledge, the guesstimates of locals were ludicrously optimistic. People here work in 'hours on a bus', seemingly adding one hour regardless of distance to convert to 'hours on a bicycle'. So, for instance, if it took four hours to travel the 87 miles to the next town in a robust old yellow school bus last week, that was the new benchmark. Do the maths and you'll quickly see that the ETA by bicycle to the same destination would be five hours. If bus time equalled two days, bike time would be scaled up to two days and one hour, maybe two. To complicate the lottery, maybe every tenth enquiry I might get a wildly accurate estimate just to keep me on my toes. The hard times were always therefore worsened by asking this question. It was those same times, however, that I desperately needed to hear blind optimism to keep me moving – I'd created my very own dry-baked, road-weary catch-22.

There is no landscape like the Sechura Desert. I had suffered in the jungles of southern Mexico, my still green body unaccustomed to the humidity, and been reduced to screaming at the wind-blown tundra in Alaska over a year before. The hills in Colombia had forced me into my smallest 'granny-gear' cog for days at a time and sucked away calories almost quicker than I could consume them. But here in the Sechura, the hatred I had for the ever-moving sand, the dry smell of chicken shit, even the deep red of the crescent-shaped dunes before sunset, was unrivalled. It had gone on for too long, grinding down any last grain of appreciation for the desolate beauty it might have possessed. Absence, they say, makes the heart grow fonder, but this sandy wasteland would have to disappear for a long, long time before I'd start missing it.

Nazca, one of the most significant patches of concentrated archaeology in the world, marked the spot where, for me, the desert ended for good. I cycled gratefully past lines etched in the desert by the Incas, or maybe those who came before them. From the ground the lines are barely discernible, but if you climb a small rise near the road, where dusty mountains had started to sprout from the plains, you can make out the outlines of animals, as if a kingdom of giant creatures had been involved in a multiple homicide in the desert, the painted outlines of the fallen corpses from a case long since closed still visible pale in the dark, stony ground.

Since travelling through the desert I'd noticed a change not so much in the landscape but in the people and the way they think. It was as if I had got far enough south to have arrived in a land where the grip of the States and the 'Western world' was weaker. North of Lima, questions from passersby inevitably focused on economy, standard of living and the cost of my equipment. Nearer Nazca, it was as likely to turn to what kind of potatoes we have in our soil in Britain, and whether I knew what donkeys look like. I was even asked on the roadside, after purchasing a melon out of the back of a battered Ford pick-up, if where I come from, we have water. On reflection, this part of Peru sees so little water that the question doesn't seem so ridiculous. And after all, I'm from England, which must be like the States, so as far as the family questioning me were concerned, it was not unlikely that we might have Coca-Cola flowing from our taps.

There are two languages widely spoken here, Castellano (Spanish) and Quechua, yet some of the farmers I encountered were mildly amused to hear that some of us speak something else.

'What does it sound like?' they would ask, steeling themselves like the old men in the Ecuadorian farmers' hostel for an inevitable giggle as soon as I spoke my mother tongue. Yet, perhaps only 12 miles away, in Nazca, savvy Peruvians entertain and rub shoulders with tourists from all over the world.

I rested in Nazca for three days, restocking on willpower and gratefully receiving archaeology lessons from another new friend (and the fount of all knowledge), Jesus, who drove me from site to site in his old, much-loved Cadillac. I relaxed, happy in the knowledge that I'd soon have company again. Diana, an Ecuadorian friend from Cuenca, was travelling south to join me on a road that headed inland once again.

From the edge of town, standing next to an old and ransacked Inca grave site, I could see two dark lines in the stony ground, running nearly parallel but eventually converging over two miles away where the plains disappeared and the grey mountains began. I asked Jesus what they were. Apparently hundreds of theories exist, of which a personal favourite is an alien landing strip, once maybe coupled to an intergalactic filling station. All I could be sure of was that the lines ended near the road which would take me once again into the pampas of the high Andes. Poring over the map I saw that the road mercilessly dropped back down into the bottom of two deep valleys, forcing me to climb the 11,500 feet I'd already gained three times if I were to arrive as planned at the 'Lost City, Home of the Incas'. It didn't look far on the map, but I'd lost the ability to be optimistic. I had a nasty feeling, as I looked up into the clouds, that this climb would be completely void of pleasure.

16

Lost city found

DAY 573: 13,399 MILES

I'd only noticed the refreshing cold, not the tendrils of mist that had crept quickly down over the slopes to envelop Diana and me and any glimpse of the desert we were leaving behind. Little drops of water collected on our clothes and visibility was reduced to about 40 feet. It was a pleasant change despite the road being steep – no impossibly distant sandy horizon to fix on, just heavy white air to brush aside a few feet at a time.

Diana pedalled with me, talking when breath allowed about what had happened in her life since that day I'd said goodbye to her in Cuenca, Ecuador. I'd been quietly looking forward to her companionship ever since. Helping me into a fresh set of hills, she was the closest I'd had to an old friend actually sitting on my bike – the first person who allowed me not to have to start all over again since northern Mexico, when another earlier acquaintance had revisited me. It was comfortable, relaxing, no more treading lightly in an effort to get used to each other's habits as I often felt obliged to do with strangers.

After two weeks, however, the mountain road had ceased to be a welcome change from the desert, thousands of feet of rain-soaked climbing had embittered me. Back then rain had been preferable to wind, but after only a few days of inoperable, moisture-ridden cameras, I had realised the only hope of drying out was for the wind to blow.

TAKE A SEAT

Diana was hoping to accompany me to Cusco, and ignoring the contour lines on the map it seemed possible in the time she had, but after 62 solidly wet uphill miles, Cusco seemed even further away and the tiny provincial buses that coughed past us in the late afternoons were an increasingly attractive option for Diana to escape the damp misery of Achilles. She kept me company for five days, rolling along the Peruvian pampas where the vicuñas – like llamas but with softer fur and more delicate – grazed, camouflaged in the browns and greens of the upland grasses over 13,000 feet above sea level. After that first night together, camped between two boulders in the claggy moonscape trying to prevent the rain from extinguishing my stove, it dawned on me that without a roof to shelter under, this stage of the journey would be permanently damp and dangerously cold. While sucking at a bowl of unfashionably wet and undercooked pasta, watching the equipment we couldn't fit in under the plastic sheet get steadily wetter in the encroaching darkness, I got to thinking that this was not what Diana had signed up for – hardly a pleasant and sun-soaked holiday for two.

I woke suddenly the next morning struggling to breathe with Diana's thick dark hair tickling my face – she'd rolled away from the downhill side of the tent, where water now pooled, and sleeping deeply, pressed me up against the wet nylon. Sitting up quickly to avoid the fat drips of water welling up on a seam above me, I unzipped the door and looked outside. The rain had stopped not long ago, and the air was still. Above us the sky was a watery blue and the weak sun made the ground glisten. Below us, where I could see for the first time sections of the road we had climbed, the mist still clung to the hillsides in slowly cresting waves, creeping upwards but spreading out in tendrils, then disappearing before it reached our sagging tent and the puddles that had formed around Achilles' wheels in the boggy soil.

Nothing we owned was dry any more, even the down in my sleeping bag clumped together, damp and useless. But the rain gave us a few hours' grace in the pampas, and in the sea of grass we found a dilapidated vicuña-monitoring station, once a well-funded German-run research post, but now almost a ruin, old empty warehouses giving us ample room to dry equipment. A local family, one of the few hardy families who live in this wilderness, kept an eye on the place, and with the caretaker clad in a heavy wool poncho, his squat, powerfully built wife and their smiling three-year-old daughter, we played a boundary-less game of high-altitude volleyball next to the bleak highway, spectators in short supply.

We met other people on this road too, all of them, including the kids, with tough, wind-burnt skin and lips creased with old, deep cracks. The children would play in the dirt next to their small adobe buildings, the families making a meager living providing food for passing travellers, mostly local buses taking the rural population and their wool to market. Diana captivated the kids with my camera, sending them squealing away and whooping with laughter at the sight of their faces on the small screen, while I ate a mountain of rice topped with two oily, fried eggs and a few dollops of mayonnaise. Ever since Ecuador this simple meal had become an easy-to-source treat, the last word in comfort food and a very practical calorie-rich meal.

I would never escape one of these windswept lunch spots without having given each child a lap on Achilles. They'd sit, like the hundreds of children before them, with their little feet perched on the higher of the two diagonal steel tubes that reinforced the tandem, leaning forward as far as they could without falling, to grasp the handlebars as we bumped over the dirt. Occasionally I'd look over my shoulder to see that one of the other kids had been unable to wait in line, draping themselves over the more child-friendly trailer like a corpse being carried by a donkey. They would shout at each other in a clipped, colloquial mixture of Spanish and Quechua. 'You're riding the gringo's bicycle!!' they'd say in shrill excitement, clapping their hands in uncomplicated delight and running after us.

Days after Diana had returned home to dry out, I'd dropped down into a small agricultural valley and found shelter in a tiny village. Moments after finding shelter in a doorway the sky, like something from the Old Testament, went black and clapped with deafening thunder. I hunkered down in the small porch, rain and hail pounding the asphalt, bouncing and exploding into a fine icy mist a few feet off the ground.

TAKE A SEAT

As I pointed my camera out at the road to film the spectacular rain, the air became charged, and for a fraction of a second I was blinded and deafened as a fizzing lightning bolt lit my LCD screen and struck the roof of the little school 50 feet ahead of me across the road. The school, thankfully, was empty – no harm done, except perhaps to my retinas.

I woke the following morning to a calm sky, but with hills dusted in snow. A night's worth of traffic sat stationary outside the small room I'd purloined, and those who hadn't disappeared into the small restaurant to sip cups of coca tea stood in heated discussion. I learned after a breakfast of more rice and eggs that there'd been a large landslide not far up the road, a layer of mud making the road impassable. The words 'You'll have to wait, no one can pass' from one of the all-knowing macho bus drivers were like a red rag to a bull, and I pedalled off, snaking through the huge line of trucks up the hill, past groups of people walking back down the road to seek refuge in the village. After two minutes of pedalling, I could see what the fuss was about. Beyond the colourful string of vehicles and at the front of a crowd of people, there was a large black scar on the hillside where grass and stones had once been. Beneath it, the road had disappeared under a sea of mud which spread down to flatter ground below.

Once I got to the back of the crowd assembled seemingly to watch the settling mud and three men wielding the only spades available, I had two options: to wait with the rest of them or disassemble Achilles and climb up around the slide. I unfastened the four pannier bags, slid the makeshift trailer locks out of their placements and put the bike gently in the gutter, in no mood to loiter in the damp air.

'Leave him, he's mad,' I heard one woman wrapped in a blanket say to the nattering throng while I hefted the heavily laden trailer onto my shoulder, the flags brushing shoulders as they bunched around, now watching the gringo spectacle. Turning away from the crowd, hopping over the mud-filled gutter and climbing unsteadily over the loose embankment, I headed up the hillside, small, muddy hollows still dripping with the water run-off responsible for the heavy slide.

It took an hour in total to shift the three loads up, over the slide area and down to the waiting crowd 500 feet further up the road. By load number three, locals and tourists alike had started to take an interest and a smattering of applause greeted me when my bike was one unit again on the uphill side of the mudslide. At that moment, with a handful of men toiling ineffectively in the mud, the emergency services arrived, and the tough faces of the crowd visibly brightened until the back of the small truck opened up. Inside were three wheelbarrows and five more spades. My brief doubts as to whether my exhausting load-hauling had been in vain vaporised; I guessed there were at least a few hundred barrow loads of muck to clear before the waiting buses could start catching me up again.

For two hours I cycled happily along, slowly up the side of the U-shaped valley and back onto the windswept pampas, where the first trucks and tour buses started to roar by, hooting enthusiastically as their warm exhaust fumes gave my face a moment's respite from the numbing cold.

That afternoon I swept quickly back down to 3,300 feet, off the pampas and into terraced farmland where wood smoke drifted out of cracks in the thatched roofs and into the damp air. Another set of hairpins took me through thin forests of pine where I held onto heavily laden gravel trucks chugging up the roads only slightly faster than Achilles, until after half a mile or so of hitching, my left arm would protest sufficiently for my grip to loosen, leaving my legs to pedal once more. As a fresh collection of thunderheads moved along the rounded spine of the nearest line of hills, dropping opaque curtains of rain, I stopped next to a small hut selling *chicharrón* – pork fried with potatoes and rosemary in a deep wok-like dish. In front of me, past the tatty beach umbrella sheltering dining truck drivers, was the city of Cusco carpeting the large valley bottom, and above it on the hillside, scraped out of the stubbly grass, were the giant words 'Viva El Peru Glorioso.' I had completed the largest section of hill-climbing to date, and was pleased to have the damp, snail's pace of mostly misery behind me.

Leaning Achilles against the cathedral, I sat on the flagstones and observed this new city, the small indigenous locals plying their trade amongst the tourists, a significant proportion of whom belonged to the dreadlocked, stripey-trousered and slightly fragrant backpacking brigade.

Looking past the thick swathe of Internet cafés, Italian restaurants and shops selling expensive tourist souvenirs, Cusco is a striking maze of small stone streets that reach out from the square like spiders' legs, up the hillsides and between the large stone buildings, the intricately carved rocks of which fit together like huge pieces of a 3D jigsaw. Away from the very core of the city are the food markets, a novelty for adventurous tourists and a practical day-to-day service center for the Cuscenos. Perhaps 20 stands selling fruit juice back onto others selling beans and squashes, frogs – skinless or whole – cows' noses, sheep heads and almost any other cut of meat you might desire. The markets provided me with a place to relax, eat cake and suck thick juice through a straw bought from whichever vendor waved their newspaper most frantically at me to attract my patronage. At night I wandered the streets some more, or frequented the touristy bars trawling for my next bicycle victim.

Two days later I succumbed to the lure of the lost city, Machu Picchu. I was tired and well into my 'rest mode' of eating and sleeping and nothing much else, but not to visit this national monument would, I felt, be almost ungrateful. Nothing in the premiere league of tourism comes cheap, however, so to avoid the $31 charge for a short train journey from the earthy coloured village of Ollantaytambo to Aguas Calientes – 'Hot Waters', the small village beneath the ruins – I set off on foot with a pint of water and a couple of bananas down the 30-mile railway track, stepping quickly to begin with between uneven sleepers to avoid twisting my ankles. Sometimes there was a track winding its way loosely alongside the railway line, joining tiny villages together in an increasingly steep-sided valley, stepped with agricultural terraces right up to the ridgeline high above me. Rain came and went as I tramped along, regretting the too-small shoes I'd bought in Ecuador a little more each time I stubbed my toe on a sleeper. When the clouds quickly rolled in, the small patch of sky framed by canyon walls and trees above me darkened, making the valley seem ominous and unfriendly. Locals stared at me from small adobe doorways, accustomed to seeing tourists framed by the aluminium surround of a train window passing swiftly and without benefit through their little world, only 25 jungled miles from one of the world's seven wonders.

Where the track ended and the rails continued uninterrupted in their gradual descent to Aguas Calientes, I stopped for a rest in a tiny earth-floored store, where a handful of villagers shot the breeze in Quechua. Throwing in a smattering of Spanish for my benefit, they questioned me as to my purpose here, and what would possibly inspire me to spend nearly two years travelling on my own, without a huge family and a house? I explained the whys and wherefores of my journey as I had done a million times before, though secretly I was finding it increasingly difficult to convince myself that I believed in the answers I gave. After five minutes of small children wandering in with a few pennies to buy sweets, an older man plonked himself on the bench next to me while the two indigenous women and baby opposite stared wide-eyed at me, a strange, blonding man with shorts and hairy legs. The man smiled at me inquisitively, his gold tooth glinting slightly in the half-light of the small room.

'Why don't you find a woman in this village?' he asked, 'I could help you tomorrow if you like,' he added willingly.

'That's very kind of you, but I must continue on this little journey of mine,' I replied, grinning.

'What do you do for work?' the man asked, obviously formulating an ensnaring plan.

'Well, I do various things, a bit of mountain guiding, I'm making a doc—' he cut me off. His eyes lit up and his cheeks creased into a triumphant smile, revealing not one gold tooth, but a whole collection.

'There, you see! You could herd cattle over there on the mountain tops with your woman, that way you would have it all!' The women across the way giggled, covering their mouths and rocking to and fro, silently applauding his insistence and cunning. A little lost for words, I left them quickly with a weak promise of my return, wondering as I walked into a light drizzle whether my self-appointed life coach and marriage consultant could have found anyone desperate enough to be my wife.

Before darkness fell, leaving me tripping more often on the tracks that sometimes spanned angry streams, I crossed paths with a local lady and her dog – they must have lived in a small habitation hidden in the trees. She strode quickly past me in the opposite direction with a huge bundle of crops wrapped in a shawl on her back, raising her brimmed hat in polite greeting as she passed. I guessed even factoring in the effect of this harsh existence on her complexion, that she was about 60, and still as tough as anything, little bare feet poking out from under her heavy skirt and propelling her uphill faster than I descended.

I arrived in Aguas Calientes just after midnight feeling broken, having lost a toenail and narrowly avoided being run over by a tourist train, whose bulging carriage sides forced me to jump blindly away from the blurring lights into a rocky ditch shoulder deep in undergrowth. The tourists in plush seats, sleepy after their complimentary snack, were blissfully unaware of their driver's attempt on my life.

After a brief, abortive hunt for a dry cave or undergrowth a short way away from the small concrete village packed shoulder to shoulder with hotel complexes, I bedded down under the corrugated roof of the 'Inca shuttle bus' fuel pump, the smell of gas permeating my mat and sleeping bag. But despite the relative discomfort of my immediate surroundings, as soon as I had become accustomed to the throbbing of feet recently liberated from tight shoes, I fell quickly into a dehydrated, dreamless sleep.

Only three hours later, at 6:50 a.m., I dragged my tired, blistered and broken body, barely able to walk after the previous day's ordeal, up to the lost – until recently – city of Machu Picchu, still cloaked in dappled cloud, allowing brief glimpses of the grey walls, forests and mossy cliffs that make up its surroundings. Having queued behind a small group of tourists – their heads buried in a French Lonely Planet guide – I gained entry and climbed up to the lofty Wayna Picchu, the towering rock and ruins that overlook the roofless city. Just then, the carpet of rippled clouds drew silently back, revealing the green terraces with ant-like people making their way along the labyrinth-like paths and terraces. The depths of the tight valleys, thick with lush green slopes and small but ferocious rivers that I had followed the night before, remained hidden under thick lakes of fog.

Sitting there, the rocks dropping steeply away beneath me and a handful of people making their way up the steep steps to the summit, I couldn't deny that this was indeed a special place, beautiful and historically astounding – a civilisation in the depths of seemingly impenetrable mountains. But my own experience had not only been slightly marred by my ridiculous walk to save $31 but also by the people. The tourists, by the time I was making my way down from the peak, were thick on the ground, but it wasn't this that upset me. It was the guards, officials, souvenir sellers and hoteliers who made up a significant proportion of the Peruvians in this valley. I felt like I was getting to know the Peruvian people after months in the saddle cycling through village after village, but this crowd was not like them, and the only reason I could find for that was intensive tourism. The guards stared at me as if I were about to take a sledgehammer to the lost city, the salesmen in the village treated me like a liar when I told them I hadn't the money to buy this jumper or that set of pipes. Even the locals who plied their trade in the center of Cusco seemed blind to anything other than dollar bills. I'm no sociologist, but perhaps this change can be seen anywhere where heavy-handed tourists wave money around in a place where that volume of wealth was previously not even conceivable for the locals. Either way, after the unquestioning hospitality of a shepherd giving up his sheepskin bedding for me to sleep on the floor of his hut, being told to piss off after closing time by a bored-looking guard is a little overwhelming.

Adam had rejoined me in Cusco, and, I'm not sure how, convinced a lovely girl by the name of Phoebe Walker that the company of two puerile Brits on the rain-swept pampas heading for Bolivia was exactly the adventure she needed, so she abandoned her friends and became my next stoker. After a week resting up it was time to roll away from the beautiful tourist enclave in search of the no-strings-attached friendliness to which I'd become accustomed. But I had one last culinary quest to complete before leaving Cusco behind. Fully loaded, and with Phoebe having passed the two-minute crash course in 'tandeming', the three of us rattled down yet more cobbled streets past young children selling finger-puppets and posing for photos next to their alpacas, to arrive weaving between drooping tarpaulins at the covered food market on the edge of town.

17

Into the land of the coca leaf

DAY 591: 13,807 MILES

I never passed up an opportunity to taste something new, and I'd skipped breakfast especially, saving my appetite for what we were looking for.

Once I'd found a wooden post to delicately lean Achilles against in the cramped and muddy alleyway, Phoebe, Adam and I perched ourselves – inconspicuous in fleeces and leggings – on a rickety wooden bench. In front of us was one of seven different stalls staffed by powerfully built women deftly juggling ladles, plates, bowls and huge cauldrons of soupy mixtures heated on primitive gas burners. The colour of this place was governed by the blue plastic sheets draped overhead, not quite providing shelter from the sporadic rain. Everything, even the usually colourful shawls of the local women, had a faded bluish tint.

The three men squeezed onto the bench opposite had their heads lowered to their bowls but eyes fixed on us as they slurped and occasionally chewed on a gristly chunk of whatever it was they were eating. I suspected as I ordered that mine would look almost identical. The big lady looked at us waiting for our order more out of etiquette than enquiry since there was only one thing on the menu here. '*Un caldo de cabeza porfa,*' I asked, smiling. I'd ordered what was apparently the local breakfast dish. Head soup is the literal translation, but just as one wouldn't expect pan-fried duck to arrive in front of you with wings and feathers, I was expecting something with all the flavour of a head but bearing no close resemblance to anything living. A large bowl of

213

steaming, muddy-coloured soup was put in front of me, the other two deciding to hold off on ordering until they'd seen my reaction. First impressions were encouraging, I was able to ID a chunk of potato and a small strip of onion amongst the floating fatty blobs. But prodding into the depths my spoon struck something hard. Scooping the foreign body up above the waterline I was greeted by a sheep's head cut clean down the middle, complete with eye, skin and one or two clinging bits of bedraggled wool. Across the way the men and the big lady looked at us unsmiling, finding nothing funny about my breakfast. I pulled theatrically at a tooth and was surprised to find it came out in my hand. With little meat to suck on I let it 'plink' back into the soup and sink to the bottom, before exploring the skull more thoroughly with a knife. I ate what little meat there was on the bone, but the only part with any real substance was the eye, which separated from the orbit with a little tug, snapping the redundant optic nerve. Tentatively biting down, I found it was moist but still chewy, like a stringy egg white, not the taste sensation I was hoping for. While I chewed I removed a soggy matt of wool from the surface of the soup, like a plug of hair that accumulates in the shower. I tried not to fuss over this meal lest I offended anyone, but after scraping what I could off the skull, I asked the lady politely if we might have some rice and eggs. I badly needed to supplement this bony breakfast, and a half-hour later, the three of us left having filled up on our staple rather than two more sinewy heads.

Along the wide open pampas of southern Peru the horizon was a distant line, sometimes snow-capped, sometimes green, but always fresh, with at least a slight cool wind reminding us that we were not all that much lower than the summits of Mont Blanc or Mount Rainier. The spiky grass continued to camouflage the vicuñas, alpacas and llamas that grazed here, looking up with their camel-like faces to see what that strange, slow, whirring noise was. Though Phoebe was more used to playing a civilised game of field hockey, or perhaps breaking into a fast canter on horseback, she rose to the challenge and helped power Achilles up the one remaining high pass that stood between us and the highest navigable lake in the world, Titicaca. On the shores of that lofty lake Phoebe still had every intention of accompanying me into Bolivia, though I had my doubts – as I had with each and every companion – as to whether her bottom would let her down after the fairly standard three-day benchmark.

The damp cold and wind chill as we descended quickly from nearly 14,000 feet necessitated the loan of my favourite socks to Phoebe to use as gloves as she hunkered down behind me trying to avoid the worst of the freezing mist and rain. The communities we sped past were tiny and few and far between, squat adobe huts clustered together in groups of four or five, home to those who worked the land, their heavy woollen ponchos protecting them against the rain at least as effectively as the thatch on their modest dwellings.

Despite my doubts, Phoebe stayed the course through the upland agriculture, past giant snaking sandstone ridge lines that grew from nothing out of the cultivated plains, to the shores of the ocean-like lake of which, the Peruvians proudly informed us, Peru owns the Titi and Bolivia the Caca. Weeks later over the border I was told that the opposite was true, and given that Bolivia is the underdog to all its neighbours, I chose to side with them.

In Puno, a city in the throes of religious festivals when we arrived, Adam left us just shy of the border with the promise of a teaching job in Bolivia beckoning him south. Despite the possibility of reuniting in the near future in La Paz where he'd be working, it was a strange feeling, having an element that had grown into a comical mainstay of my journey removed overnight. As one would expect, having experienced everything from maddening desert to painfully miserable Andean snow together, we'd grown close enough to share jokes that no one else found funny. We recognised each obscure gripe of the other, knowing the best ways in which to bypass or exacerbate them. We'd developed our favourite foods together – shopping for supplies had become a fluent and efficient process, centring on the all-important after-dinner treat which we spent many weeks isolating from a large array of possible regional and international contenders. In the end the uncontested winner, and something we searched for hopefully in even the most isolated mountain *tiendas*, was the blocky chocolate quite rightly named 'Sublime'. Adam and I had in fact grown so close that on a number of occasions, cold and hungry but with only one silver-foiled Sublime between us, we'd shared it.

Thanks to the family of friends I'd made in the coastal deserts near Lima over New Year, I rolled with Phoebe into a family home, sharing a spacious room in the Romero household with an armadillo (only a few of which I'd seen on my journey, and mostly in 2D, flattened on the roads of Mexico). From this base we explored the city and the islands constructed from dead reeds that had floated and been added to on the lake for centuries, home to a community of indigenous fishermen and now a popular tourist destination. Then, not 12 hours after arriving, Phoebe and I were wedged in the back of an old Dodge pick-up with the rest of the extended Romero family sheltering under heavy canvas as we bounced along a muddy track to a tiny homestead in the hills above the lake. As we climbed away from its shore, we could see the snowy peaks of the Cordillera between the storm clouds on the far side of the lake, across the invisible Bolivian border.

Once a year in these parts it is customary to give thanks to Pachamama – Mother Nature – for the crops and livestock provided by her, and to bless the current stock in order to ensure abundance for the coming year – a sensible custom in a world where a few dead cows could mean something a lot more serious than another trip to the supermarket or mortgage advisor.

In this desolate yet stunningly beautiful landscape the family all played a part in herding alpacas, cows and sheep together to conduct a ceremony of thanks. The resident shepherd who lived in one room of the small homestead, the only structure in this rolling grassland, conducted the ceremony, sprinkling watery mixtures of maize and other grains symbolising a myriad of things on the corralled animals. The shepherd's son, only four years old, with his own tiny poncho and small whip, showed no fear amongst the llamas and cows towering over him, walking amongst them, nudging them through the small corral entrance.

At the heart of the ceremonies was the coca leaf, chewed, shared and rubbed on the backs of the animals as a blessing, a time-honoured custom. I'd never seen such a meticulous and beautiful ceremony in churches back home, let alone outdoors. I only remember settling for the slightly more apathetic tradition of leaving a couple of cans of baked beans next to the altar at the local harvest festival.

Of course, like any good ceremony, alcohol was involved, barely diluted and stinging as it flowed hot down my throat, making my eyes water. The small gathering chuckled on seeing my sensitivity and I stared back at them, wiping my watering eyes. I didn't see even the slightest wince on any of their lined faces as each in turn tipped back a shot of the dangerously clear liquor. Pachamama wasn't forgotten when drinking either, each of us dribbling a few drops of moonshine onto the earth by way of thanks.

A week or so earlier I had witnessed a similar custom at close quarters. Approaching the entrance of a small bar with Phoebe and Adam I had looked up to see, in the half-light inside, a man striding forward with the action of a ten-pin bowler, letting his straight arm swing forward near the ground to send a small amount of Coke from his plastic cup flying in globules out into the dusty road, missing me by inches. The other two men did likewise, one of them catching me a glancing blow that dried an hour later, leaving a sticky deposit on my shirt. I adopted the custom, only too happy to throw drinks around.

The border crossing was the calmest I had come across, perhaps with the exception of Gold Rush Creek up in the hills that had led me from Alaska to Canada. That was a million miles away in every sense. Here at least there were people other than the sleepy immigration police sitting in their small room proudly emblazoned with the Bolivian crest. A cart half full of candy and assorted cheap cigarettes rested on its props like a wheelbarrow next to the steps that led down to the building. A taxi driver lay on the hood of his car, looking up hopefully when Phoebe and I arrived, then lying back down on seeing the bike. The thin-leafed shady tree the cart's owner was dozing under had a Mediterranean feel to it, but if you looked past the glare of the sun, the dark corners of this spartan border post were punctuated with poverty. An old lady sat deep in the shade of a tiny doorway with a child, far too big to be carried, draped across her bony little lap. A man of a similar age sat on a small whitewashed boulder outside a hut nearby. His large, strong-looking dark hands clutching a stick in front of him looked out of proportion now the rest of him had shrunk, dried and weathered by time. He wore one laceless shoe, and the other foot was bare and clay-like, the road's dust having stuck to it.

Getting my now worn and creased passport stamped next to Phoebe's comparatively new one, we rolled into Copacabana, a restful though touristy village 6 miles further along the shores of the lake. That day the debilitating cold of the mountains that had necessitated the donning of every shred of clothing seemed like a distant and unlikely dream, as the high-altitude sun heated the thin air and began to burn another layer off my already delicate nose and dry lips.

The following day, with Phoebe and a new Chilean friend I lay sleeping a few feet from the lakeshore, the windless air only causing gentle ripples too weak to harry the sand in the shallows. I woke and swam in the warm water occasionally, the warmest water I'd ever felt at over 13,000 feet above sea level. Then I slept again, forgetting the strength of the sun and waking up with a hard-edged and reddening tan line around my shorts that made it look as if I'd been constructed by a colour-blind mannequin maker.

Thankfully, as well as a small collection of touristy bars and cafés, this tiny village had a market servicing the local population, which I found for breakfast the following morning. One constant in markets, or busy streets of any size from Ecuador to here, was the sight and sound of music videos being played on a small TV, usually hung under a plastic sheet on a cart selling bootleg DVDs on the street. This cart became an entrancing hotspot for dozens of people, eyes glued to the tiny screen flanked by large speakers, all powered by a couple of car batteries on a shelf underneath.

These were no ordinary music videos, they were in fact the very best of local legends singing in a manner that my Western ears were not attuned to. Strangling a cat is an overused and clichéd phrase, I know, but there is honestly no better way to describe how they sounded to me. The focus of the video would normally be an indigenous girl in full traditional dress singing and backed by a small group of musicians perhaps in cheap suits, jigging in a field like a misplaced, aging boy band. The diabolical image quality only added to viewing pleasure as the picture jumped from the musicians to a fairly standard collection of stock clips including a shaky Trafalgar Square, an elderly man getting knocked over by a sheep (or goat, depending on the region), onlookers watching someone dancing in a field, and then bang, back to the dancing girl and the backing musicians jigging around trying to avoid cow pats.

Slightly resentful of my own nagging voice telling me to push on, I dragged myself back onto the bike helped by a new stoker. The novelty of Achilles had worn off for Phoebe – she had done what she had said she would and got me over the border. From here Giannina, a Chilean on holiday from Santiago, stepped into the breach – she was travelling to La Paz, and why not on a bicycle?

The two days we spent together took us from the restful surrounds of the lake over its narrowest part by means of a dangerously flexing overloaded wooden ferry into a more representative Bolivia. The lake imposed its own personality on its surroundings, seemingly more relaxed, with a quality of life that decreased as distance from its shoreline grew bigger. Giannina, only occasionally admitting to needing a rest from the saddle, was the first Chilean stoker I'd had, and the first South American who had accompanied me any distance since before Cusco. It was good to be conversing in Spanish again, though Gianinna's Chilean dialect took me by surprise, and it took a while to interpret what is commonly known as the most difficult Spanish tongue in the world. With the lake left well behind us on the other side of a low band of hills, we sought refuge in a small town on the Altiplano, dirtier and drier than the pampas I'd left on the other side of the border. Tired and wanting to find a cheap hostel rather than a filthy yard to camp in, I became increasingly irritated as we cycled around a town whose entire community seemed to be drunk, celebrating, by the looks of it, some kind of carnival. I nudged Achilles through crowds, Giannina now walking by my side looking in vain for some kind of establishment that wasn't closed up for the festivities. An old man clutching a beer suddenly leaned towards me and sent a fine mist of spit flying into my face as he slurred out the words 'Take me on a ride.' He got on surprisingly quickly but I was too irritated to appreciate this fairly harmless interlude. I stamped on the pedals, accelerating through the narrow gaps in the crowd and ignoring the shouts of the drunk to slow down. '*Puta madre, estas loco!*' he'd say, while trying desperately not to spill a drop from his bottle. He staggered off as soon as I crunched to a halt a minute later and I pedalled off towards Giannina, waiting conspicuously on a street corner ahead of me. After another more aggressive drunken encounter, we stopped in a small store back on the edge of the main road to get supplies for camping further away, and in doing so met the only sober family in town. After buying sardines, pasta and a bottle of highly chemical mayonnaise, Giannina and I found ourselves wheeling Achilles through a flimsy metal gate and into the half-finished concrete courtyard behind the store. I ducked beneath the washing line strung across the yard and only then noticed two fleshy corpses hung from it with bailing twine. Once the family had kindly pointed us to a spare room stacked with sheepskins I took a closer look at the objects on the line. They were piglets, except they weren't, they were the fairly developed fetuses of pigs, hung by their necks and drying slowly. Wary of offending the family that was harbouring us, I asked no questions until I stopped in La Paz, where I later gleaned a little information about this apparently common grotesque custom.

La Paz sits overflowing out of the bottom of a deep valley, more than 3,200 feet below the Altiplano that surrounds it. On the northerly side near the airport the city's impoverished edges have spread onto the uplands to form El Alto, home to the majority of the working class, where the houses sit on top of each other and the streets are clogged with the fumes of decrepit cross-country buses arriving in the capital.

By the time Giannina and I had rattled down the dangerously potholed concrete road into the center, the harsh sun and wind had reddened the tip of my nose and my lips had become cracked and ulcerated, making it painful to speak. Gianinna had, after two days, reached her pedalling goal and planned to rejoin her friends in the city.

By this time I was only too willing to stop, despite the fact that I'd rested only days before on the shores of Lake Titicaca. This vibrant and colourful city was all the excuse I needed and I quickly found a job at the popular English Pub to somehow justify pausing here. The stress of travel had taken its toll. Physically I'd changed. The mountain weather and sun, when it had appeared, had caused wrinkles to appear when I smiled, and my skin flaked off in dry chunks, often getting stuck in my long, sun-bleached hair. With slight alarm I realised, looking in the mirror one morning, that I looked a little like a Brazilian footballer who had fallen on hard times. Mentally though, I was done, stopping at every available opportunity, and rolling south again a little more sluggishly every time, loath to be leaving what stability I found myself building within hours of stopping somewhere.

My walk to work took me first past Plaza España, where I would stop, do chin-ups on the climbing frame and watch small children battle it out on the wonky table football tables that live every night under the slide until an elderly man arrives to ready them for action. Down the steep cobbled streets I'd walk, past the policeman, arms casually folded over his shotgun, onto the main street suddenly hit by a turbulent stream of interesting faces, from large indigenous women (*cholitas*) toting huge amounts of booty or a child or both wrapped in a shawl, to sophisticated businessmen talking on their mobile phones, or fashionable students loitering with their friends outside a pizza parlour.

By the time I'd reached the pub each day, I'd seen shoelace salesmen, old ladies selling spoons, a million pirated DVD stands and the accompanying music videos, policemen in big white gloves trying in vain to direct traffic, a Chinese restaurant called Jackie Chan and a small stall selling my favourite biscuits, which I would inevitably make a stop at before entering the confines of work, quiet, early in the day.

Only when I re-routed one day did I encounter the Witches' Market, given its name by the tourist trade due to the weird and wonderful objects on sale. It was here that I came across dried llama fetuses, and recounting my pig memories to the saleswoman she explained to me that the custom of burying particular animal fetuses under your house or in the yard was thought of as good luck. A little further down the hill I found my spiritual home, the culinary heart of the great city, not far from the cathedral, where under the Lord's watchful eye I would regularly recharge on at least four sausage sandwiches and a litre of freshly blended fruit juice.

Travellers had informed me that the people of Bolivia, in comparison to their neighbours, are squat and ugly. While many of them are indeed on the short side, I didn't find the ugliness to be true. In fact the bar became a particularly agreeable place to work in due in part to the girls who worked with me, with their beautiful jet-black hair, warm-coloured skin and infectious smiles. Coupled with the flirtatiousness of the Latin culture, it became a hard place to escape from willingly. However, after making a short foray away from the city to become the first tandem to cycle from the jungled base to the top of the cloud-cushioned precipitous track commonly dubbed the world's most dangerous road, I did escape, after a couple of weeks, clad in the guise of a super-hero and with the gap-toothed Lancastrian pub landlord Ollie in a similar outfit sweating back up to the Altiplano behind me.

That had been his condition – he'd accompany me for a day or two, but only if, for the duration, we wore two Spiderman outfits he kept for fancy dress parties. There was no way I was going to let a mask and some tight-fitting material get in the way of potential companionship, and so for a day and a half the drink-addled Ollie, once a keen biker, helped me along the long, straight roads south, the sustenance in each small grubby village becoming less varied and dirtier. Ollie's strength came largely from the small bag of what I can only assume was tobacco, which would be ceremoniously unpacked and drawn from at each rest stop. After a bland lunch on the second day he left me, having had enough and wanting to return to the cozy gringo confines of his pub. He waved and walked over to a small bus, which sped off once he'd boarded in his felt hat and one-piece Lycra suit, revealing a large gathering of people in the plaza.

In the time it took me to finish my rehydrated black potatoes –

common in these parts – and a generously boiled piece of mutton, what had seemed to be a pleasant gathering in the tiny plaza had transformed, swollen across the highway into an animated road block of weathered faces nodding or shouting in time with a solid little woman wielding a megaphone. Others busily carried rocks or tires into the road to stop the traffic. People had warned me about the localised political volatility of Bolivia, every small municipality fighting for indigenous rights in a disjointed display of nationalist passion.

I gingerly approached the backs of the *campesinos* focused on the powerful woman in charge. One or two grinned, and others ushered me past while the rest of the traffic remained stopped behind boulders, burning tires and the throng of people. I dared to think that I was in the clear, edging my way slowly through the mud next to the makeshift podium, when from behind me I heard an angry voice shouting out.

'Why are you flying the Bolivian flag?? You're not Bolivian!'

Until now, flying the flag of the country through which I travelled above that of my own had done me nothing but favours. But now it seemed my act of diplomacy was backfiring. The woman's megaphone fell silent, the chanting died out, and all eyes turned on me. Suddenly, feeling the prickle of adrenaline, I frantically looked out at the crowd, trying to guess the answer that would prevent me from becoming a capitalist straw man to be thrown on the burning tires like Guy Fawkes. It must have only been seconds later when I shouted back equally aggressively and instinctively, 'Because I love your country!'

As quickly as they'd flared, nostrils relaxed, questioning brows softened and cheeks creased into smiles as the sea of little hats and long shiny braids parted for me. A smattering of applause followed me down the highway for 20 yards south of the gathering before the megaphone swung into action once more, and I wiped the sweat from my face. Only then did I look down to see my red, web-encrusted legs powering Achilles away from the mob – it dawned on me that the entire drama had been conducted in my new one-piece Spiderman costume.

Strangely though, I remembered more questioning looks when wearing my normal cycling garb, so I was forced to assume that either Spiderman passes through this part of the Altiplano frequently, or that the locals regard the get-up as a very practical, if slightly snug, weather-repelling suit.

Alone again and with no more road blocks, the roads quickly got emptier and turned to dirt. As the mountains that hemmed in La Paz grew distant the sky got bigger and the customary afternoon cloud bank often never came. The mountains never completely disappeared, but travelling on a high plateau meant everything but their summits was below me. The sky seemed to roll down past the horizon exaggerating the curvature of the earth, and the snowy skyline, like the Cordillera further north, was replaced by distant dusty volcanoes. There was no longer moisture in the air as there had been on the pampas, and the washboard roads were dry enough for the light dust to linger in the air when a vehicle passed.

Rarely was there anyone to talk to here, but every 30 miles or so there was a village, brown and dusty like the road. In between the settlements the road sometimes passed over a shallow river, where I'd stop and wash the dust off my body and tuck into the plentiful supply of bread I'd bought in preparation for long stretches of nothing. At the rivers it was common to find a boy or a young brother and sister sitting playing never far away from their herd of llamas or alpacas grazing in the short, spiky grass. I'd relish their company, sitting nearby and greeting them, after which talking would be scarce, the sociological gap between us seemingly too large to breach in just a few minutes together. Once I passed an elderly man riding a bicycle in the opposite direction. There was nothing for miles and the tires of his antiquated bicycle had thick pieces of square rubber stuck on the outside, presumably primitive patches.

With increasing distance from the tiny settlements the road would disappear under deep, drifting sand with growing frequency. After getting bogged down a few times, wheels spinning and kicking sand up into the chain and pedals, I found that if I travelled at speed I could, providing the sand trap didn't last long, barrel through to the other side, skidding without steerage through the powdery trenches thanks to the weight of Achilles.

INTO THE LAND OF THE COCA LEAF

Edging closer to a large white lake marked on my map, I passed moonscapes with the ruined carcasses of abandoned adobe settlements. I stopped to explore the remains of a modest church, intricate designs in the crumbling mud walls still visible. In the musty darkness inside I made out an altar, collapsed under a couple of crude joists from the roof. The only sounds were the buzzing of a large fly and the persistent breeze that made my flags flutter noisily outside. Other than that there was nothing. The air almost felt dead. I left quickly, feeling uneasy, as if something bad had once happened here. The occupied villages only felt marginally more alive, the main differences being a functioning water pump allowing me to restock and a new sign warning drivers to watch for schoolchildren crossing. Rolling through these places, the lack of cars and children made these signs – new and clean – look comical and out of place.

After four days of this upland desert with the road worsening, I rolled over a small rise to see the lake, El Salar de Uyuni (the biggest salt lake in the world), for the first time. The white, shimmering landscape seemed to brand itself on my eyes enough for me to have to squint. With the haze blurring its boundaries, the white seemed almost endless, only separated from the sky by a rippling line of barely visible mountains. I had wanted to see this place for months, and the view charged me with the tolerance and energy needed to continue the 12 remaining miles, through the dirty and distinctly salty village of Colchani to the next oasis, Uyuni. The washboard troughs saved the worst for last, almost big enough to swallow the trailer wheel. Achilles and I bounced forward stressfully like the bobbing head of a pigeon, close to stopping each time the anchor-like trailer dragged over the sandy ridges. And then herringbone bricks took over on the outskirts of town and I rolled gratefully into what looked like the set of a Mad Max movie. A small town in the middle of nowhere, bordered by salt on one side and sand on the other. Harsh describes the landscape here, beautiful but harsh. From the rusted hulks of a hundred old steam engines listing heavily on their sides in the desert, to the bright partially water-filled salt plains, the horizon constantly muddled between surface and sky.

TAKE A SEAT

Not really knowing where to look to best take it all in, I cycled slowly down a street and stopped next to a ripped sign advertising a *pension* down a lopsided alleyway beneath a tangle of electrical wires.

Cycling across that vast expanse of salt, I'd decided, would be a spectacular experience, and despite the fact I'd in all likelihood have to make a round trip from Uyuni to pick up a navigable road south, it seemed like an opportunity too good to miss. During my first evening in the small town, I found via email that Adam now had a telephone number. I called it, unable to think of a better companion on Achilles for a ride across El Salar. As his phone rang, I silently prayed that he'd be able to take a couple of days from teaching at the language school to join me.

18

The salt leads south

DAY 630: 14,512 MILES

I'd urged Adam to replace his one dollar 'Gucci' glasses with something of better quality before he joined me. I hadn't thought about it until hearing about a Dutch cyclist found by the Bolivian army cycling in huge wavering circles out on the salt flats, apparently totally disorientated. He'd been blinded by the glare of brilliant white and, but for the chance encounter with the army, would have been left to dry up in what must be the most dehydrating place on Earth.

Retracing our steps to the dishevelled village of Colchani, Adam grumbled about the ruts that had aggravated me two days before, and more than once warned me that if I carried on over the washboards my rear saddle would disappear up his rectum. I grinned to myself sadistically, until I turned round to see that despite my advice Adam was bouncing along with the same knock-off glasses. He told me not to worry, he had another pair he'd bought especially.

Turning left off the main road after buying two warm beers and three blackened and lonely looking bananas, the road changed. The dust got paler and the washboard disappeared. On either side, large white tide marks in the earth appeared, matching those on my shirt after days of sweating. Then the pale earth was replaced with water, saline pools sometimes more than a foot deep covering the salt each side of the small causeway we rode on. The whole environment became a bluish white, like a Bounty Bar advertisement without the refreshing

227

coconut palms, and with harsh cubic salt crystals crunching under the tires instead of sand.

I propped Achilles on the broomstick I'd purchased especially to counter the lack of parking facilities in this 2D wilderness, and surveyed the road ahead where it disappeared for perhaps 600 yards under a blue mirror of water. Adam rummaged in his pouch behind the back seat and retrieved a pair of glasses. They looked suspiciously cheap – reflective aviators that had La Paz flea market written all over them. As if to confirm my suspicions, Adam proudly put them on without taking the others off. He smiled, waiting for my response.

'Can you see anything?' I said, suppressing a laugh.

'I can see most things, in outline – my eyes aren't burning as much any more,' he said, still grinning, obviously pleased with his economical though bulky eye protection.

Feeling the sharp crystals digging into our now bare feet, we set off, carrying the equipment as we waded across the shallows to the dry salt. The salt punished us more the softer our feet got, causing us to adopt an awkward gait, like cartoon characters attempting to creep up on their enemies.

A gaggle of Land Cruisers packed with tourists had arrived on the shores of the Salar now, and they drove by plowing a V of ripples through the water, passengers staring and clicking cameras at us, the animals in this spartan safari park. The pain of carrying Achilles through the salty water was, unfortunately, necessary. I arrived on dry salt with a dent in my shoulder from the bike's weighty frame, but secure in the knowledge that I'd saved Achilles from the rotting effect of the heavily saline water, the splashes of which were already drying white and crusty on my legs and shorts.

Arriving on the other side of the shallows and getting back on the bike, Adam and I cycled past a field of chest-high soggy white conical mounds. The salt was being shovelled into these piles by two men, wearing ragged balaclavas to protect their faces from the burning glare. The salt, Colchani's currency, would be loaded onto a truck to be taken and processed for consumption.

Slowly the white surface got firmer as we pedalled away from 'dry land'. The tire tracks from the Land Cruisers gradually disappeared into nothing and cracked crystalline polygons took over, the raised edges of each catching the sun as it sank lower in the sky.

When it eventually dipped below the horizon, the sun's dry, oppressive heat was replaced by a void of cold. The salt hemorrhaged heat like the air, no warm ground to lounge on admiring the view, just a sudden bitter cold and a building wind pushing smudges of lenticular cloud over the distant mountains. Darkness in this place was only relative, with the ground glowing with what light the stars offered. But as Adam and I cooked pasta clad in all the clothes we had, the distant mountains disappeared, only visible in the regular and silent flashes of lightning that traced the edges of the Salar. Those distant storms made me worry quietly about the road ahead. I knew the roads – or lack of them – taking me to Chile would be a challenge without violent storms thrown in at over 16,000 feet above sea level.

Other than the friendly roar of the stove and the fluttering of tight tent fabric, it was quiet. The tourists had returned to Uyuni, and now our tent and Achilles propped on my broom handle were the only objects protruding from the flats until the salt met the shores of Fish Island, 25 miles to our west. We needed to reach the island the following day to replenish our water supplies. Late that day we had been unable to distinguish the island from the band of peaks on the horizon. If we couldn't find it, with nothing to orientate ourselves by, we'd start to dry up pretty quickly, like the Dutch cyclist I'd read about.

Adam shivered violently next to me during the night, the salt offering little insulation. He even threatened to squeeze himself into my bag and put his feet in my armpits some time before dawn. But as soon as the sky began to redden with morning, we got up and shook the blood back into our extremities on the salt, still covered by the long blueish shadows of the distant mountains.

In the first immediately searing rays of the high-altitude sun, the faint tire-tracks of a jeep caught the light where they crushed the edges of the salt polygons. Following them, we reached the island's shores two and a half hours later, tired, dry and down to our emergency biscuits. The cold of the night had quickly turned into a mouth-watering memory as the salty sweat stung our eyes, Adam's still covered by his two pairs of shades, the second of which slipped off the end of his nose regularly. On rounding the dark cactus-choked peninsula, an unexpected and incongruous sight greeted us.

Fifteen Land Cruisers were parked up on the browning salt near the 'beach'. A group of shirtless and reddening tourists played an expansive game of football and behind them, an area of cacti had been cut back on the island to house five stone buildings, a hostel and a restaurant among them. Usually I'd have had something to say about this scar on an otherwise pristine landscape, but I was too hot and thirsty to care, besides I'd relieved myself on the salt earlier that morning, destroying any chance of 'taking only pictures and leaving only footprints'...

After eating and drinking and topping off a litre of guzzled water with a celebratory beer, we wandered through the maze of cacti to the island's highest point, where in every direction salt stretched away for at least 40 miles. But after 24 hours looking at this incomprehensibly beautiful environment, it had become unpleasantly harsh. The crunching rattle of the salt as we rode and the solid grip of dry heat had burnt us into submission. Adam's half-Pakistani skin had turned dark and my hair, freshly bleached by the salty sun, stuck to my cracked lips when the wind blew. Using the dribbling tap behind the hostel we filled up our five water bottles and headed back to Achilles resting on the beach next to the trucks, not looking forward to the gruelling return journey but now hungry for the dusty track that existed on the far side of the salt.

The next day, having to teach English to his class of Bolivian students in La Paz, Adam left. The day after that, after stocking up with six days of provisions and a new broomstick (the last had shaken out of the trailer on the washboard road), I left Uyuni in the opposite direction, alone again.

I was alone by choice, there being no shortage of tourists in the little town of Uyuni who were keen to hop on the back. I heard from other riders further north about the Lipez region I was about to ride into. It was hard, they said, covered in deep sand and climbing high enough to get sick with the altitude. At night, Christophe had told me, it could drop to below -4°F, and what little precipitation there might be would fall as snow or hail. However, more than a companion's ability to handle this shock to the system, I feared for the failing strength of Achilles' rear wheel. The rough roads leading here had taken their toll, and I'd regularly found myself replacing snapped spokes in the dust, as the rear rim slowly deformed with the stress of each bump. Putting another 132 pounds on that wheel I thought might destroy it altogether with no hope of being able to replace it for over 600 miles, the distance I'd have to cover to cross the nothingness of the Atacama desert.

Lipez stretches to the very bottom corner of Bolivia, and 60 miles south of Uyuni villages disappear altogether. Some days I travelled less than 20 miles, the sand clawing at my tires as I crawled upwards, leaving me regularly floundering and struggling to push Achilles back onto equally frustrating rocks and pebbles. This degree of physical difficulty had in almost every instance in the past reduced me to a frustrated, screaming rage. But in the thin air of Lipez it was different. The landscape, more than the dramatic Cordillera Blanca or the tunnels of Duck Canyon, hypnotised me into a state of tirelessness, keen to find out what was to come, what would reveal itself around the next corner.

First in a harsh headwind there was a wide flat valley where the red sand was dotted perfectly regularly with mushroom-like clumps of hardy grass between which I camped. On the next slow climb, a tiny stream was fringed with such intense greens they looked fake against a backdrop of ultramarine skies and rust-coloured rocks. Then I sped down towards 'Laguna Colorada', a blood-red lake where from a distance I could make out the vivid pink dots of flamingos standing spindly legged in the shallows. I cycled up into mountains the colours of which I'd never seen outside garish urban advertising or primary-school finger-painting. I guess that's why they call this place Dali's desert. Melting clocks and elephants with huge obelisks on their backs were all that was missing. Huge jet-black boulders sat, hard to say how far away, in a sea of rich yellow sand. The sand was backed by mountains laid down in beds of a million shades of greys, red and browns, like a glass rolling pin I once saw in my childhood with all the different sands of the Isle of Wight inside, stacked on top of each other. One thing didn't change though while I cycled through these Technicolor landscapes. Every morning I would wake up and wait for the sun to reach me. Even then it would take a half-hour for the ice to slide off the tent fabric, and an hour for any water bottles I hadn't kept in my sleeping bag to thaw. Without the sun, and with insufficient air to trap heat, this place turned into a freezer.

At the end of one long day, gales having tried to beat me back the way I had come, snow was beginning to come down, stinging my face as I topped out on what looked like the last draining hill of the day, well over 3 miles above the distant sea. Before me lay a confused mess of sandy vehicle tracks leading off between a similarly muddled collection of sand dunes. I desperately needed to shelter from the encroaching weather, made harsher by the altitude, and so blindly followed the most prominent of the ruts over a lip in the dune bank and into the next watershed. Half a minute later, in the wind shadow of the darkening mountain, I was looking over a valley like no other. Below me, a collection of geysers fumed slowly in the cold air and the setting sun had suddenly turned the primeval valley floor a glowing amber. The dense plumes of sulphurous steam cut blurry-edged shadows in the hummocky sand, and out of the wind the only sound I could hear was the hissing of one of the vents on the valley floor. I camped that night amongst these craters, but, while bubbling ominously, the smell of rotten eggs forcing its way through my tent fabric, the heat from them didn't stave off a temperature of a brittle -13°F in the moonlit crystal-clear air.

It had been a week now since I'd bought fresh food, and I was craving something juicy to supplement the pasta and mayonnaise that were keeping me going – and could do so for another week if things went pear-shaped. Despite the landscape's fortifying effect on me, my body was wearing down, losing weight little by little with every day I survived on the basic rations in my bag. I was getting close to the border, two, maybe three days away at most, depending on the sand. On the Chilean side of the border the roads changed, I'd been told. Tire tracks in the sand on the Bolivian side apparently transformed into smooth asphalt after the checkpoint. The best news, though, was that the road descended non-stop for almost 30 miles, to arrive in the wealthy tourist-filled town of San Pedro de Atacama, which sits on one of the driest desert plains in the world. After eating my pasta I played my harmonica and wrote, fantasising about the foods I would eat and the parties I'd have once back in civilisation. It was always like this – the next town was always that highly sought-after oasis of people and food, encompassing everything I craved so badly during periods of isolation. During those times, even after more than a year and a half of getting used to it, loneliness and that all too familiar feeling of missing the life I'd just left behind me would slowly invade as I sat in my little glowing tent, it being too cold and dark to go outside but too early for my eyelids to start drooping.

I slept in all my clothes that night, buried deep in my sleeping bag with the drawstring pulled tight over my head. Even then I woke regularly, shivering until by tensing and relaxing my muscles I warmed up enough to drop back into a fitful sleep.

19

Towards the Pastors' Passage

DAY 636: 14,891 MILES

The next morning I filmed the bubbling geysers, while desperately trying to massage blood back into my hands. Even the camera was feeling the cold, flashing messages warning me that ice was crystallising on the tape heads. Juggling it between my hands, I struggled to cope with the numbing pain of the freezing metal casing while the sun crept down the vapour columns towards the frozen flags hanging stiffly from my trailer.

Two days on I lay in the orange glow of a street light, a mangy dog loitering nearby eyeing up my dirty pots and a small block of cheese. I'd arrived in San Pedro after a long, long day of struggling to the border on the pass between two volcanos. The road did change as I'd been told, and despite exhaustion after the harsh sandy tracks, the tarmac encouraged me and I descended in the darkness. I didn't want to spend another night up there, not when I could see the twinkling lights of San Pedro 5,000 feet below me in the encroaching darkness. The two shivering Bolivian policemen at the tumbledown checkpoint next to the confused collection of desert tracks wished me well and I pedalled off up the remaining gravelly sand, past a weathered sign. 'Welcome to Chile' it read, the letters faded by years of alternating desert sun and frost.

The dog got up sluggishly and ambled closer to the remains of my supper. I smacked my arm heavily on the ground, the only movement I'd made for a while. He backed off to the scraggily dry tree in the corner of the yard and sulkily lay down again, smacking his lips. I'd found the cheapest campsite in town after searching with the last shreds of energy I had. I was too tired to try to make friends that night, though it was around 10 p.m. and the tourists were wandering lazily through the neatly swept streets after supper. I had no resources left with which to smile or converse, and a quick look into a doorway at a menu depressed me. The money I could survive on for two weeks in Bolivia would barely last a day here. Brimming over with self-pity, I'd got directions to this dusty courtyard from a kid in the street and laid down my sleeping mat and collapsed after eating the remains of my pasta. Any hopes and dreams I'd had of sumptuous banquets had been dashed by Chile's massively inflated prices.

I woke early, a deep sweaty sleep having allowed me to recharge on optimism. I packed up and wheeled my bike through the dust, past two dead trees and the now sleeping dog. Past the local chicken coop, through the wooden gate hanging bent off its hinges and into the cobbled streets, still cool and fresh, where I sat with my back against the cool white walls of a small colonial church. In front of me was the small, rich square where a couple of early-bird tourists took a stroll before breakfast. In the middle of the square was a large, leafy tree. I hadn't seen anything like that since the downtown tree-lined streets of La Paz.

My mood got slowly better. I picked up a lovingly prepared care package full of nuts, maps and books that a girl I'd met in Uyuni had left at a hostel for me, then I made my way down to a café she'd told me about. There, without much of an introduction, Christian Tarantola, the owner, made me his assistant, making juices and pizzas for those that had the cash.

I lived with Christian, and I ate for nearly free, sating my desire for fresh fruit and vegetables. For nearly ten days I lounged in this desert oasis, often sitting after work in front of an oil-drum fire in his yard on the poorer edge of town. We'd sit together in two old sofas left outside, drinking whisky and staring through the drifting sparks at Licancabur, the volcano I'd cycled past to get here. We compared notes in the darkness from the comfort of these couches – Christian had, like me, arrived to relax for a few days on a bicycle adventure of his own. That was a few years back. Now he lived in this bohemian paradise patronised by tourists. As much as I revelled in a string of bonfire parties, rubbing shoulders with new and beautiful friends from Santiago, I could see that San Pedro was the land of the lotus-eaters. It was strangely addictive, an artificial oasis in the desert that allowed outsiders to escape the pressures of the real world and live a life cushioned by a stark beauty and the safety net of the tourist trade. Christian's dream was to explore unknown ancient cities in the mountains further south, near his family home. He talked about the roots of his dream; as a child he'd wandered amongst ancient remains far from the gaze of archaeologists, and planned to go back. It felt to me though that those dreams were slowly decomposing while the hypnotic stupor of San Pedro strengthened its grip on him.

As soon as I felt its stranglehold on me I escaped the oasis, first bathing in the concrete conduit that brings the town water from the mountains. I left before dawn, and as the heat returned I had already crept from under the shadow of the majestic Licancabur, and into the full strength of the desert sun. Christian had his café to run, and the tourists in the village were on a schedule. Despite my best efforts to find a companion, I left San Pedro alone.

Twelve miles from town, once San Pedro had disappeared behind fluted dusty hills, I became a little intimidated by the Atacama Desert. The endless reddish stony land is a harsh, unforgiving desert. The broken wooden crosses of forgotten cemeteries half buried in sand creak in the wind; if you look hard into the searing opaque haze, you might see a bleached plastic bag rolling as if caught in the spokes of an invisible wheel, or a tattered length of toilet paper skittering along near the road, snake-like, before a stone or lonely twig snags its forward progress. Like the ocean's filter feeders, the brittle fingers of the desert shrubs seem as effective at collecting desert garbage as they are at sucking up what water exists in the parched earth.

The distance of the desert horizon and the straight black roads left me ample room for thought. My mind would wander in a super-heated stupor, making up rhymes or conjuring up dreamscapes of refreshing oceans or misty waterfalls. If I became aware of a truck or bus closing in on me I'd hug the white line, keeping the distance between me and the high-sided vehicle to a minimum and basking momentarily in a warm but refreshing turbulent wake of air. Sharing my life intimately with traffic for nearly two years had deadened any fear of fast-moving juggernauts.

Once, I looked up after the half-second refreshment had washed over me to see the back of a luxury coach. There was a picture of the driver, looking relaxed and smiling. Squinting hard I made out the words next to it – 'semi-coma'.

My mind wandered again and I grinned, imagining an only partially conscious driver weaving from side to side on the road, knocking down cyclists like bowling pins as he went: all drivers were required to be in a semi-comatose state before travel – it was the tour operator's rule. Rather than admitting to myself that the words were actually 'semi-cama' explaining the bus seats reclined comfortably, I chose to continue the little sketch show in my head to occupy time as my feet revolved mindlessly beneath me.

At night I would camp a little distance from the road, always in the open, no need to worry about moisture, since not even the lightest morning dew fell here. I tried, after a strong afternoon wind had surprised me the first day here, to rise early and take advantage of the still mornings. At 5 a.m. the hard light of the moon gave every little stone and twig a hard-edged shadow, making everything even more visible than during the day.

Then, after days of desert and only a handful of eerily dilapidated truck stops, moisture returned to the air and the smell of the sea came with it. The sea is cold here, but it didn't matter. Rolling from bone-dry mud hills to a small bay home to a handful of seasonal fishermen, I leaned the bike up against a stone wall and walked into the waves.

I continued to try to rise early, since the wind only strengthened on the coast and never came from the north. But mornings became cold and damp, making my early rises more of an effort than before. Sometimes the road ahead was dimly lit by the occasional lamp post as well as the spreading smudge of dark blue on the horizon. The heavy salty air seemed to dampen the sound of the lazy breakers chastising the rocks below me, and the white dotted line ahead disappeared over a small series of rolling bluffs. Sometimes I was awake enough to notice white splodges, hazard areas demarcated by the seabirds sitting on the lamp posts or overhead cables. I steered a drunken line avoiding these strong-smelling drop zones, not wanting to fall foul of an early morning turd from the sleepy guillemots.

Despite the damp, I enjoyed the novelty of the coast – rolling breakers, sea breeze and cool water on hand to refresh. Green became common, sand became a pleasure rather than an overwhelming backdrop, and the sun returned to being a welcome companion, fighting with the wet, frigid sea mist in the mornings. By 8 a.m. each day it had won and the mist had executed a silent retreat into the depths of small valleys and hollows until it disappeared altogether, allowing my stiff fingers to defrost.

Nearing La Serena – a popular place in the summer and the point on the coast that marked the start of the wealthy second-home paradise of those who lived in Santiago – after a long and tiring day of short, steep rolling hills, I pulled off the road in the late afternoon high above the coast on a beautiful scrubby headland. It was dotted with giant boulders, the occasional horse or donkey grazing at their bases. I cycled down a sandy track, excited at the prospect of camping in the middle of this rock garden, a climber's playground, and soon found the largest, most sheltering stone, parking Achilles at its foot.

It wasn't the first time I'd felt disappointment on this journey, but it was the first time in Chile. Around me, in every direction, were the remains of picnics, bathroom fittings, children's toys, even floral arrangements – presumably from funerals or cemeteries. There was garbage, broken, ripped and ugly, in every fissure and bush. It was something I'd expected in Bolivia and Peru, countries that have not yet solidified an infrastructure for collection and processing of waste. But Chile? It's practically 'first world', at times making the England of my now-fading memories seem old-fashioned and outdated. Chile has garbage trucks, it's got recycling, and I sometimes saw wind turbines on the horizon, or houses with entirely solar-panelled roofs. So why did a seemingly large number of people feel the need to travel some distance from their home to a beautiful, comparatively untouched area and dump their rubbish? It made me angry, not least because I couldn't pitch my tent without clearing space amongst used diapers or paper plates.

Instead of climbing, I built a fire and set about burning a mountain of rubbish. It was like trying to sweep the nearby beaches clean of sand armed with a toothbrush, but by the time the sun had dipped below a line of advancing sea mist, I had at least created a space in which to live and cook free of bleached bottles and cigarette butts.

The long, straight roads of northern Chile had allowed me to progress quickly, as planned, and with the quality and availability of bread, butter and chocolate milk stepping up as soon as I crossed the Chilean border, I even managed to gain a little weight. But the Atacama had starved me of one vital ingredient. Company. So it was with anticipation that I rolled into La Serena, knowing there was a chance Philippa, an Achilles veteran who had ridden with me already in Peru, was waiting to join me again. I walked into the first Internet café I came to and found I had a few new emails, but the most recent one was from Philippa. She said she would be waiting on the street I was on, next to a bakery. I swivelled round in my chair and looked across the street where I'd clocked a bakery, making a mental note to buy breakfast there. In front of it was Philippa. As she waved and crossed the street to greet me, I registered a fleeting look of worry, the sight of Achilles no doubt triggering the pain receptors in her bottom.

The look of worry turned out not to be unfounded. Burning the candle at both ends for a large chunk of her gap year had weakened her system sufficiently for Philippa to suffer in a big way not long after we left La Serena, having set off as soon as we met. Initially though, travelling in tandem again was everything I'd dreamed of in the desert. I even found a shower in a service station, and the girlie smell of Philippa's shampoo made me feel cleaner than I had for months. What with that, a new pair of socks she'd given me and the ocean road, things had quickly become rosy.

TAKE A SEAT

We journeyed nearly 100 miles together before, in the shelter of a small and deserted fishing harbour one morning as the sun shed its first light on the water, she announced that she had been broken by Achilles once more. During the night she'd lost her voice and coughed violently when she sucked in the damp air. An hour later, we said goodbye for the last time on my journey, as she hobbled onto a bus bound for Santiago.

Though her stay in my rolling hostel was short, she'd provided me with the burst of companionship I'd needed. I'd had no idea until the first night sleeping on the beach with Philippa how unaccustomed I'd become to company, but at 2 a.m., waking from a deep sleep, I found out. I stirred, lulled into semi-consciousness by the breaking waves on the darkly shining sand. There was, however, another noise, closer than the waves. I lifted my head and looked out of the open tent vestibule. There, a black dog was licking the dirty sides of my new pot, a much valued addition to my cooking set since it could easily accommodate enough pasta for two hungry cyclists.

Once I registered that the utensil was in some kind of danger, I let out a flustered bellow followed by a small flurry of swearing. The dog, pot gripped firmly in its jaws, disappeared, swallowed up by the darkness as it made its escape. A second or two later, still trying to wake up and orientate myself, something stirred next to me in my tent. 'SHIT!!' I thought. 'There's another thieving mutt in the tent!' Completely disorientated and confused now, I swiped at the moving object and let out a much less coherent and slightly scared 'Blaaaaugh!' noise. This whole episode flashed past in seconds. It took my brain another moment to register the face that had appeared at one end of what was in fact a sleeping bag. Philippa asked why I'd hit her. I tried to explain, my heart still racing, that it was because I'd thought she was a dog, though I knew as soon as the words left my mouth I'd dug a hole from which I couldn't escape.

Philippa was made of tough stuff, however, and sustained no lasting damage; and the pot was recovered a mile further down the beach the following morning, found next to a pile of broken beer bottles.

* * *

TOWARDS THE PASTORS' PASSAGE

Well before I reached Santiago I was embraced by friendship once again, extending its hand from Chile's capital 124 miles inland. As I was picking bits of my cheese and avocado sandwich, carelessly dropped, out of the sandy grass next to a tent full of surfers, four cyclists introducing themselves as Omar, Mauricio, Christian and Pamela arrived on shiny bicycles, questioned me about my journey and, on hearing I was homeless, without hesitation whisked me away to a rented house with a spare bed waiting for me! It was with this happy bunch that I journeyed to Santiago, Mauricio (also slightly worryingly known as Kamikaze) stoking for me from the coast, up the last hills and through two tunnels to the city, where we were expected.

Gersom Rodriguez, having learned of my journey, had emailed to say he would meet us on the outskirts and guide us in. From the moment we rendezvoused, I began to get wrapped up in a blanket of new friends from Santiago. I rested up surrounded by cycling enthusiasts who paid regular visits to my new home, the Rodriguez house behind the local church, inviting me to barbecues or shepherding me around interviews with the local news. This close-knit group of unpretentious pedallers – they called themselves the 'furious cyclists' – played off one another, each with a humorous idiosyncrasy that set them apart from the others as they rolled around promoting cycling as a mode of transport. Unlike them, I chose to ride on the metro, making new friends and allowing my legs to recharge for the last stretch of my journey south.

Two weeks later, yet again finding it hard to rip myself away from the quickly laid foundations of a new life, I left Santiago with Horacio, one of the 'furiosos'. He'd decided to give making beautiful ceramic masks and sculptures a rest for a week and sample a life on the road. We quickly tired of Ruta 5, the main north–south highway in Chile, and hung a left into the rolling hills and forests near San Javier, one of the principal forestry areas in the country. Memories of Oregon and northern California came flooding back as we cycled happily through the fresh, still air of autumn, pines, eucalyptus and native oaks colouring the folded hills with yellows and rusty browns.

Horacio seemed to fit in here too, his long hair flowing behind us and unkempt beard hiding the chin strap of his helmet.

A couple of days south of the city we reached Chile's vineyards, where tall, expensive gates hiding car ports and swimming pools made camping difficult. At the bottom of a nearby hill covered with pines, we found a track winding away into the trees. It looked promising, but after 300 yards a house emerged, a large, romantically dishevelled house. Horacio and I parked the bike and stood some distance away shouting, 'Hooolllaaa, is anybody there?' while trying to smile politely at the small band of dogs eyeing us suspiciously.

Half an hour later, after a lady had appeared tentatively in her slippers from a doorway partly obscured by wisteria, we were sitting in the classic high-ceilinged kitchen warmed by a large wood-burning stove, drinking tea and eating bread and avocado. The Astaburuaga family – part of Chile's aristocracy – had ushered us into their incredible home, awash with gleaming wooden floors and antiques that would make a museum curator jealous. On no account, we were told, were we permitted to camp outside that night.

Never on this journey had I slept in such luxury, another small wood stove at the foot of my bed, crackling soothingly in the otherwise silent house, generations of books sitting dormant in the library, and polished leather horse saddles hanging like figureheads on the walls in the darkness.

The next night Horacio and I were camped outside a quiet gas station, back to normal again, the palatial quarters of the night before becoming a distant dream, the physical remains of which was a bottle of the family's fine wine, which we sipped out of plastic mugs while cooking pasta in the damp air.

Only 12 hours later we were looked after again, but this time within the confines of the Busto family home, more basic but no less inviting. The two sons and their elderly father were building an extension to their squat adobe house, set in a large stand of pine trees, and had invited us in for tea after we'd pitched our tent under the trees nearby.

'It's OK, you can come in,' they said, 'our women have gone to town for the week.'

I asked what relevance this had, and they replied as if I should already know the answer. 'Foreigners always steal our women.'

The dry, smooth mud walls radiated heat from the stove-top crammed with simmering stews and boiling potatoes as we chatted and drank generous servings of *pipeño*, their potent homemade wine. Rather than expensive antiques, it was three beautiful strings of red chillies hanging to dry above the stove that added the colour to the Bustos' house.

As we pedalled between a brilliantly varied bunch of camping spots and hosts, the sharp cold of the mornings made me think about the road south. It was late autumn, and although snow rarely fell on the lowlands at these latitudes, it would be falling already all over Patagonia. The snippets of news I received from passing travellers or by email told me that other cyclists were hightailing it north again or heading home to avoid the vicious southern winter. If I had been sensible I'd have sped up, or refrained from resting for prolonged periods in order at least to try to beat the worst of the weather to Ushuaia. I was getting tired of travel, constant pedalling and mentally unsustainable transience. If conditions got too testing, I worried about my ability to push through, let alone get a stoker on board in less than inviting icy wind and snow. But when we were escorted into Concepción by the students of DUOC, a technical college that kindly offered me hospitality, I stalled again. Cordon bleu cuisine was waiting for me in the gastronomy department, as well as state-of-the-art edit suites to order my film footage in the audiovisual department, along with a plentiful audience, including the press, to listen to and publicise my voyage. Though a willing host and surrogate family with whom to spend my time were largely responsible for my stalling, the rain didn't help. It hadn't proved a problem in my journey for more than a couple of days at a time up until now – it would simply get me and my kit wet, forcing me to dry out when my skin became white and wrinkled. Normally traffic didn't bother me either, but on the lovely dry 'route of the Conquistadors' south of Santiago, I'd developed a healthy respect for the logging truck, with its playful and unpredictable second trailer. A number of these vehicles had whooshed past Horacio and me, causing even the pines flanking the road to bow lightly in their turbulence. We would feel the barrage of air shunted ahead by the flat-fronted cab, then the seemingly airless void as the first trailer blurred past our left cheeks. Then, sucking at the large surface area of Achilles and his two passengers, the second weaving trailer would pull us into the road for an instant before disappearing, fish-tailing well over the white line of the hard shoulder in a happy-go-lucky salute.

So, in the knowledge that there were 60 mph winds, standing water and no hard shoulder on the road south, I decided to wait 'until tomorrow' for a week, until the weather forecast didn't have anything negative to say about the following day. Then I left Concepción with a heavy heart and minus Horacio, my wanderlust having rekindled little strength during my rest. But I wasn't alone.

With a plentiful supply of students at DUOC willing to pedal, I'd snagged my first peace-loving, practising Rastafarian to ride Achilles. Of course, being a practising Rasta, Fernando wouldn't touch the tins of tuna and the mayonnaise that had become my staple diet.

We travelled south past the poorest city in Chile, Lota, where a disused and cavernous coal mine sits surrounded by the depression of sooty poverty, seemingly the last industrial barrier before the true south. Deep in the surrounding plantations, in pockets of still lingering native woodlands, we found the ghosts of a bygone era, our tarpaulin strung between the fly wheels of a traction engine slowly rotting into a carpet of yellowing leaves. We'd be woken in the mornings by the drone of logging trucks and the annoying whine of chainsaws felling pine to feed the construction industry.

Fernando was a very earnest character, only 20-something but looking older and behaving way older than his years. He rarely laughed, and occasional smiles were well-hidden by his thick beard. He was an ambassador of all things pure, and during a long, rambling conversation as we cycled along a road where the trees had given way on one side to the coast, he pointed out to me that we were travelling into the heart of the Mapuche region, the only recognised indigenous area left in Chile. Back in Santiago I'd made a point of buying a symbol of the indigenous people after my close shave in Bolivia, and now, as Achilles rolled on, my tattered and faded Union Jack fluttered weakly beneath the vibrant Mapuche flag.

I had chosen once again not to take the Pan-American Highway south. The only other sensible option was the coast, where I ended up with Fernando, stormy winds sending bands of frothing waves spilling onto the dark sand. After two days and with bad weather rolling in, Fernando bowed out, his knees troubling him and the predicted rain not exactly filling him with enthusiasm. I can't say I was upset. When a stoker no longer enjoyed their journey I could feel it. Pain or mental anguish lessened their power and I was left with more work to do. Fernando had been a brief and interesting companion, but I left him at a corrugated iron bus stop, content to be alone again.

In the small depressed fishing village of Tirua, the asphalt disappeared into puddles, giving way to *ripio* tracks (dirt – usually with uncomfortable washboard ruts) that took me up and down short, steep hills. The track was sometimes hedged in by immature plantations and at other times it followed a tranquil lake shore, occasionally passing a *ruca*, the beautiful traditional thatched dwellings of the Mapuche people. Miles back, near the Biobio River that marks the Mapuche border, I had been welcomed into their region not by a quaint touristy sign notifying me that this was the home of the 'Indians', but by some careless graffiti sprayed on the side of a small bus shelter. 'Indians, fuck off and die' it read in badly spelt Spanish with a swastika scrawled underneath. It struck me as odd that a small proportion of misguided Chileans use this sign as a licence to hate whatever they want, in this case alienating a significant proportion of their own ancestry.

My heart sank over the next few days as I began to realise the story of the dwindling First Nations blood in North America is not very different from the one here at the other end of the continent.

Apparently even today, kids can be heard laughing at Mapuche names read out in their class register, and well-meaning white folk often urged me to take care in these parts, for there are 'Mapuche' here, they warned, as if doing me a great service.

Needless to say, only a day after hearing these words of warning I found myself in freezing weather lodged in the cozy kitchen of a beautiful Mapuche family gobbling *cochayuyo* – a soup of seaweed and spices – and sipping on a bottle of moonshine filled with *chupones*, sugary flowers that had been left to flavour this spirit for the last year. The family talked in their native tongue, Mapudungun, a language rarely heard these days.

The plantations continued as I rolled south on forestry tracks, sometimes camping in garden shed-type bus shelters along the isolated roads. I began to notice the frost settling on my bike each night getting slowly heavier, causing me to tuck my water bottles in my sleeping bag again to keep them from freezing. Traction engines were increasingly abundant, not only left to rust in the forest but used as decorations in the small towns and villages that have grown up around the logging industry. They would line the streets, an open-air exhibit of the last century of iron workhorses.

I eventually popped out of the coastal plantations just short of the Germanic and beautiful town of Valdivia, where DUOC friends spent the weekend with me eating empanadas and sipping hot chocolate at German cafés. From there I journeyed into a land that most tourists know for its beautiful lakes surrounding the Fuji-like Osorno volcano. It was the start of what I came to know as 'the Pastors' Passage'. This doesn't refer to any kind of religious proctology, but rather the string of pastors who opened their doors to me, thanks to a kindly acquaintance back in Blighty. This part of Chile is evangelist-heavy and I benefited from this directly as each clergyman hooked me up with a fellow pastor a day or two further south.

It was in the town of Osorno that I experienced this heavenly hospitality for the first time, and the pastor's son took me to talk at his local university. INACAP was similar to DUOC in every way, including the response to my journey from the students. But rather than escorting me into their city, they escorted me out in the driving rain, and rode with me for two days, Marco the footballer stepping up to the stoking plate and five of his friends following along with a hurriedly assembled collection of bikes and luggage. One of the lads wore his climbing helmet and carried a heavy and unwieldy tent, sleeping bag and stove in a backpack that towered above his head as he rode. But the group's party atmosphere and high spirits kept me smiling despite the weather, and Marco's powerful thighs kept us moving quickly on a road made of sharp volcanic rock skirting the base of the volcano. At first, as we pedalled through forests stunted by centuries of eruptions, I thought it was just the bumpy road and Marco's heavy frame that were causing rear wheel spokes to snap frequently. Twice it happened within 20 miles of our turning onto the ash-strewn road, and the second time when I turned the bike upside down to set about replacing the spoke, I examined the rim. Looking carefully I saw the problem. It was nothing to do with weight or the cheap Chinese spokes I'd picked up back in Bolivia. The central strip of extruded aluminium was being subtly ripped out by the tensioned spokes, causing them to stress and snap. This problem was irreparable without building a new wheel, and that would be a hard thing to do down here. It wasn't easy to tell how much longer I could run on it for, but one thing was for sure, the less weight I had on it the better.

In Puerto Montt, where, after two days and a night's 'base camp' party in a lakeside forest, Marco and his crew of friends headed north again. I couldn't get a rim in town for love nor money, not one that was anywhere near strong enough for Achilles. The road further south wouldn't improve, and it wasn't long before I'd hit the famous Carretera Austral, an unpaved track snaking its way beneath the ice fields of Patagonia. If I broke down again there as a result of an unsuitable wheel, my journey would be finished.

The only way was to get something sent from Santiago, but that would take time, maybe a little over a week. Winter could advance a lot in a week, I thought, unwilling to suffer more cold than I had to. So instead I chose to carry on alone, loading the trailer with as much as I could to save the wheel, and arranging to pick a new one up in a week when I would return quickly by bus.

The island of Chiloé had been recommended to me as a place worth a visit, apparently full of tradition and legend based around isolated fishing communities where the houses are built on stilts above the waves. A short ferry ride took me over the straits to the northern tip of the island during a brief spell of blue skies. But soon the rain came down in sheets as I cycled along a road submerged under 6 inches of water for perhaps a mile at a time, soaking my legs and shoes with a heavy spray.

It was here I discovered that after two years of constant use the waterproof properties of my technical rain gear were left wanting. While riding through squalls when rain was blown horizontally, my jacket acted as a kind of one-way colander, allowing water in but never out until I emptied gallons at a time from my sleeve. It was because of my failing equipment that I was especially grateful for hospitality from at least a couple of pastors, who rescued me from cold, damp days of pedalling after nights sheltering in fishermen's sheds or damp cowfields. Even then I was lucky, able to find some wood dry enough to make fire in an old abandoned stove, or share hot tea with fishermen in the fairy-tale estuaries and bays.

Like other southern communities, life on the island revolves around well-fuelled cozy wood stoves, from where, to my delight, fresh bread was regularly produced while my dripping clothes hung on the rack above the hot plate, muddy water dropping and fizzing on the cast-iron surface. As I sat warm and content in the kitchen with various families, I'd watch the local news or read a paper.

For nearly two months by this time, every time I saw a TV set I'd hear about Chaitén, a volcano near Futaleufú that had been smouldering threateningly and spilling ash onto the surrounding villages. It was directly in my path and the whole area had been sealed off when I was all the way back in Santiago, temporarily severing the only road south in the country. I paid little attention however, never imagining that the effects of an eruption would last more than a week or two, but in Puerto Montt I learned that the region was still carpeted in ash, mud slides and suffocating smog, causing people to abandon their homes until the volcano had done its worst.

So, with little choice, after making a speedy return journey to Puerto Montt to build a new wheel, I boarded a freight ferry that supplies the deep south with fruit, vegetables and shellfish from the marine farms, embarking on a 35-hour journey through the channels and islands south-west of the affected village of Chaitén. The journey was in every way a breath of fresh air, giving me distant but tantalising glimpses of unclimbed peaks and precipitous fjords disappearing deep into the mountains on both sides. In the darkness I retired to the cramped saloon where truckers sat dozing or catching up with friends who often made this route. Achilles was lashed on the deck to prevent the waves that sometimes broke over the hinged bows from carrying him away.

As a large crate of bivalves gurgled and hissed, stacked on the deck next to Achilles, I thought about the two years and two days I'd spent on the road. During quiet moments like this I thought about the people I had met and then cycled away from. While my brain was full of beautiful experiences, I still felt somehow unfulfilled. I was getting close to the end, but my permanently pedalling away from stability detracted from my enjoyment of the present. I experienced a regularly recurring state of regret, and it was completely exhausting.

I arrived in Puerto Aisen sleepy and depressed, but snapped awake by 14°F and clear skies. I'd landed in a different world, as if, during the night, the boat had crossed into a place where the real cold lived. I was surrounded by a world of snow and ice, the pale blue of hanging glaciers poking out from valleys above me. While my progress seemed to be slowing, and from the permanently damp saddle of Achilles, Tierra del Fuego never seemed to get closer, this place felt geographically and psychologically like it might just be the beginning of the end.

20

· ·

Together come cold and company

DAY 720: 17,041 MILES

From Puerto Aisen I cycled inland to Coyhaique, the last stop on the 'Pastors' Passage', surrounded by freezing but sun-kissed limestone escarpments. I made good progress, inspired by the clean, cold air and the growing fringe of icy mountains, but my optimism ebbed away each day with the setting sun, when the cold bit deeper and my water began to film with ice.

The young *carabiñero* in the small police station at El Blanco saw me unpacking my stove in the bus shelter nearby and from across the road beckoned me into the guard room, where the chair and electric heater left just enough room for me to lay my sleeping bag out on the floor. Once the warmth had brought my nose and cheeks back to life I was unwilling to venture outside to retrieve my cooking gear, so dined instead on marinated chillies and a fruit juice I'd been given that I'd kept in my pocket. I slept deeply with the electric heating whirring near my face, but by the first light of morning my water, still outside in bottles on Achilles, had frozen solid. I stuffed some peanuts and half a mandarin in my mouth and pedalled off, trying to combat the bitter cold with an explosive bout of cycling.

The next village beneath the peak of Cerro Castillo was guarded by a high, ice-encrusted pass, but as I pedalled upward the sun and a lull in the wind rekindled my enthusiasm from the day before. I climbed up above the snowline, passing thick icicles that affirmed the fact that winter had very definitely caught up with me in Patagonia. Although I'd rolled in to what is regarded as Patagonia before reaching Puerto Montt – it apparently starts at 39° south if you're west of the Andes – this notch in the mountains felt more like the vision I had had in mind of this legendary region.

Stopping to rest and lean on a slightly sun-warmed metal barrier, I took in the clean, snowy landscape, sparkling like a festive window display. Behind me, in between the frozen waterfalls and the road thick with packed snow, a stream gurgled, hidden under an inch of ice. While the sun shone and the air was still, this potentially painful environment was beautiful riding territory, with enough traction on the snow as long as I took care, and views that constantly drew my eyes up to the serrated peaks.

But as soon as I reached the village, the tarmac ended and the wind began, putting an end to the winter wonderland experience. The road became bumpy and irritating but the snow and ice had stayed behind on the higher ground. It was June 24, the eve of my birthday again, and it seemed unlikely that this one would in any way resemble the last, in the sweltering yard of a fire station back in Panama.

The sharp, powerful headwind brought clouds scudding quickly back into the clean blue sky, and soon I was pummelling my way through it along the left side of a giant river, where I'd shelter in trees every time wind-driven raindrops threatened to blind me. As the weather closed in I rolled out of the river valley and into a dank, dead-looking forest. The thick cloud meant night encroached quickly, and any hope of camping in comfort faded when I arrived at a roadside shack only to find it full of long since extinguished candles, a once glowing shrine to St. Sebastian. A mist hung in the leafless branches of the trees as I pushed Achilles up an old and overgrown logging road and pitched my tent between a cluster of small trunks that allowed me to hang my plastic sheet between them.

For the millionth time the immediate surroundings, depressing already, were made worse by loneliness. In the darkness I was serenaded by the dripping of rain from the branches onto the plastic sheet, and when I woke in the grey misty light, the rain had stopped but the dripping continued, tapping out an irregular beat over which I sang myself – mostly for the benefit of the camera – an irony-saturated Happy Birthday.

It was as if the murky, Tolkienesque forest harboured the miserable weather, for as soon as I escaped from it blue skies promised to return, shedding shards of cold sunbeams onto the string of lakes I was following. But sunlight came and went in the tiniest of windows, and in heavy rain only an hour later I began to lose traction on a muddy climb. Then without warning my wheel spun and I went careening backwards, jack-knifing my machine and being forced to push as the light faded and the rain forced its way through my layers. Long after dark I arrived at the village of Villa Tranquillo and quickly scuttled into the tiny covered shack in the middle of the waterlogged park in a far from tranquil mood. From where I stood dripping I could see a light bulb lighting up a hostel sign. A birthday treat to myself? No, I decided, trying to feel tough. I had a dry spot here in this open-sided shed, and it was free. This far south everything was expensive and I was beginning to worry about stretching the seams of my home improvement loan to bursting point.

Having wedged Achilles into the shelter and walked to the small police post to request permission to camp there, the sergeant seated in front of a crackling wood stove was threatening and unfriendly. He told me in no uncertain terms that they didn't like vagrants in this village and that if I wasn't out before first light he'd see to it that I was punished. This sudden display of unfriendliness after months of the opposite struck me hard and I wandered back to my miserable wooden hut feeling a very special kind of birthday dejection. He'd even taken my passport to check I wasn't Israeli. Apparently he had a problem with Israelis . . .

Despite the weather remaining unchanged, my spirit was lifted marginally the next day when I found the only Internet connection in town before I departed. I had an email from Joselyn Moreno – a girl who had noticed Achilles way back in Concepción, and who I remembered meeting outside the university. Her email said she was coming – she'd get down to the town of Cochrane in a few days, about the same time as I would, I guessed, and having not considered it a possibility before, I was surprised and pleased that company in this wild and unforgiving environment was not so out of the question. Returning to my shack, I gobbled down my birthday meal of rapidly cooling pasta with a grin on my face. My clothes wouldn't dry here and my feet were white and flaky, but the good news buoyed my spirit.

The following day, wetter than the one before, I was rescued by a shepherd, Stefan. Beaten early by the rain, I'd made towards his small cabin in a field and he'd opened his small barn that smelt of saddle leather and dry hay. He lit a fire in an old oil drum before drifting wordlessly away, leaving me to hang up my clothes and sit in my shorts next to his dog, staring at the flames. I felt pathetic, I'd gone all of five miles before the rain had halted me again. I knew it wouldn't stop. This was Patagonia, famous for some of the world's worst weather. I beat myself up sufficiently to get up after two hours and retrieve my clothes, now half dry and smelling sweetly of woodsmoke. Before backing Achilles out of the barn I trotted across the boggy grass to Stefan's cabin to thank him and say goodbye.

'But I just made soup for us both,' he said matter-of-factly once I'd given my speech. All at once the policeman's unfriendliness of the night before was forgotten and I closed the door of Stefan's cosy two-roomed house behind me, unable to turn down hospitality.

Stefan was everything a Patagonian shepherd should be. He was a handsome man, tall, with a black moustache and a beret-like *boina*, the traditional headgear of the southern gauchos. He showed me the braided leather horse reins he'd made during long lonely evenings and told me stories of other travellers he'd met on this road. Once, he said, he'd returned from the fields during a freak summer snowstorm to find a 6 foot 3 German cyclist sitting on the floor, having let himself in, and drying his socks on the stove. Not wanting to scare the soaking giant, Stefan had walked quietly in and sat in the corner – I could imagine him calmly chewing on his pipe, just watching the intruder respectfully. Neither spoke the other's language, but within an hour he had made the German welcome and they sat as we did, albeit silently, sucking maté out of a wooden cup with a straw and keeping a small kettle simmering on the stove-top. I slept that night where the lofty impostor had barely fitted, on sheepskins stretched out in front of the stove, twice sitting up to feed the dying fire with another log.

In the morning Stefan made a small mountain of fried bread – *sopapillas* – which he emptied into a pillowcase for me to take, assuring me that this would last at least four days and keep me on the road. I realised, as I cycled over now frost-hardened mud under clear skies, that it was only the uncomplicated company of people like Stefan that was keeping me on the road. Most of the rest of the time I was becoming dejected, hoping that I'd roll up to the doorstep of someone like him. Often I did, and always, seemingly, just as I was about to give up my last reserves of hope.

A quarter of the contents of my pillowcase disappeared that day as I happily cycled along the track that criss-crossed the turquoise river, the surrounding mountains getting whiter. I made good progress and soon dropped down to the tiny harbour of Puerto Bertrand, the gateway to the ice fields that existed a little way down the fjord to the west. On the far side of the tiny community I found a pleasant meadow on the banks of the river. There were two old fire rings, presumably from travellers like me who had passed this way in the more forgiving weather of late summer. Soon I had a fire going in one of them and moved some stones into the flames on which to cook. It was freezing but beautiful, and the smoke from the fire billowed diagonally across the meadow pushed by a lazy breath of wind. I ate before the sun disappeared, stealing the warmth away with it, then crawled into my tent, kneading my cold feet in my sleeping bag. Tomorrow I could get to Cochrane if the weather stayed like this, I thought, where Joselyn would join me and the journey would become an unadulterated pleasure again. Once I'd massaged warmth back into my bones and as the nylon above me stiffened with the ice of a starry night, I drifted off to sleep.

At about 4 a.m. my journey changed. Up to this point I'd cycled over bits of snow or ice here and there, but it was the snow of weeks past, well packed and dry. Now I woke to the gentle sound of snowflakes airily collecting on my tent. It was an unmistakable sound I'd heard on countless climbing trips, and with it came an ominous glow outside as the dark landscape turned white. I carefully unzipped the vestibule and peered out. A small avalanche of snow fell onto the back of my head as I emerged, but I realised as I looked at Achilles, an inch of snow piled delicately on the top tubes and saddles, that I was excited. This change would make my journey difficult for sure, but it was different, spectacular, there would be a fresh bout of brilliant photo opportunities that would keep me fired up.

There were no tire tracks on the road, four inches deep in wet powder by the time I'd packed up. I gingerly experimented with pedalling and found that, providing I didn't put too much pressure on the pedals, I could make slow but significant progress on the flat and the snow crunched pleasantly as I went. But when the track took on an almost imperceptible increase in gradient, the back wheel suddenly started to spin. I tried again and again and the same thing happened, the whole bike slipping sideways, the shallow treads on my tires not digging deeply enough into the growing mat of snow. After a few minutes of pushing and slipping over every second step, the novelty of the snow had more than worn off. I'd been in it for less than half an hour.

As the hills grew again I resorted to walking up each one three times with a separate load, as I had done on the very first climb of my journey. Even then, with panniers slung over my shoulders, I slipped regularly, my summer shoes caked with snow and gripping less than my tires. I started shouting irritably into the flat light. The snow deadened the sound like a heavy curtain, making me feel smaller and more useless than ever. Cochrane seemed to grow further away, the slippery snow adding hours, maybe days, to my journey.

I saw one bus that morning, sliding crab-wise dangerously out of control down the hill I was walking up, a handful of terrified passengers looking out at the drop below them. At the top of the same hill I let Achilles fall into the snow and quietly despaired. Looking through the heavy flakes I saw a cow silently watching me on the other side of the bus's disappearing tire tracks. In a sudden fit of rage I hurriedly made a snowball and hurled it. I missed the cow, and hurled another which disintegrated in the air. The cow sniffed the air with lazy indifference before wandering off, plowing two lines in the snow, now nearly a foot deep.

The downhill was worse – my brakes were frozen and my feet lacked sufficient traction to stop Achilles gaining momentum. Together we'd fall down hills before I dragged him up the next. Darkness fell and I was still pushing, it was the only way to keep the blood flowing through my soaking feet. Stopping in this weather, I realised, would be dangerous.

I reached Cochrane that night after hours of sulky pushing, the white light of my head torch freeze-framing snowflakes in mid-air. Having forked out for a hostel to dry out and warm up in, I learned that the bus I'd seen was to be the last one for a while due to the snow. So that was it. The possibility of Joselyn's company had been suffocated by the onset of winter.

After a two-day rest, and restocking my exhausted supply of *sopapillas* with help from the kindly Tita Gomez, a schoolteacher in the village, I pushed on. The snow had been rolled flat by the odd vehicle and I was once again able to cycle, a new sun having occasionally burned through the snow to the gravel beneath. After escaping more or less unscathed from a dangerous sliding crash down a steep, icy hill – the result of getting a little overconfident – I camped in a forest, and found my stove pump had broken in the accident. Mercifully, the forest floor was just dry enough to provide ignitable kindling and I built a weak fire to cook with, which hissed as moisture escaped from the twigs and blackened my small pot.

The next day it snowed again, and the day after that it rained hard, then snowed. Patagonia seemed to be trying to stop me in my tracks. After three more days of alternately soaking and freezing travel, I found what looked like an abandoned army camp and collapsed in one of the dry, empty buildings, making it my home while the rain melted the remaining snow.

I felt by this stage almost numb with indifference. The weather had now destroyed and rebuilt my hopes so many times I no longer cared, and I treated this old army outpost like my home as the weather did its worst.

Rooting around the remains of life there, I found two candles and stood them on the crude wooden table, where they shed enough light to write by. I could hear, over the metallic rattle of hail and snow on the tin roof, a mouse exploring an old plastic bag full of powdered milk next door. The in situ 45-gallon stove crackled as I wrote and doodled, passing the time in the late afternoon darkness. I wasn't waiting for tomorrow so much as waiting to finish the journey. Any feeling of being close to the end was fading fast as yet another flurry of wet snow blanketed the landscape. I'd already learned that to fight for a pitiful amount of headway in this would result only in slippery frustration. Back in Cochrane I'd tried to make a pair of snow chains for my shoes, but all they seemed to do was cut off the circulation in my feet. I was very definitely paying the price for trying to forge ahead in a Patagonian winter.

I knew now that Joselyn would never arrive. She would have been something like partner number 265, I'd lost count exactly, but who'd wait long for another bus knowing they were heading into an icy misery?

I found an old, crumpled copy of *El Condorito*, Latin America's favourite children's comic, and sat for a while reading it, edging my chair closer and closer to the stove as the night wrapped its icy fingers around the abandoned building. I could hear, more than see, the consistency of the precipitation changing from snow to something wetter, no doubt leaving a translucent layer of dangerous slush on the track 200 yards away. If that refroze later, I'd be stuck here.

Looking at my dimly lit reflection in a broken mirror, I found I looked tired, with the dark rings around my eyes pronounced and puffy. Not so much lack of sleep I thought, rather lack of any reliable warmth, since damp constantly sucked it from my body.

After 48 stationary hours I found it difficult to find things to keep me occupied. I'd already swept the place, cleaning it for no reason. I'd read the comic and a scrap of porn mag I'd found while cleaning, and I'd drunk enough coffee to give me the shakes. Boredom rather than hunger caused me to empty another pack of porridge into my mug. I didn't have much food, but enough oats, I thought, to last me a few more days.

I found a sharpening stone amongst some rotting onions and a few jars of ancient condiments now home to a diverse variety of fungi. My knife was sharp, but I made it sharper, the methodical movement hiding my caffeine shake as my mind drifted out of Patagonia and into the past.

I was in banana plantations, or underneath coconut palms, and I could still just about conjure up the smell and images of sweet, putrefying mangoes while struggling to control the bike as kids jumped on like rodeo clowns. The only thing my mind struggled to reconstruct was how sweating heavily in a Central American 104°F heat under an ineffective mosquito net could ever have been unpleasant. I began to shiver and turned my chair around to lean on the stove, absorbing what little heat there was left before crawling into my sleeping bag.

I left my tent – pitched in an empty room – once in the night to relieve myself outside. The sleet had stopped and I could see a roof of stars. But before morning it had begun to rain, not hard enough to destroy the slush, only make it slushier. By the time I emerged again, the continual drip of rainwater in the grey light had formed a large puddle on the floor next to my tent. I packed, emotionless and cold, and plodded along, or cycled where thinning slush allowed me to. A mist hung over the ancient and dead-looking *lenga* trees and I walked with head bowed, not alive enough to appreciate the land I was inching through. The wonder and curiosity that I'd once had for every unfolding vista had been destroyed. Within minutes the clothes I'd painstakingly dried, smashing up a broken chair to provide fuel for the fire, were wet again.

I passed the odd group of road workers starting the work that would apparently see this wilderness road paved within a year to allow dams and electricity pylons to be built. I used to care about this controversial exploitation of Patagonia, but now I was more interested in whether I might scrounge a hot lunch off the workers or sit for a few minutes around their oil burner. When that happened I'd chat politely and gratefully accept hot stew or warm drinks, but I was emotionally detached, dreading launching myself onto the road again.

At Lake Chacabuco, with the help of a marine survey crew, I succeeded in fixing the fuel pump for my stove, replacing the crucial seal that I found had split. Lucky, since in another forest camp where more snow fell, the dead wood was too damp to light. But this time the snow was forgiving – there was less, and it didn't completely halt my progress. The road became a little flatter as I crawled towards the large coastal inlet that marked the end of this highway, and the wind, too, seemed to have taken pity, not blowing as hard, letting me travel calmly through straight black and white avenues of tall dark trees. After one more night on the soft comfort of sheepskins in the cottage of another life-saving shepherd I reached the village of Villa O'Higgins, the last outpost on the Chilean mainland.

As I approached the first buildings and a slight breeze rippled the small unfrozen patches of open water in the lake, a well-cleaned police truck approached me then crunched to a halt in the dirt. The window wound down and a smart young *carabiñero* leaned out, and as if to confirm what his eyes saw in front of him, asked, 'Sir, you're the man on a double bike expecting to meet a girl here?'

I'd written off any possibility that Joselyn might still be trying to join me, but answered him enthusiastically, daring to think that company on the road ahead was back in the frame again. Apparently she'd been held up for two days waiting for buses that had got stuck in the snow, but the cops had received a message instructing me to wait in Villa O'Higgins that night and possibly the next, until she arrived. I smiled at him, the bearer of glad tidings, and confirmed that I'd be happy to hunker down until she made it here. He sped off north, and I rolled into town, needing only a small, cheap hostel to top off my contentedness. Nice weather, the promise of company, a warm shower and some fresh bread and butter would, I thought, put the pain of the preceding days behind me. It was too bad that, as had been the case with the other tiny communities along this isolated gravel road, the people didn't possess that warm, welcoming Latin spirit I was used to, in fact their temperament for the most part mirrored the weather – cold.

In summer this place is crowded with adventurous travellers, but when I arrived it was deserted save for one man weaving drunkenly on his bicycle and shouting expletives into the wind next to a giant empty runway. After filling up at a small bakery-cum-hostel, I trundled down to the far end of the village, past six or seven bland timber houses to a nice cottage surrounded by trees, the police station. On the way I was spotted by the village drunk and, guessing I needed somewhere to stay, he wobbled after me on his own squeaking bicycle.

'Where are you going? Turn around, I'll take you to my house, five luca per night.'

'Do you have hot water?' I asked, wanting nothing more than a shower.

'No – yes,' the man stuttered, unsure, 'but my house is the other way, turn around!' he said. I doubted he had a shower at all, let alone a spare bedroom.

'I'm going to the police station,' I said, now only 100 yards away from the small white building.

'Aah, OK, I'll lead you there,' the drunk answered, taking charge and weaving in front of me in a sudden bid for first place.

A minute later I was sitting down, explaining who I was while the police told me what they knew about Joselyn's predicted arrival time. While the official talked he looked questioningly at the drunk who sat squeezed up next to me on the cramped sofa. Something told me he'd been in here before, but mostly on the other side of the small metal door on the opposite wall. After an awkward silence he looked up and registered the cop's expression.

'I guided this man to you,' he said weakly, ethanol vapour filling up the small room as he spoke. Then, losing his Dutch courage in an instant, he stood up unsteadily and walked out. The rotund cop smiled at me briefly, silently apologising for the mild intrusion, before instructing me, like the first officer, to stay here tonight and await the arrival of my 'friend'. Each time he said the word 'friend' he looked at me as if he knew otherwise. In Chile, a one-night stand or a casual bed partner is referred to as a 'hot water bottle with toenails'. Rather than try and convince the man that my sleeping bag was warm enough I let it go, smiling back at him as if to say he was in on my 'little secret'.

Grateful that the drunk seemed to have cycled off, I went back to the bread lady's hostel and lugged my defrosting muddy bags into the living room before showering, eating more bread and heading out again. I walked slowly around the tiny village, buying some snacks and supplies from a small convenience store and checking my email in the minute public library.

Joselyn didn't arrive that day, and I was grateful as it gave me a credible excuse to stay and rest in town for one more day – I was enjoying fresh bread and butter after a little too long subsisting on deep-fried produce. On the second day, I wandered up a series of wooden steps to a small viewpoint on the hill overlooking Villa O'Higgins. The village and airstrip sat flat and ordered looking on the valley floor. To its left lay the O'Higgins Lake and to the right, another smaller lake and the highway on which I had come nestled between the snowy peaks, some with glaciers bulging over steep drops, waiting to topple into patches of forest when the sun warmed the ice in the summer.

Villa O'Higgins, named after the first outsider to push into this territory, was the last village on the Carretera Austral. It was the end of the road, where Chile is split for the last time by the sea that cuts it off from the tooth-like peaks of Fitzroy and Torres del Paine.

I shouldn't have been here. It wasn't sensible. The summer's tourism had long since disappeared, and the winter weather had moved in to take its place. Things only got worse when I began to inquire about boat timetables to head south across the lake. I was nervous about the price, thinking the lowered demand might hike up the cost to extortionate levels. I needn't have worried. Not about that anyway.

'Boat?' a shopkeeper repeated at my enquiry. 'Boat? Ummm, no, I think they stopped a couple of months ago, and they start again in November perhaps, yeah, in about four or five months.'

'Shit,' I thought, before returning to the police station and confirming that this was true. There was no boat to the border crossing.

'So, what are the options then?' I asked desperately, flooding with miserable thoughts of backtracking along the road I'd sweated blood to come in on. The two policemen had a brief discussion before picking up a radio.

'Paso Mayer, Paso Mayer come in!' the man spoke into the radio handset. After a second or two of static the reply came through, 'Paso

Mayer, Paso Mayer, *mande.*' A crackly conversation ensued in which it became apparent to me that in winter, the only way south is to cross a rarely travelled pass to the north into Argentina, known as Paso Mayer. I had no choice.

By the time the dark-haired Joselyn arrived the next day, the bad weather had come in again, laying a fresh carpet of snow on the track we skidded up. But her boisterous company, coupled with the fact that some kindly gauchos crossing the border later that day had taken our heavy kit in their truck, made the ride manageable. Joselyn proved to be tough, she was a ski guide and seemed to relish the snow through which we cycled. Later in the day the skies cleared and revealed a pristine landscape, fresh, soft snow sparkling and providing more traction than usual.

Before sunset we reached the border, a small wooden cottage with a horse tethered outside. Inside was a policeman, who like those we'd met at O'Higgins was pleased to see a female, inviting Joselyn more than me to sit on the sofa and watch a badly dubbed Sylvester Stallone movie. Not long after the drowsy heat of the checkpoint started pulling at my eyelids, the gauchos arrived. I shook myself into action and went out to the truck to retrieve our stuff, but the largest of them stopped me.

'What are you doing?' he asked, genuinely confused.

'We can ride from here,' I said, smiling but suddenly realising I had no idea what this valley offered in terms of roads. Apparently there were none. Freezing rivers, he said, but no roads. I was too tired to dispute our riding ability and put my trailer back down in the bed of the pick-up. It was late and we wouldn't have got far before having to camp.

While there were occasionally the deep ruts in refrozen mud that the Argentinian gauchos had laid down on their way into Chile, there was nothing that resembled a road. The two vehicles travelled close together, waiting at the banks of each river before ramming the ice away bit by bit, forcing their way through. It wasn't the first time during my journey I was pleased to be sitting in a truck and not to be riding Achilles, and I felt decidedly guilt-free about the use of powered assistance.

That night we stayed with the three Argentinians in their isolated homestead surrounded by snowy peaks hidden by the night. The Fernet was broken out, a lamb stew was created within an hour and we ate and drank happily in front of a roaring pot-bellied stove.

All too soon, after an affectionate welcome to Argentina, Joselyn and I left, pedalling east for the first time in Argentina in the teeth-chattering cold of morning. The road hadn't improved, we pushed on stretches where frozen tussocks put up brittle barriers, and unlike the trucks the day before, we balanced delicately across any rivers we met, the ice fracturing loudly and perilously as we went. Joselyn would go first, tiptoeing across giggling, before I followed in her footsteps, teetering across with Achilles.

It didn't take long for my rebuilt wheels to feel the effects of the frozen ruts and shattered ice that plucked at the spokes when we broke through it. Punctures began to get common, and only when fixing them with numb hands did I find out that the new wheel had been badly built, with the overly long spokes poking at the inner tube within the rim until holes appeared. One night, having let ourselves into a deserted barn hung with carcasses of sheep, I did my best to fix the problem, wrapping old strips of rubber around the rim to protect the inner tube. On these tracks though, I knew it was only a matter of time before regular punctures came back, exhausting my already dwindling supply of patches.

Then one day the ice disappeared. The temperature had graciously risen, allowing us to cycle without wearing every thread of clothing we had. After porridge that morning outside another police checkpoint Joselyn and I cycled off, keen to take advantage of the dirt road free of sheet ice. Six, twelve, fifteen miles crept by in high spirits. I was even learning to understand Joselyn's rapid and mumbled Chilean Spanish without saying 'What?' every fifth word. The sky was blue and things looked good.

Then the increasing temperature caused a change that suddenly made ice preferable. Within the space of 100 yards on a stretch of isolated road, the mud went from semi-frozen to completely thawed. Achilles dragged and slowed to a barely operable speed. Thirty yards further on, with mud having clogged the wheels and chain into a semi-solid lump, we ground to a halt. Joselyn, who until then had worn a pretty smile, began to frown. It wasn't the muddy predicament we were in that caused this, it was the fact that she recognised the onset of my bad mood before I did. We cleared the wheels and chain of clay-like mud and started again. Within 15 yards we were forced to a halt again. The third time I lost it, and Joselyn hung back, allowing me to let off steam wrestling the bike forward alone, on foot. It didn't take much these days for me to transform into a short-tempered idiot.

It was getting dark, and beneath my angry carapace I felt guilty for putting Joselyn through this. I instructed her to take her backpack and walk on ahead to try to find a truck to pick us up. If we carried on like this the mud would snap the chain and probably the spokes. Doubtless keen to put some space between us she headed off, her headlamp bobbing off into the distance as I desperately tried to push Achilles. After 20 minutes on my own I gave up, shoving the bike and 90 pounds of sticky mud into the ditch on the edge of the track. I shouldered everything I could carry and marched off, Joselyn's light having disappeared round a bend in the darkness.

We walked 10 miles before finding the dim light of a road-maintenance trailer. The kindly Argentine duo inside needed no convincing to fire up the grading machine and trundle at a snail's pace back down the road to pick Achilles up with the digger arm on the back.

Thankfully that was the last day of mud we saw, and we cleaned the bike properly in El Calafate, another tourist stronghold not far from the translucent blue ice of the Perito Moreno Glacier and the Patagonian mountains. The same day as we arrived in Calafate, we'd cycled past the junction that would take us to the fang-like Torres del Paine just visible on the horizon. Despite having spent the best part of ten years dreaming about climbing those peaks, no amount of pristine summits would convince me to turn onto the track that led there. I was exhausted and that dream had, for the time being, been put on hold.

Two days later, a few miles after spotting a small flock of flamingos standing on the banks of a white and frozen river, we arrived again at the Chilean border. It had begun to snow heavily which, coupled with thick black ice, had already caused a few spills that day. The Chilean police did themselves proud at the checkpoint. They wanted to search my entire luggage for illegal agricultural produce. I couldn't believe it, and I smiled at them, assuming they were joking. They weren't. They failed to understand my rising anger as I chucked my belongings on the ground, fuming and swearing at the agriculture fascists. To make things worse, I haplessly unpacked a head of garlic. They snatched it from me looking pleased with themselves. I vaguely remembered having bought that garlic in the Chilean Villa O'Higgins, but I didn't bother trying to fight any more, packing up and riding gingerly through the thickening snow, falling twice still within sight of the border guards.

Despite worsening weather, frayed nerves and a repulsive mood, the border allowed me to feel that we were close now. The next time we crossed back into Argentina we would be within a few days of the end. Furthermore, with Joselyn due to leave soon, I had the company of Alonso to look forward to, a happy-go-lucky acquaintance from Concepción and an old friend of Joselyn. I hoped that, like Adam, Alonso had the clown-like tendencies it would take to see me through to the end of this journey.

But before arriving in Punta Arenas on Achilles with dignity intact, the rubber strips protecting my rim were breached again as we tried in vain to remain upright on an endless sheet of black ice, only 30 miles from the Magellan Straits. When Joselyn and I heard the 'ppffsssssss' of the back wheel blowing out for the third time in an hour, I put Achilles down in the snow, looked at Joselyn and gave her a hug. I was smiling now despite our predicament. My foul mood had cost me too much energy to maintain, and I'd abandoned it that morning in the fire station we'd camped in. Now, in this nearly Antarctic wasteland, with a road that resembled a mirror, the situation seemed pathetically comical. We swallowed any remaining pride and while I unhitched the trailer and took off pannier bags, Joselyn stuck out her thumb as a lorry rumbled slowly into view behind us.

The dirty white seven-and-a-half tonner pulled up slowly in the snow. The dwarf-like driver hopped down and greeted us with a cheerful smile. There was no question that he would come to our aid and he began unlocking the tailgate, opening it to reveal stacks of fishy smelling crates. On our asking what he was carrying, he reached into the closest crate and dropped something on the floor, stepping on it lightly and causing whatever it was to crack. After sheep's head, guinea pigs, locusts and an unsavoury cow's stomach soup, sea urchin added itself to the ranks of culinary firsts as I stood with the driver and Joselyn sheltered from the worst of the wind by the truck, scooping orange goo out of a broken shell. The sulphurous, gelatinous flesh was just about palatable, but for once, cold and feeling slightly feverish, I wasn't in much of a mood to sample anything. After polishing the delicacy off, we gratefully climbed aboard, with Achilles safely stashed with the crates. After a few minutes of polite but exhausted conversation I succumbed to the heaven of the hot, fogged-up confines of the cab. My head sagged onto my chest and I began to dribble.

21

The frigid land of fire

DAY 774: 18,156 MILES

I'd heard countless hollow promises from people saying they'd join me on my way south; Alonso was one of the few who was true to his word. Mostly people made their excuses when the time came, and sometimes they'd just fail to keep in touch. Even when Alonso had told me of his intentions months before, I didn't embrace the chance of his company despite the fact we got on well. He was a big guy, and I wasn't sure I wanted the worry of a weak back wheel and a generously proportioned stoker.

But after having the wheel rebuilt and a few days relaxing with Joselyn in the house of a good friend of hers in Punta Arenas, he appeared, all 217 pounds of him – I knew because we checked on the scales. Alonso had laughed, exposing his stomach and shaking his head, insisting the scales were lying. They weren't, and I immediately went to the garage and set about packing as much of the contents of the rear panniers as I could into the trailer in a futile attempt to spread the load.

After the black ice and mile upon mile of snow that Joselyn and I had travelled through, I'd reached the end of my slipping-and-falling-over fuse. With Joselyn's help I found remedy for more of the same in the form of a pair of nearly new studded tires stored hidden at the back of a garage full of adventure racing equipment. Those, combined with Alonso's downward force would, I thought, make Achilles unstoppable . . . or immovable.

TAKE A SEAT

Joselyn was so keen to accompany the two of us that she purloined a bike for herself, but our first attempt to leave was hampered by a high fever I'd developed quickly after stopping in Punta Arenas. My body seemed to be getting increasingly worn out. I felt a little as if I was in the so-called Death Zone at high altitude, where insufficient oxygen prevents your body from recharging or regenerating. In my case, however, the problem was more psychological – I was running on fumes when it came to motivation, and my body took advantage of this, becoming sluggish and weak, forcing me to curl up in the comfort of a bed for a bit longer.

But two days later the fever passed, and the three of us cycled the short distance over ice-rink roads to the ferry that would take us to Tierra del Fuego – the land of fire (given the name due to the cooking fires seen burning on the beaches by Magellan and his crew). With Alonso in the stoker's seat, we didn't accelerate quickly – we lumbered like a tank – but we did have traction.

The Magellan Straits have a reputation, and they didn't disappoint. Though only Joselyn lost her breakfast in the saloon bin, Alonso and I had to swallow hard between giggles to prevent ourselves doing the same as the car ferry rolled heavily and the horizon disappeared from view.

On the south side of the Straits the black ice had disappeared and the damp wind pushed the three of us south along a road that quickly turned from tarmac to washboard track. With Alonso keeping Joselyn and me amused with an incessant stream of mostly nonsensical babble, we cycled past a moorland artillery range, a line of burned-out tanks and one lone soldier crouching in the brown grass as exploding mortar shells showered the brow of the hill in dirt. It was a barren place. On one side the drab moorland and on the other, a dark beach with wind-strafed waves that looked even colder than they were.

As the road turned slightly inland the wind begin to hinder us and the ice returned, causing me to steer aggressively, sometimes directly into large potholes, in an effort to avoid slippery patches. Alonso's chat was silenced abruptly each time the back wheel dropped off the lip of the hole and he felt the full force of Achilles shock his coccyx and, rattle through him. I couldn't help but giggle each time he groaned and let out a *'puta madre'* in a breathy, urgent voice. He begged me to stop after half an hour of this, explaining that his 'hole' hurt so much it was as if he'd been violated. Alonso's constant joking made it difficult to take him seriously, but he was never as serious as on this rest, when he extracted his hat from his bag. It was of course a stupid hat, a fleece one that had holes cut out for the eyes and a tail like a dinosaur. He folded it carefully twice, then wedged it with a degree of precision into his underwear between his legs before experimenting, sitting tentatively on the unsympathetic saddle. It did the trick and Alonso began to chat again as the weather worsened and the wind sent hard flakes of snow stinging into the left side of our faces. That hat would have been useful Alonso said, squinting into the wind with a numbing forehead, but there was no way he was going to retrieve it now.

We found shelter before dark in a small empty farm cottage. The owner was nearby and unlocked the door, telling us it was empty but there was fresh firewood next to the stove. We should make ourselves at home he said. Saved, again, and just as the weather was ramping up into a full-blown Patagonian squall. Looking out of the window as the panes rattled violently, I realised that any nights stuck outside in this kind of weather would not only be sleepless, but stressful and dangerously cold.

The evening was spent thawing out once the stove had warmed up, and the three of us sat huddled around it in our thermals, conversations mostly revolving around the state of Alonso's arse and the dwindling possibility of using the dinosaur hat as a hat ever again. It got dark early, about four or earlier, on stormy days like this one, and the longer the evenings of inactivity became, the more I appreciated having not just one, but two companions. Any tensions of the day caused by cycling-induced stress were diluted. If I felt like writing or sorting camera equipment that was again getting problematically wet, there was no longer any awkward silence or pressure to socialise, since the others could carry on talking happily without me. And it did seem pretty happy. Alonso had got over an early bout of expedition nerves and the initial very real shock of the saddle, Joselyn had been reunited with an old friend and I was happy to be stuck in the middle of these good-natured Chileans.

I woke with my alarm early the next morning, before first light. Despite this I registered a light coming through the window that could only mean more snow had fallen. I got up and snapped awake in the freezing room as the other two dozed, and surveyed the fresh white landscape with dread. More snow fell, which in waves of wind-whipped spindrift attacked the building and peppered the glass, rattling the loose panes. At least now there were no real hills, Achilles was equipped with studded tires, and most importantly I had company. Thinking back to Adam and Barney, I remembered that shared misery was manageable compared with any unpleasantness I'd had to deal with alone.

Once the others were up and we'd made the most of the stove to make porridge and coffee for breakfast, we ventured back onto the road to find that the wind was in fact with us and the snow had all but stopped. When we were pedalling it was as if there was no wind at all, my tattered flags waving only slightly as we kept pace with the southerly gale. It was still cold though, so the necessary stops for Alonso to massage his buttocks and reposition the rapidly thinning hat between his thighs were bone-chilling. So much so that rather than get cold I adopted the role of a slave-driver, the same behaviour my father had complained so bitterly about in Colombia, not allowing a stop until Alonso's almost constant laughter or jovial expletives were interspersed with very real screams of pain. This cruel strategy meant we made good progress along the shore of another desolate bay until mid afternoon, 37 miles into the day when the temperature even while pedalling became cold and Alonso was suffering from the 'second day blues'. Usually day three was the clincher, but Alonso's premature exhaustion matched a strengthening theory I'd been developing for months. It was a simple flow chart in my head, a chain of yes–no questions.

Is my new stoker a cyclist/sportsman? No? Then three days is the stoking life expectancy, a period only increased by a hardy few or those who enjoyed my company enough to overcome the trauma. Not many. But in time I had added another question: does stoker complain of bottom pain within the first hour? Yes? Then stoking life expectancy can be reduced by 24 hours. This was the category in which Alonso fell, but in this case, he had no option but to carry on. There was no bus stop or train station to save him here.

So, as he flagged and I began to struggle with his dead weight it looked like we'd be caught in the open that night, with no homestead – *estancia* – visible on our side of the distant, nearly flat horizon. It would be cold, even colder now I'd lost every ounce of the macho bravado that used to insulate me, and it could be the last straw for Alonso. But then Joselyn saw a horseman, probably a shepherd, a few hundred yards away slowly trotting towards us.

Still 30 feet away the man greeted us as his horse skittered sideways, nervous of Achilles and his cargo. He wore the same kind of hat – a boina – that the other shepherds wore and he had dark, unkempt hair and a craggy, strong face. In response to our question shouted above the wind, Ivan told us there were no estancias for miles, but smiling timidly, he invited us to follow him to his small house, hidden by a rise behind us. As we looked back we could hear the faint and wind-snatched barking of dogs that had caught the scent of the horse or their master, or Alonso's sweaty hat.

We fought our way against the building headwind back up the track to a small gate and over frozen ground to a tiny corrugated iron hut, Ivan's home.

Three steaming plates of stew were placed in front of us almost immediately once the four of us had wedged ourselves gratefully inside, all but filling his one and only room. No sooner had I cleaned my plate than a rack of Patagonian sheep was produced and Ivan began cutting and sawing the shell of meat into manageable chunks. The big folds of tender fat tasted sweet, almost better than the meat itself – perhaps it was my body's way of ensuring I lost no more weight and had maximum protection from the cold. We ate well, filling the tiny remaining gaps in our stomachs with bread Joselyn made before she curled up under a sheepskin blanket Ivan lent her. While she got the blanket, on hearing about Alonso's predicament Ivan presented him with a strong-smelling tincture designed for cowboy saddle sore. The noises coming from the freezing outhouse as Alonso applied the medication indicated that the potion stung a little.

Before reclaiming his bed from Joselyn, Ivan told us he used to be a telephone engineer in Santiago but in a sudden reaction to the hustle and bustle of city life, he chose the opposite and moved down to this corner of a ranch, where he looked after 2,000 head of sheep, one of which he killed every week to feed himself and his dogs. He'd never had anyone stay in his house before. It got lonely sometimes, he admitted shyly, his kind, weathered face smiling at us as the cold enshrouded the metal hut, crystalline fingers of ice spreading across the tiny window panes. Once our sleeping bags were laid out, there was no floor space left. Ivan tripped over me during the night when stepping out for a leak, and Alonso kicked me in the head by accident while he slept. It didn't matter though, it was a tiny price to pay for some of the very best Patagonian hospitality I'd received, and the life-saving warmth it provided.

The next day dawned crystal clear and bitterly cold. Achilles had frozen to the small wood pile he was leaning against, and as I freed him and rolled across the rigid grass, ice pinged off the chain, the cog's teeth forcing it from the links. Then, as the three of us saddled up, waving at Ivan and sad to be leaving so soon, I twisted the shifter with my gloved hand to get into the lowest gear. There was a snapping sound and the shifter went slack as the gear cable fractured in the cold. Achilles was as tired as we were, and the -5°F that night had proved too much for the well-used wire. I dismounted, swearing, while Alonso held Achilles steady in his double-gloved hands. I guessed at a suitable gear, changed it manually with a spanner and we rolled slowly off on the mercifully flat track, the frozen dirt crackling under the wheels.

That day we crossed our last border, back into Argentina. The weather was kind, with barely a breath of wind and a sun that almost felt like there was warmth in it. The fence line running parallel to the road was hung at regular intervals with signs warning us of land mines, a hangover from the Falklands War as well as constant friction with Chile. Neither the llama-like guanacos nor the odd fox seemed to heed the warnings though, and once the skull and crossbones sign was dwarfed by a pair of enormous owls perched on the wooden fence post. As we crackled closer they spread their wings and glided silently over the road and out of sight.

The sun sank low and stretched our shadows across the brown grass as we left Chile and pedalled along the 8 or 9 miles of no-man's-land. We stopped once where two Argentine freight trucks were pulled up in the dirt. The drivers were setting up a gas burner and a big kettle on the bumper of the second truck and they beckoned us over to share maté, a social custom I was getting used to and fully appreciated. Before we left again, Carlos, one of the drivers, had climbed into his cab and retrieved a small Argentine flag for me to fly on the trailer. It was my last flag of the voyage, and it looked ceremonial hanging above my Union Jack, the tattered half of it that remained, faded and spattered with mud.

Alonso had gone quieter now and Joselyn cycled a little way ahead. When I turned around my stoker was no longer smiling or sniggering as he usually did. He looked drained and he frowned as he tried to overcome the stress of riding. The Argentine checkpoint was a welcome sight as the setting sun made the white sign glow and the temperature plummet. The roofed structure was adorned in stickers that said in no uncertain terms that 'The Falkland Islands are Argentine and always will be.' For me the Falklands War was a conflict of which all I could remember were headlines in the paper that I was too young to understand, but I was mildly concerned that the soldiers who manned this border might have a problem with me. After all, most families down here had had a relative killed in that ridiculous conflict. My anxiety so far on this trip had mostly been unnecessary, and with smiling squaddies beckoning us into the warm waiting room, the border crossing was no exception. They took it in turns to come and chat with us, obviously a little more enamoured of Joselyn than either Alonso or me, so while she fielded their advances we set about cooking and changing our studded tires for the normal ones now the worst of the snow had disappeared and the road south of the border was tarmac once more.

Alonso recovered a little of his clownish self as we got warm and filled up on pasta and soup, but it was as if a small part of him had ebbed away. A good night's sleep didn't seem to help, and during the following morning's ride he was almost silent. We stopped with increasing frequency for Alonso to sit by the side of the road with his head between his legs and for me to change gears if a small hill lay ahead of us. But by the time we reached the grey of the Atlantic just to the north of Rio Grande, Alonso seemed almost to have lost the will to live. All 210 pounds of him – I reckoned he'd lost at least 6 pounds during the last few days – sat limply on Achilles, unable to inject any power into the pedals at all as we struggled into town, where we stopped at the first place likely to sell fatty food. It was an empty fast food joint, not a patch on the Patagonian lamb we'd become used to, but sufficient for Alonso to struggle off the bike and shuffle inside, homing in on the smell of the deep-fat fryer. I sat opposite him and noticed he'd got paler and his eyes were bloodshot. We were, I guessed, two days from Ushuaia and I was glumly unsure as to whether he'd make it. I found out on a trip to the toilets that I didn't look much better. The rings I'd developed around my eyes in the first snows hadn't disappeared, and snot was slowly melting out of my moth-eaten moustache. My hair, on the other hand, looked fit for some kind of shampoo advertisement, blond at the tips and shiny, falling fashionably unkempt around my shoulders. As we sat there on the plastic chairs – the type that come with the table and bolted to the floor – we silently crammed our faces with cheap-tasting chips, the bubbling of boiling oil not quite drowning out our open-mouthed chewing noises.

We stopped in Rio Grande for two days in an expensive hostel while it snowed and rained, everything in the small, squat city disconcertingly grey. Alonso slept and ate, trying to regain just enough elusive charge to finish this journey with me. We met Alejandro, a policeman from Buenos Aires who had brought his young family to discover the southernmost tip of their country for the first time. We cooked and ate together and I begrudgingly remounted Achilles and gave the children rides around the parking lot when windows in the rain and snow meant only a light drizzle fell. When they asked to ride the bike, I felt like telling them to leave me alone, I'd had enough. But I stopped myself, just. Doing that would have been to spurn one of the reasons for this journey – to invite people to get involved and perhaps to give a fraction of what I was taking back.

With the help of a group of kids on BMXs, I found a MacGyver-like bicycle mechanic, who after an hour of tinkering with grub screws and wire cutters in a brilliantly cluttered workshop saw to it that my frayed gear cable was serviceable enough, I thought, to see me up the few steep hills that I knew remained between here and Ushuaia.

It was raining the next morning when we reluctantly left. A cold, sleety rain that seemed to dig in and freeze you from the inside out. Just occasionally it let up and revealed gnarled dead trees in the monochrome landscape. Despite the rain, the pampas was still a frozen white and damp mist hung low like dry ice, half submerging the black and spartan forests. My rear wheel began to show signs of wear again. The new wheel built back in Puerto Montt and again in Punta Arenas was cheap, and I was impressed that it had held up on the washboard roads for this long. But now spokes began to snap again, numbing my hands in the damp sub-zero air as I fumbled with tools and replacements.

Two spokes down and being soaked by sleet that froze our jackets, we bumped onto the slushy back road of Tolhuin after 70 miles of head-bowed, painful silence from Alonso, doing his best to assist. We waited irritably for Joselyn to catch up in what was quickly becoming a whiteout. Now, even she – owner of the toughest bottom ever to grace the back seat of Achilles – was struggling with pain and exhaustion. With the weary hope of desperation we headed directly for the fire station over the rutted wet ice. I no longer cared about steering a sympathetic line to save the bike or Alonso's bottom and we grated painfully across half-frozen tire tracks, not knowing whether there'd be a bed or a floor or anything waiting for us.

Almost immediately on our arrival a reassuringly tubby man rolled open the heavy metal shutter and beckoned us in out of the snow. Achilles and Joselyn's borrowed bike joined 13 other vehicles in the huge station thanks to Hugo the fire chief, who shook us each by the hand once he'd shut out the weather again. Five minutes later we were sipping maté and watching *The Simpsons* with a handful of volunteers who treated the station like a second home. Then even before we'd properly thawed out, smells began to emanate from the far side of the large living area. Hugo was preparing dinner, three huge pots of *puchero*, Patagonian lamb and steaming vegetables. We devoured it sitting at a long table with the firefighters and their families, Alonso and I sharing satisfied glances after seconds and thirds from the stew pot.

That was before one of the friendly, giggling firemen mentioned something about a 'fireman's baptism'. They talked excitedly about treating us to it, whatever it was, and thoughts of rugby team initiation ceremonies galloped worryingly through my mind.

I was told to don an old fireman's jacket and boots and the men and women chattered excitedly, as agitated as a pack of dogs before feeding time. How could I get out of this? They'd trapped me with a lovely meal, and Joselyn and Alonso weren't going to help me out. Assuming this was perhaps a treatment reserved for gringos, they were enjoying my predicament as much as the firemen were. Maybe as far as they were concerned it was payback for all my mood swings and the times I'd lost it with the wind or balance or lack of progress.

'Do you want to go voluntarily or do we have to force you ...? I suggest voluntarily,' the biggest of the rosy-checked firemen said, smiling down at me. I marched outside obediently while the congregation, including some local families, sniggered and jostled me outside, the children now geed up into a Coca-Cola-fuelled frenzy. A particularly deep patch of slush was found, and after being told to lie down, armfuls of snow were showered over me and wedged into my jacket, face, boots and mouth, filled within seconds by the scrum of *bomberos*. And so it was that I was baptised, *bombero*-style. A few minutes later, after I'd been triumphantly escorted back inside and I'd emptied most of the snow from my shirt, Alonso was caught hiding behind an engine and given the same treatment, as was Joselyn, though the lads went easy on her. Then, back in the warm kitchen, as if we'd passed an exam and needed a reward, we were congratulated by all members of the station and presented with a key to a nearby house in which to sleep.

I hadn't drunk a drop that night, yet I felt tipsy. Maybe it was the sudden adrenalin of the baptism coupled with the food and exhaustion, but whatever it was I was happy and I'd truly let my guard down. I'd forgotten about the stress of the last weeks, and looking at Alonso's face he felt the same – he was smiling his big, broad mischievous grin for the first time in days. As we crawled into the little beds in the cabin we talked sleepily but enthusiastically about the following day. The last day, we kept saying. The last day.

Morning came too soon, and a short, deep sleep made the previous night's high spirits feel like a pleasant dream. We reluctantly creaked out of our bunks and trudged out in the dawn light together, slush soaking our shoes and wet snow specking our clothes before we'd covered the short distance to the fire station and breakfast.

As we left the shelter of the large vehicle warehouse, the radio crackled over the station loudspeakers, and a minute later the smallest of the emergency trucks lit up and backed out into the snow with us. Apparently there'd been an accident on the road between Tolhuin and Ushuaia, up on the high pass where the snow was falling quicker than the ploughs could clear it. We looked at each other, still sheltering under the eaves of the building. We had at least to have a go at fighting through the weather. Besides, it was unlikely to get much better at this time of year. The night before I'd put our studded tires back on Achilles, but the studs had all but worn out on the miles of bare wet tarmac the previous day.

Everything got slowly worse as we climbed gradually and for the last time over what remained of the Andes, with thick sheets of snow reducing visibility to a few yards and blanketing the camera the instant I got it out to hurriedly film the final hours of the ride. It was Alonso's turn to provide the driving force of our progress, and he did so, head still bowed behind me but gritting his teeth as I squinted half-blind into the flat whiteness.

As I cycled I thought numbly about where I was. Over the last two years I'd dreamt countless times about these final miles. I'd imagined how satisfied I'd feel, I thought about filming different conclusions, perhaps jumping with joy into the Beagle Channel, or finding a local policeman or granny to ride the last few yards into town with me. So many of the people I'd met had wistfully mentioned the possibility of meeting me in Ushuaia to crowd the finish line and give me a hero's welcome. The thought of reuniting with an eclectic bunch of friends from all over the Americas had filled me with excitement in months gone by. But I'd lived my journey often in a little egocentric bubble – I'd been naive. Weeks after I left, new friends' lives would invariably overtake them again, and my plans understandably became secondary or were forgotten altogether. Besides, I no longer seemed to care.

Alonso and I, with Joselyn a little way behind, arrived at Ushuaia's signpost tired, very wet and half numb with cold. We'd pedalled through nearly 70 miles of heavy snow, wind whipping the crystals painfully into my eyes as I'd tried to pick a line with the hardest snow pack free of floundering heavy goods vehicles. I was wearing the Spiderman outfit I'd promised Olly, its owner, I'd wear on the last day, but it was buried under two more layers of damp fleece, with only the blue and red Lycra leggings showing, dirty and baggy after a prolonged soaking.

We posed for the obligatory photo next to the sign. 'The most southerly city in the world' it stated proudly, in letters carved deeply into damp wood, yet when I read it I felt almost no emotion at all. I leaned heavily on Alonso as we hugged, tired but weakly grateful for his company. I could think of no one more positive to share those last yards with, but my gratitude and camaraderie had been submerged, for now, by a wretched flood of exhaustion and indifference. Trudging fairly solemnly back to Achilles, leaning heavily on a wet snow drift, we cycled into town and found shelter in a hostel with a handful of other tourists.

The next day, after a night of lamb chops and a sleepy rather than ecstatic drunkenness, we rode Achilles to where the road ended on the Lapataya Peninsula. For those 20 miles we experienced the worst weather I'd ever ridden in, the wind twice as aggressive as the day before and the snow twice as deep. But within a stone's throw of the small bay, the wind did eventually die and the cloud dispersed as if we'd somehow been pardoned. The sun shone cold but clear on the tranquil glassy Antarctic water, and the shark's tooth peak of Mount Olivia gleamed in fresh white snow behind us.

Alonso removed the doubtless unpleasantly fragrant dinosaur hat from his boxer shorts and put it on to accompany my Spiderman suit, now fully exposed as I hung upside down for a photo on the last signpost on the continent. 'Alaska: 17,848 kilometres' it said – that was 11,090 miles. Over the last two years, one month and twenty-two days, with the help of about two hundred and seventy companions, I'd done nearly double that. I got down from the sign, rejoined my companions, and we headed slowly back up the snow-covered track the way we had come. This time, though, I pushed Achilles, who rolled with a tired rattle and a slight grating sound. As I walked, feeling empty and a little lost, I became aware of the desire never to ride my beloved bicycle ever again.

A deep-blue shadow now covered the steep south face of Mount Olivia and the sun became nothing more than a glow behind it. The mountain shared the name of my sister, who would give birth to her second child any day now.

I'd left the UK before Gabhran, my first nephew, had developed any memories of me. To him, I wasn't Uncle Dominic at all; I was 'the man on the bicycle'. Weeks back I'd thought that name had a heroic sound to it. Now it just sounded hollow, a little sad, lacking family connection. I walked through the silently falling snow, reflecting on the alternating peaks and troughs of over two years of intoxicating friendships and heartbreaking loneliness that had created an indifference I found unnerving, and I thought it was perhaps time to go home. But 'stability' had a terrifying ring to it. It was going to take some getting used to.

Epilogue

DAY 782: 18,449 MILES

Staying still was nice. I was dry, I had a bed, and the icy blue sky was reflected in the now mirror-like Beagle Channel. For a few pleasant days before Alonso and Joselyn headed home on northbound goods vehicles, my alarm no longer forced us from the warmth of our beds. There was no need to take advantage of what little winter daylight existed in these latitudes. Time and daylight no longer mattered. I was at the end of my journey. I'd finished. However I said it, it sounded strange.

It took months to recover physically from the weather-induced exhaustion of that Patagonian winter, but the painful memories of those last few days immediately began to soften, my brain filing the sensations in an archive deep enough to ignore. After a week lazily wandering the streets in Buenos Aires, having had to fly there before flying home, I was dimly aware of a new embryonic thirst for adventure growing inside me, and I didn't like it. I suppose I'd hoped that this journey might have purged my system of a craving for the new and exciting. One big adventure to sate my appetite and allow me to 'settle down' and enjoy the life of a 'grown-up'. Even before the British Airways flight lifted me off Argentinian tarmac to fly home, I realised that I'd been naive.

Had I succeeded? I suppose so, geographically speaking, but the importance of that had receded somewhat the further south I'd cycled.

EPILOGUE

I began the journey full of machismo, hungry to prove that I could do it, come what may. But slowly, ever so slowly, my priorities had changed and I learned the real worth of the journey. Company. Sharing. Faith in those around you wherever you are, despite the largely negative scare stories that plagued the world when I left and continue to do so now. Thanks to the spare seat on Achilles, I was able to learn a little more than I might have done otherwise. I could really physically share my journey with people, many people who would never normally have dreamed of travelling on a bicycle. I wasn't aware of it at the time, but when I set out on June 16, 2006, on Achilles the tandem bicycle, I was giving myself the opportunity not only to be inspired, but to inspire.

A week after returning to the UK, a small article about my journey was published in the *Metro* newspaper, read on almost every city bus and train in the country.

As a result, I got a pleasant swathe of well-wishers emailing to congratulate me on my two-and-a-bit-year endeavour cycling a heavily laden tandem bicycle from the cold, windy north of Alaska to the cold, windy south of Argentina.

Once back in England, it became obvious that I'd changed. The last two years had disproportionately shaped my life, my goals, my future dreams, as if I'd skipped like a stylus into a groove of a different track. That sounds dangerously like I thought I'd 'reshaped my destiny', but I don't believe in destiny . . . at least I don't think I do.

Days after the last tumbling shreds of that newspaper article had been cleared from Tube station platforms, I was checking my email, looking forward to perhaps another message from one of the hundreds of people I'd rubbed shoulders with somewhere along the length of the Americas. I casually scanned the screen, noting with mild alarm that the number of invitations to buy Viagra seemed to be increasing. After deleting each one of them in turn (vaguely wondering whether I should save a promising-looking one to consider a few years down the line) my eye rested on an email from someone called Bonnie Putt.

'Bonnie Putt?' I blurted out, as a flood of memories from primary school washed into my travel-weathered brain. She was my first 'girlfriend'! On the first family holiday I remember, in Crete, my mother had teased me about her and playfully encouraged me to buy her a little silver ring shaped like a dolphin. It was beautiful, but looking back on it I'm not at all sure why she was encouraging a seven year old more interested in drowning ants in honey to buy a ring for a little girl. But that's what I did. Needless to say – and I haven't changed that much – when I returned to school I remember pausing outside our classroom (the same classroom where I wet myself twice, the second time making it marginally closer to the toilet door but not quite close enough to deem it a near miss) and realising that I was far too shy to give this little ring to Bonnie. The obvious alternative was to drop it into what I thought was her satchel, one of the 18 hanging in the cloakroom, so that was what I did. So for 21 years I have never known whether Bonnie ever got the ring, whether it was her satchel I put it in or, perhaps, Russell's, the only boy who I seem to remember wetting himself more than I did. And at that moment, looking at Bonnie's email, I realised my curiosity could be satisfied once and for all.

I met her a few weeks later in London after another day editing the hundreds of hours of video footage from my journey. We caught up on the last 21 years, and I found to my dismay, though I wasn't surprised, that she never did get the ring. She did however remind me of something a little more peculiar.

I remember singing a duet with her, 'Tea for Two', on the little stage in front of the whole school and doubtless a small crowd of cooing parents. Bonnie also reminded me that after 'Tea for Two' we sang 'Daisy Bell'.

> There is a flower within my heart
> Daisy, Daisy
> Planted one day by a glancing dart
> Planted by Daisy Bell

So far, nothing strange, though I'm sure if I'd understood the oh-so-sweet lyrics at the time I might have walked off stage. But, listen closely. If we move swiftly on to the second verse, there's something a touch prophetic.

EPILOGUE

It won't be a stylish marriage
I can't afford a carriage
But you'll look sweet upon the seat
Of a bicycle built for two

If I ever get married the wedding, as the song predicts, most likely
won't be packed to the rafters with style; a bicycle built for two, though?
What are the chances of singing about the machine that has propelled
me through two such radically different years of my life, 20-odd years
before the event (albeit without Bonnie). Well, I suppose a statistician
would say the probability is actually quite high, and that if you factor in
the number of times one breaks into song, and the number of times any
given tune mentions bicycles, and then – OK, all right. But I thought,
just for an instant, that this fact was peculiar enough, in a fairy-tale
kind of way, to give destiny a fighting chance . . .

Index

INDEX

INDEX

INDEX